Praise for The Survival Guide

M000032270

If you're like most dads, you're facing an impossible tug of war between work and home. My advice? Read this book. In this smart, charming, and actionable guide, Scott Behson offers a practical toolkit for thriving in both domains. You'll discover how to make family time more memorable, how to negotiate more flexibility with your boss, and why you should pack at least one stuffed animal on every business trip. Behson is the rare writer who can communicate everything you need to know, while making you feel like you're just chatting over a beer with a good friend at a barbeque.

> - Ron Friedman, PhD, author of *The Best Place to Work: The Art and Science of Creating an Extraordinary Workplace*

Finally! This is the book dads juggling work and family have been waiting for.

In my work over the past 15 years as the director of the Boston College Center for Work and Family I have seen the challenges faced by working fathers move from a fringe topic to one that is front of mind for business leaders. Our Center has been striving to make the case that supporting working dads helps everyone - fathers, their spouses and children, their employers and society. Finally, it seems real progress is being made on this important issue.

While we are pleased with this progress. there has been a persistent gap that *The Working Dad's Survival Guide* addresses head-on: How can dads themselves better analyze their priorities and take actions, at home and at work, to maximize their effectiveness? Behson's book is full of great insights, perspectives and advice that will help dads be more successful on all fronts.

- Brad Harrington, PhD, Executive Director of the Boston College Center for Work and Family

In *The Working Dad's Survival Guide*, Scott Behson sets out to do one simple – but not at all easy – thing; help men feel confident and successful in both their work life and family life. Using the perfect combination of exercises, stories, insights, and practical strategies he accomplishes that goal with flying colors. There's no magic pill that will make you the best dad you can be. But with commitment, hard work, and Scott's guidance, you're well on your way.

- Armin Brott, author of *The Expectant Father* and *The New Father: A Dad's Guide to the First Year*

The Working Dads Survival Guide combines success stories of real working dads with practical advice that finally gives new and expecting fathers a resource for navigating tough conversations with our parenting partners and our employers. Cheers to Scott Behson for providing the 21st century working dad a roadmap for career and parenting success.

- Matt Schneider and Lance Somerfeld, Co-Founders, City Dads Group.

In *The Working Dad's Survival Guide*, Scott Behson, tears down the "wall of silence" that has surrounded a generation of men who are seeking to redefine what it means to be a good father and a good man. Filled with the heart-felt voices of dozens of fathers struggling to juggle it all, Behson's imminently practical book lays out new ways of thinking, and helpful exercises, tools and strategies for how to be successful both at work and at home. If you're a working father who's felt alone, the Survival Guide is truly that - operating instructions to find your network and navigate this confusing yet exciting time.

- Brigid Schulte, author *Overwhelmed:*
Work, Love and Play when No One has the Time

In my experience as the Founder/CEO of FlexJobs, a job search service that helps professionals find legitimate flexible work, I've seen first-hand how eager all professionals, dads included, are to find better ways to balance their careers with their family lives. That's why I'm so glad Scott wrote this book, because he not only clearly shows the conflicts faced by many working dads, but he also provides actionable advice that will help dads find better solutions at work and at home.

The stories, exercises, and concrete tips Scott offers in *The Working Dad's Survival Guide* bring clarity, focus, and motivation for readers to tackle these issues in their own lives. As a working mom myself (married to a wonderful working dad!), I understand so many of the same thoughts, frustrations, and hopes we all feel when it comes to work-life balance. Scott's experience, and positivity, are a welcomed relief!

- Sara Sutton Fell, Founder & CEO of FlexJobs

I wish I had this book when I was taking heat in the corporate world for being an active parent. The suggestions and exercises would have made a big difference, to both support the choices I was making, and help me build a community of other working dads so I would not feel alone.

Behson unapologetically writes that men do not parent like women, and that sitting around sharing feelings is not our thing. But we can get together and talk man to man about the complex reality we face. He offers practical solutions and anecdotes that cover a wide variety of real life situations that working dads face today.

If you are a working dad who wants to spend more time with your family, or are feeling unappreciated at home for the work you are already doing, this book is a must read!

- Greg Marcus, PhD, author of *Busting Your Corporate Idol:*
Self-Help for the Chronically Overworked

In the early 1990's when I first conducted open discussion groups for dads, I invited the dads to share one thing they learned from the other dads in the room. The number one answer, "I learned I'm not alone. That other dads have similar challenges."

Behson's assessment of today's modern dad is accurate and confirmed by the stories I collected in my book, *Dads Behaving Dadly: 67 Truths, Tears and Triumphs of Modern Fatherhood*, which is a collection of stories written by a wide variety of dads, who share their honest, sincere feelings about their struggles and rewards of being a modern dad.

Behson's book provides valuable, concise, practical information that will help so many dads balance their work and family lives. *The Working Dad's Survival Guide* is a well-designed game plan for dads on how to be successful fathers as well as productive employees.

– Hogan Hilling, author, *Dads Behaving Dadly I* and *Dadly II*.

Scott Behson stands prominently at the fulcrum point of an important social and political discussion in America. As an expert, and father himself, Scott is working diligently to give fathers the opportunity to engage more with their children by stoking debate over the working and personal lives of men. More and more fathers are asking questions of their employers, themselves, and their roles in parenting. While the conversation of 'leaning in' and 'opting out' play out for women, Scott is blazing trails for men who want to participate more in their children's lives and shift the consciousness of the business world.

- Charlie Capen, co-author, *How to Be a Dad* and
The Guide to Baby Sleep Positions.

The juggling act required to balance work and family has for too long been marginalized as a women's issue and more specifically a mom's issue. It's incredibly exciting to have Scott's strong male voice helping to finally shift this narrative.

The Working Dad's Survival Guide will no doubt give fathers everywhere the courage to speak out about the fact that the "traditional" workplace model is broken for them as well as for moms. Navigating the intersection of work and family is a complex task for both men and women, and Scott's recommended tools and strategies will not only help fathers but also ultimately help all parents find common ground and solutions to succeed at work and at home.

As we work to bring the benefits of work flexibility to more companies and people across the country, the 1 Million for Work Flexibility movement is proud to have Scott's support and involvement.

- Emma Plumb, Director of 1 Million for Work Flexibility

The Working Dad's Survival Guide does an excellent job of clarifying the changing expectations of working fathers and what this means in terms of mindset and practical shifts from generations past. I most appreciate that it emphasizes the critical impact of time management and financial decisions and the importance of taking care of yourself and cultivating a support network. This is a solid toolbox of strategies for working dads who really care about their careers and their families and want to figure out how they can succeed in both arenas.

- Elizabeth Grace Saunders, author of
How to Invest Your Time Like Money

Being an equal partner and involved father leads to a more meaningful, balanced life. Lots of guys knows this, often having learned the hard way from their own fathers, but not everyone knows how to pioneer a new role. Scott Behson draws brilliantly from his life and research to provide the stories, tips, and tools we need to become the fathers we want to be.

- Jeremy Adam Smith, author *The Daddy Shift*

We hear a lot of stories that men are changing, becoming more engaged and active fathers. Scott Behson's book is for us -- we who want to be more engaged but don't exactly know how to do it. We who try to balance being involved dads with pursuing success in our careers. With clear insights, examples and strategies, Behson breaks it down and enables each of us to reconstruct fatherhood as a deep and glorious connection to our kids.

- Michael Kimmel, PhD, author, *Guyland:*
The Perilous World Where Boys Become Men

There is a revolution taking place – one that's going to improve the lives of men, women and children. Scott's book is an important part of this movement for change. *The Working Dad's Survival Guide* provides a step-by-step resource to help men feel successful at work *and* at home - whether it's his chapter on negotiating changes at work, creating more "memorable" times at home, or making sure involved dads take care of themselves (including having some fun with their spouses!) You might be a new dad who is craving this information, or an experienced dad interested in making a change, either way, Scott's words of wisdom and friendly tone will help guide you to a solution that's just right for you.

- Jessica DeGroot, Founder & President, ThirdPath Institute

A portion of the royalties from this book is donated to A Better Balance.

A Better Balance (ABB) is a national legal advocacy organization fighting to give American workers the time and flexibility they need to care for their families without risking their economic security. ABB works to promote equality and expand choices for men and women at all income levels, leading the charge for policies that help families, such as sick leave, family leave, fair and flexible work, and stronger legal protections for caregivers. ABB's efforts help people who work outside and inside the home achieve a better balance between providing for their families and caring for them. Visit ABB at http://abetterbalance.org.

THE WORKING DAD'S SURVIVAL GUIDE

How to Succeed at Work and at Home

SCOTT BEHSON, PhD

MOtivational PRESS®
LEADERS IN GLOBAL PUBLISHING

Published by Motivational Press
1777 Aurora Road
Melbourne, Florida, 32935
www.MotivationalPress.com

Manufactured in the United States of America.

ISBN: 978-1-62865-194-2

Contents

Dedication

To my amazing family, Amy and Nick. The best thing I ever did was marry Amy Griffin, and the best thing I'll ever be is Nick's dad. You are the joys of my life.

To all the busy, involved working dads out there. You are the unsung heroes that hold it all together.

To my Dad and Mom, Joe and Grace, for showing me how it's done.

FOREWORD TO THE WORKING DAD'S SURVIVAL GUIDE

Stewart Friedman, PhD

When I started in the field of work and life in 1987, rocked by the birth of my first child, no one would have thought to pen *The Working Dad's Survival Guide: How to Succeed at Work and at Home*. Men were fathers then too, of course, but it wasn't a central concern, a primary social role. Indeed, my colleagues and mentors at Wharton, who truly had my best interests at heart, urged me stick with leadership development as my core professional focus and were incredulous that I'd opt to pivot to the "women's" field of work and life. I am thrilled to say that now the need for such a book is great because men, especially younger men, expect to be and want to be involved fathers – the significance of this role in all aspects of life has changed.

Over twenty years ago the Wharton Work/Life Integration Project launched a longitudinal research program, surveying thousands of men and women about their choices and aspirations for their lives.

One output was the book I co-authored in 2000 with Drexel University's Jeff Greenhaus, *Work and Family — Allies or Enemies? What Happens When Business Professionals Confront*

Life Choices. We detailed an action agenda that is still relevant today. Based on our findings we recommended:

- Reshaping the division of labor at home.
- Changing society's gender ideology through education and socialization.
- Helping young people choose careers that fit their values.
- Teaching employees how to generate support from others.
- Investing in what employees do outside of work.
- Creating work environments that value employees as whole people.
- Training managers to take a new look at work processes.
- Demonstrating the economic value of investing in family-friendliness.
- Authorizing employees to think and act like entrepreneurs.
- Expanding childcare options, including through public-private partnerships.

Out of this research and other initiatives we undertook at Wharton in the '90s grew a program designed to enable change for individuals, organizations, and society. To make it easier for men to tackle the challenges of integrating work and the rest of life, the program – which I called Total Leadership and founded while I was on leave from Wharton in the late '90s, serving as the senior executive responsible for leadership development worldwide at Ford Motor – uses language that men could comfortably use: "performance," "measurable results," "attainable goals," and "leadership." These terms, and the merging of leadership development methods with what we'd been learning from field research about how to integrate work and the rest of life, helped CEOs, Human Resource executives, managers, and others in organizations to use the Total Leadership approach for men and women, at all career stages and at all levels, interested in learning what they could do personally to create meaningful, sustainable change as leaders in all aspects of their lives.

This approach has now been used by thousands of Wharton students, over 130,000 students in a world-wide Massive Open Online Course (MOOC), by hundreds of organizations across the nation and overseas, and has been the focus of an NIH-funded multi-year study on improving the careers and lives of women in medicine. The book based on the program has been translated into seven languages and has been an international bestseller. This is a proven method, involving peer-to-peer coaching, that debunks the zero-sum mentality of "work/life balance," which presumes tradeoffs and sacrifice, and relies instead on what I call "four-way-wins." And the metaphor is not scales in balance but, rather, a jazz quartet. You want to achieve harmony, not a balance. Sometimes only one instrument dominates. Together and over the course of the piece, beautiful music can take place. The Total Leadership model is a mindset of looking for ways to capitalize on synergies among the spheres of work, home, community and the private self (mind, body and spirit). You start with a *diagnosis* – examining and clarifying your values; then undertake *dialogues* with key stakeholders at work, home and in your community about your mutual expectations; and finally *discover* new ways of trying to meet expectations while living your values through continual experimentation and innovation.

In 2012, The Wharton Work/Life Integration Project surveyed two groups, some of the same people who responded to our survey as graduating Wharton seniors in 1992 and a new cohort of our graduates, the Class of 2012. Thus we were able to compare men and women at about age 20 in 1992 and again at about age 40 in 2012, and we were able compare how young people, men and women, responded in 1992 compared to the cohort coming of age in 2012.

As this book by Scott Behson demonstrates, things have changed. In 1992, men were much more likely than women to agree that dual career relationships work best when one partner is more advanced in their career than the other. And they were also more likely to agree that dual-career relationships work best when one partner is less involved in his or her career. In 2012, however, we found a convergence of attitudes about two-career relationships. Now men are less likely to agree with both those statements than they were 20 years ago. Compared to graduates 20 years ago, young men graduating today are more egalitarian in their views.

Men and women today are more likely than the previous generation to share the same values and ideas about what it takes to make dual-career relationships work. One implication of this finding is that there is greater solidarity among men and women and therefore more flexibility about the roles that both men and women can legitimately take in society. There is now a greater sense of shared responsibility for domestic life. Men and women are now more aligned about how to navigate *who* in a dual-career relationship should focus on their careers and *when* they should do so. Today's young men don't merely accept women in the workforce, they *expect* to see women as peers. And men are now more cognizant of the difficulties they themselves will face in resolving conflicts between work and family in their own lives.

Because men now expect greater parity in career opportunities and commitments, they are increasingly motivated to experiment with new models for how both partners can have more of what each wants in life. Traditional gender stereotypes are prisons for men too and hold many back from trying new approaches to work and family life. There is whole new industry of stay-at-home-dad (SAHD) bloggers, new Web sites for fathers, books about fatherhood, and articles by and for SAHDs and gatherings where they are exploring in nuanced and poignant detail what they are struggling with and reveling in as they try to weave a new social fabric that combines the roles of breadwinning with caregiving.

Men need help navigating these new waterways. Today's male hero—key to the cultural changes needed to enable greater freedom for women in all spheres of life—is not the gallant warrior but the nurturing caretaker, what I like to call the New Knight in Shining Armor. Much has been said about how to help women succeed, but a new kind of bravery in men *must* be as much a part of the story as the career-triumphant woman.

The Working Dad's Survival Guide: How to Succeed at Work and at Home provides detailed and specific exercises that men can use to help them navigate this strange new world. This book offers a section – in four chapters – on success at home focusing on the family unit, the importance of taking care of yourself and of building webs of support. And there's an entire chapter on paternity leave. In 1987 that phrase, "paternity leave," like "stay-at-home-dad" was not part of the common vernacular!

I'm thrilled to say that, at last, the time is ripe for a working dad's survival guide. Thanks to Scott Behson for providing it.

Stew Friedman is the Practice Professor of Management at the Wharton School, where he founded both the Wharton Leadership Program and the Wharton Work/Life Integration Project. For two years, he served as the senior executive for leadership development at Ford Motor Co. Stew's most recent book is *Leading the Life You Want: Skills for Integrating Work and Life* (Harvard Business, 2014), a *Wall Street Journal* bestseller. His

Total Leadership program is used worldwide. He was chosen by *Working Mother* as one of America's 25 most influential men to have made things better for working parents, by Thinkers50 as one of the world's top 50 business thinkers, and by *HR Magazine* as one of the Most Influential Thinkers 2014. The Families and Work Institute honored him with a Work Life Legacy Award. Follow on LinkedIn and Twitter @StewFriedman and tune in to Stew's show, *Work and Life*, on SiriusXM 111, *Business Radio Powered by Wharton*, Tuesdays at 7:00 p.m. (ET).

INTRODUCTION: HEY DAD, YOU ARE NOT ALONE!

▌ Here are four dads, in their own words:

My wife is an environmental scientist and is away at a conference. So, this week, I'm a solo dad — I'm leaving work a little before 3pm, rushing to pick up my daughter from pre-school and then rushing to meet my son's school bus. Tonight, homework, meals, baths and bedtime are totally on me. After the kids are asleep, I'm back on my computer to finish up work. It's a long week, man.

· ·

My wife went back to work after our daughter started first grade. I was downsized a few months ago, but landed a contract IT job and now I work mostly from home. After years of being the breadwinner and my wife doing the rest, now I have to do my share, and it's tough figuring out work time and daddy time when I'm working from home with my daughter around and my wife out on a sales call. I know my wife is pissed- she feels she still does so much at home even after a full day of work. It's pretty stressful right now feeling our way through this transition. I'm worried things are not getting better.

· ·

I have a pretty high-octane career in international finance. I confess I work very long hours, travel a lot and have a killer commute. My job pays really well, but it's stressful because so much depends on my yearly performance bonus- I have to be "on" for work all the time. One Sunday, I remember bringing my son to his friend's birthday party. I was exhausted from a huge workweek and looking forward to relaxing. Then I got calls on both my Blackberries about a client emergency, and had to go into the office. I think I'm a great dad when I'm around, but my kids and wife sometimes don't get enough of me.

• •

My wife's been in a long-running Off-Broadway show for almost three years. It's great and I totally support her career. But the world is not set up for help with young kids on evenings and weekends, so the night shift is always on me. My wife's great, and around during the day, but this week, she has a voice lesson, dance class and several auditions. So, after I teach my classes, I have to leave the office early to get my son from school, and then I have the homework, daytime and dinner shift too. I'm a really active dad, but right now, I'm running low on energy.

Do any of these dads seem familiar?

The first three are my friends. And, yes, the last one is me. I suspect you, your friends, coworkers and neighbors could all tell similar stories.

While everyone's details are different, the themes are similar. Virtually every working dad I know struggles with balancing the time and effort required to be a good financial provider with the time and effort needed to be a present, involved, loving father.

I certainly struggle. I bet you do, as well. There are only 24 hours in a day and we only have so much energy.

We all deal with this work-family challenge in different ways – and it is never easy. But we have struggled, seemingly alone, for too long. As a society, we don't talk enough about the work-family challenges fathers confront, and we fail to recognize that so many dads are running themselves ragged to succeed both in their careers and in their families. A little support from employers, public policy and society would be nice.

It's time that our most important life challenge – success in both our careers and in our families – is finally recognized as an important issue. It's time that we, as fathers, start discussing our struggles. It's time for some encouragement, information and advice for busy dads trying to succeed in our careers and as fathers. That's what this book is all about.

Consider these six facts:

1. **This generation of fathers works as hard and for as many hours as prior generations**. We face at least as many financial pressures and a world with less job and financial security than dads who have come before. The 2013 Pew Research Study found that, even with the rise of breadwinner moms and dual-income couples, fathers are the sole or primary providers for 85 percent of dual-parent households.

2. **Fathers today aspire to career success**. 76 percent of those surveyed in Boston College's New Dad studies wish to be promoted to positions of greater responsibility and 58 percent express a strong desire to move into senior management.

3. **Today's dad has tripled the time he spends caring for his children and does twice the housework, compared to fathers of a generation ago.** 65 percent of dads see their role as both provider and caretaker, and 85 percent aspire to fully sharing parenting with their spouses (however, only about 30 percent report that they do so). But maybe we're being too hard on ourselves – according to a recent American Time Use Survey, when you combine time at work, housework and parenting time, moms and dads carry just about an equal workload.

4. **Workplaces and corporate cultures have not kept up with these changes**. Because dads' struggles are not commonly discussed, companies have not had to confront our work-family concerns. In fact, a series of studies from UC Hastings College of the Law showed that men who use common forms of workplace flexibility, such as flextime,

telecommuting or parental leave, are seen as insufficiently committed to their work and "unmanly," facing disrespect and career consequences. Men are expected to be "all in" for work even when they are far more involved at home.

5. **50 percent of working dads say they find it very or somewhat difficult to balance work and family responsibilities**. In fact, about two-thirds of fathers today report work-family conflict and stress. According to a recent Families & Work Institute survey, this is an even higher rate than reported by working moms!

6. **When dads are able to succeed at work and be involved at home, families and children benefit**. Research shows that kids with dads who are involved in their lives from the start have better health, better grades, and higher rates of graduation, as well as lower rates of incarceration and teen pregnancy. Girls with involved dads are more likely to pursue a wider range of careers, including traditionally male-dominated ones, like engineering and science.

You would think that, considering these facts, society would recognize the critical need to support working dads, and that employers and spouses would step up for us. You'd expect fathers to get together to share ideas, advice and encouragement because we all face a similar huge challenge, and so much depends on us. Unfortunately, you'd be wrong.

There is a strange "wall of silence" that has built up over the issue of involved fathers who work hard to juggle work and family demands. So, if you have ever felt that all your efforts in attaining career success while also making the time to be an involved dad have been overlooked, you, my friend, are not alone.

If so many of us deal with the same issues, why do we feel alone?

First, many men who are really busy with work and family don't have the time to devote to making new friends and seeing old ones. If we had networks of fellow dads, we'd begin to see that our friends, co-workers and neighbors are struggling just like we are, and that many of them have developed techniques and strategies that work well for them. We could borrow each other's ideas. At the very least, we'd have peers with whom we could share our frustrations.

Society, thankfully, has some supports for moms. Mommy and Me classes and various Mommy groups are staples of most neighborhoods and communities. Most of the time dads are technically allowed in these groups, but are not always tolerated or welcomed. In fact, I have a friend who was asked to leave a play group because they (I kid you not) "couldn't take the risk that a man could be a sexual predator." And just where are the Daddy and Me classes or Dads' Groups?

But, let's get real, even if these groups existed, how many of us would join them? We're too busy juggling work and home. Also, we're not joiners, and, for many of us, sitting in circles singing children's songs and talking about our feelings is not exactly our bag.

Even if we wanted to join these groups, who has the time? Men work more hours after we have children – not fewer. Increased financial pressures, combined with the likelihood that our spouses downshift or temporarily leave the workforce, mean more financial responsibility falls to us. And our workplaces, by and large, do not accommodate our family needs.

Women face many struggles and barriers in the workplace, but workplaces tend to be at least somewhat understanding when women need to work more flexibly or take time off to handle family responsibilities[1]. As mentioned before, for dads, there is an extra stigma because men who accommodate work to family are not only violating 'work-first' corporate culture but also societal norms of masculinity. As a result, most men cannot be open about their family lives at work, and need to keep their work-family concerns largely invisible in the workplace.

Until very recently, TV, advertising and other media depicted dads almost exclusively as lazy and incompetent, or as immature overgrown kids themselves. I love Homer Simpson and Peter Griffin, but, too many times, commercials and TV shows portray "doofus dads" as the punchline. Case in point – a few years ago, Huggies ran an infamously patronizing ad in which they assumed leaving a dad to change a diaper was "the ultimate test" because, of course, dads let their kids sit in their own filth while they watch football and then do terrible jobs when they finally, reluctantly change them[2]. This lowers the bar for the next generation of dads and implicitly tells women that they need to be responsible for everything.

Shifting Expectations

Another reason we often feel alone is that our generation of dads is caught in the crosswinds of changing expectations of what it means to be a good father. Our dads and other role models did it differently.

My father is a wonderful guy and was a great dad to me and my sister. He was a constant, loving presence in our lives, and I always knew he was there for me. However, my dad's role was far more straightforward than mine. My dad was the sole wage earner for much of my childhood (and was always the primary earner), and my mom was the main caretaker. My dad was a great role model and took an active interest in my education and activities, but there are a lot of things I do that were never expected of him.

He pretty much only cooked at backyard barbecues and occasional "pancake Sundays." He rarely prepared meals, cleaned the house, went food shopping or did laundry. Of course he mowed the lawn, took care of the car, and did minor house repairs, but he rarely changed diapers, supervised bath time, or drove me to activities (except baseball – that was our thing together). He was never expected to do these things, but he was awesome at everything that was expected of him. Actually, in many ways he was ahead of his time. He supported my mother as she earned her bachelor's and master's degrees part-time and often went well out of his way to mentor several of my friends and baseball teammates. I don't mean to slag on my dad – I'd consider myself a success if I'm half the dad he is. But he is also a product of his time and of the much clearer expectations past generations had for good fathers.

Dads in those days could be more laser-focused on their careers and providing for the family, knowing they had wives at home who would take care of the rest. In today's era of dual-career couples and egalitarian relationships (not to mention single-parent families), the strict division of labor has eroded. Both parents – dads and moms – are now focused on both earning and parenting. Today, we face a different set of expectations.

■ Conflicting Expectations

More accurately, we face several sets of expectations all at once. The vast majority of dads are still relied upon to be the primary earners, but we are also expected to support our spouses' careers. We are expected to do much more child-care and parenting than our dads did, but how much can we do with our work demands and without stepping on our spouses' turf at home? We do far more housework, but still less than our wives (and a lot of them are keeping track!).

Some people see us as "superdads" when we are simply doing ordinary, everyday things – going grocery shopping or walking our kids to the bus stop. Some think we're slackers when we don't do exactly 50 percent of house tasks or if we don't parent the way moms do.

Some people think it's cute when we're playing "Mr. Mom" or "babysitting" our kids at the playground; others eye us suspiciously when we do. When we're out and need to change a diaper, most men's bathrooms still don't have changing stations (I wish I could erase the memories I have of changing my son's diaper on those gross gas station bathroom floors!).

Some see us as unmanly if we put family time ahead of career; others see us as neglectful parents when work sometimes has to come first. It's all very fluid, shifting and confusing.

To use some TV examples, Ward Cleaver (*Leave it to Beaver*) was expected to provide, leaving the house and kids to June. Tim Taylor (*Home Improvement*) was involved with his kids, but left the heavy lifting to his wife. They had it comparatively easy. Phil Dunphy (*Modern Family*) is more like us (OK, he's a bit goofier than we are, but still...), pursuing a successful career, providing the primary income while supporting his wife's career, and being a fully equal parent. Even for a fictional character, that's a lot to handle.

In, *Home Game*, his memoir about fatherhood, Michael Lewis perfectly described the confusing set of expectations that today's non-fiction dads face:

> [We are in] a kind of Dark Age of Fatherhood. Obviously, we're in the midst of some long unhappy transition between the model of fatherhood practiced by my father and some ideal model, approved by all, to be practiced with ease by the fathers of the future.

But for now, there's an unsettling absence of universal, or even local, standards of behavior. Within a few miles of my house I can find perfectly sane men and women who regard me as a Neanderthal who should do more to help my poor wife with the kids, and just shut up about it. But I can also find other sane men and women who view me as a Truly Modern Man and marvel aloud at my ability to be both breadwinner and domestic dervish – doer of approximately 31.5 percent of all parenting.

I don't know if we're really in a "Dark Age." After all, in many ways it is a great time to be a dad – there are fewer gender restrictions placed on us and our new roles, while sometimes confusing, do allow us to form potentially more emotionally rich relationships with our children.

But Lewis' point remains: The unclear set of expectations placed upon us – by society, our spouses, our kids, our families, our employers and ourselves – means that finding a balance between career and family that works for us is more difficult than ever before.

Celebrity Dads

Several manly celebrity dads, such as Brad Pitt, David Beckham, Mark Wahlberg, Terry Crews and Jeremy Renner, have been front and center discussing what being a good dad today really means. Yes, they have more money and better abs than the rest of us, but their public statements and actions are helping change society's image of what it means to be a "real man." We're starting to say goodbye to the "strong silent type" and starting to say hello to a more modern approach – a dad equally comfortable carrying a briefcase and a diaper bag.

▌ We Do It To Ourselves, Too

However, as much as we can pin blame on societal signals and unsupportive employers – if we are being fully honest, we also contribute to our own predicament.

- How many of us have thought through our life priorities while assessing both family and career concerns?
- How many have reassessed the career paths we chose out of college way before spouse and baby made three?
- How often do we take a hard look at our finances to see if we're trapping ourselves with unnecessary commitments?
- Have we examined our weekly time use to see if we are using time productively and protecting family time?
- How many recognize if we've ceded parenting to our wives and work to correct the situation (as opposed to settling for less)?
- How many push back against unrealistic employer expectations?
- How many of us stay connected 24/7 to work, even during family time?
- How many seem attached to our smartphones?
- How many of us say, "I'll make more time for family next year... next year... next year"?

Many of us have internalized rigid expectations of what it takes to be a "real man." As a result, we stay strong and silent, and just continue to plod along on our own to do all we are relied upon to do.

With all of this, it is totally natural that we look around and think "I know I struggle with balancing work and family and would love to ask for help – but no other guy I know looks like he is struggling. I'll look weak if I do." Another brick in the "wall of silence."

It's time that we recognized that, in order to succeed at work and at home, we can't just rely on society or workplaces to change. We need to recognize the important challenge we face, and do what we can both to gather support and to act more in accordance with our priorities. I believe that we can achieve success in our careers while also being the involved, loving dads we always wanted to be.

For now, the first step to succeeding as both a father and a provider is knowing that you, dad, are not alone.

▌ Our Plan of Attack

Like you, I am a busy dad. I put in the work every day to raise my son, pursue career success, and balance this all with my wife's demanding and idiosyncratic career as a stage actress. Sometimes, I find the sweet spot. Very often, I fail. But, like you, I keep on trying.

There's no one best way to manage family and career, and there's certainly no instruction manual (if only there were!). But a book of encouragement, support and advice from a fellow dad, I think, would be useful. That's why I wrote this book, and, I guess, is why you've picked it up.

My fellow management professors have an expression that says, "It's hard to understand one thing without understanding some of everything." I think this is especially true for understanding work and family. Career and fatherhood intersect and affect each other in so many ways. For too long, they have been discussed separately.

In writing this book, I consulted dozens of books on parenting and fatherhood. Many of them are really useful, but none give more than a cursory treatment to how work affects family and vice versa. Considering that our two main goals are to be a good provider through a successful career and a loving, present dad, this seems odd to me. I also consulted dozens of books on careers and business self-help. Virtually none mention family or other life concerns, except for a vague call for balance tossed off as an afterthought. This also seems unsatisfactory to me.

So, I saw a need for a book that discusses both work and family in tandem, and figured who better to write it than someone with a firm foothold in both worlds? My career as a business school professor and consultant is focused on researching work-family balance and helping both dads and employers find solutions. But, more importantly, I'm a busy working dad who aspires to both career success and being a highly involved, loving dad and husband.

Over the next 250 pages or so, I'll discuss personal stories, share some advice, and provide you with some ways to think through life priorities. Together, we'll develop strategies so we can be more efficient at work, we can be more effective at home, we can take better care of ourselves, and we can build our own informal dad support networks. *The Working Dad's Survival Guide* contains five major themes that have emerged in my research, writing and professional work in work-family for fathers, as well as my own busy work-family juggle and the experiences of other dads I know.

We just covered the first theme - **knowing that most other dads struggle with the same issues you do**. Simply knowing this makes us feel less alone and more comfortable in seeking support.

The second theme involves **consciously thinking through our work, life and financial priorities** so that we have a better understanding of what is important in our lives. By setting and discussing our career, family and financial priorities, we can create a roadmap to better align our actions with our priorities. This roadmap will spark ideas, large and small, of how we can change our actions and work out arrangements with our employers and families so everyone's needs are met.

The third theme focuses on **things we can do at our workplace** to free up time and mental resources to balance work and family while also attaining professional success. We can do this by understanding the family-friendliness of our employers and supervisors, being more efficient at work, utilizing workplace flexibility, negotiating with our supervisors, expanding the set of criteria we use when conducting a career search, and perhaps even by standing up to make our workplaces more amenable to family concerns.

The fourth theme involves **what we can do in our family lives to maximize our effectiveness as fathers**. We can learn to focus on the most important things, protect family time from the creeping demands of work, make the best use of our family time, and make sure to tend to our own mental and physical well-being.

The fifth theme is **my call for Informal Fatherhood Networks.** In my neighborhood, a dozen or so local dads gather every so often for a backyard campfire and some beers- we call this "Beer Fire!" I encourage you to create small neighborhood or workplace fatherhood networks that would afford you some social time and opportunities to talk with other dads who face the same challenges as you. I'll share some ideas on how you can get started.

The book is organized so you can read it straight through, read a chapter each night before going to bed, or jump ahead to read individual chapters or subsections of interest. Each chapter contains many quotes and anecdotes from real dads[3] and ends with a few short exercises to help us think through our work-family issues and develop action plans to enhance our success. I'll also provide a list of sources and helpful resources at the end of the book.

Finally, while we all share the same central challenge, I realize that every dad's situation is unique. Some have jobs that lend themselves to flexibility – others don't. Some are climbing the corporate ladder, others have decided to slow their careers down, and others find it hard to find stable employment. Some serve in our military and are stationed far away from their families for long stretches of time. Some have money to burn, others live paycheck to paycheck. Some have one kid; others have seven!

Our kids are at different ages and stages and, of course, infants become toddlers, who become pre-schoolers, who become kids, who become adolescents, who become *gasp* teenagers. Some dads have awesome supportive spouses who do their share – others aren't that lucky. Some dads are married, some are divorced. Some are married to other dads. Some divorces are amicable and represent good parenting partnerships. Others are disasters. Some dads, in addition to work and family, are also responsible for caring for aging parents. Some of us have kids with special needs or serious medical conditions; others have been lucky to avoid these troubles. We all have different sets of cultural and religious values.

In this book, I'll try to provide ideas applicable to the widest variety of situations. I intentionally sought out dads in different circumstances when writing the book and soliciting the quotes and anecdotes you see throughout. I hope that, whatever your specific circumstances, you find advice and encouragement you can use.

▍Thanks in Advance

Thank you so much for reading this book. It has long been a dream of mine to write it.

As fathers, our two most important roles are being a successful financial provider and being an active, loving dad. It is my hope that *The Working Dad's Survival Guide* will help you feel more confident in succeeding at both.

So much depends on us. We'll never be perfect. But I think the success lies in the trying. If you care and do your best, I think you will, indeed, succeed at work and at home.

Finally, I invite you to keep this conversation going. Please join me back at my website, Fathers, Work and Family (http://FathersWorkandFamily.com). All the exercises you see in this book, plus new ones from time to time, are compiled for you to download and use at http://WorkingDadsSurvivalGuide.com. Now, let's get to work.

OPENING EXERCISES

1. Generational Expectations

I'd like you to quickly brainstorm a list of what was expected of dads of your father's generation in order to be considered a 'good dad'. Next, brainstorm a list of the expectations you feel are placed upon you by these various sources. Finally take a few minutes to compare the lists. Notice any patterns? In what ways are things better today? In which ways are things harder? Keep these thoughts in mind as you read future chapters.

Expectations of	Our Dads' Generation	Our Generation
Spouse		
Employer/Boss		
Kids		
Society		
Extended Family		
Other:		

2. Start Gathering Your 'Informal Dad Support Network'

Remember- you are not alone! Your fellow dads can be sources of both emotional and tangible support for your work-family challenges. I encourage you to talk to other dads. I bet you'll find that you are indeed not alone, and that by sharing common experiences, you will figure out ways to be more successful in balancing work and family. As a start, please brainstorm a list of 3-5 fellow dads who face a similar work-family situation. These could be your brothers, cousins, neighbors, friends or some guys you've seen at your daughter's soccer field but haven't yet talked to.

Potential Dads for my 'Informal Dad Support Network'

Extra Credit- If you're feeling motivated, here are a few questions you can use to begin conversations with your fellow dads:

1. Tell me about a time you really struggled with work-family balance.

2. Tell me about a time you felt you were successful in balancing work and family.

3. In a perfect world, how would you want to allocate your time and mental energy between work and family? What gets in the way of doing this?

4. How many people do you have that you can talk to about fatherhood issues? (Finally, tell them they now have one more!)

PART 1

———

Setting Work and Family Priorities

In his classic book, *The Seven Habits of Highly Successful People*, Steven Covey tells a great story about identifying and setting priorities. You've probably heard some version of this before, so I'll quickly summarize.

A teacher stood in front of a class with a large glass jar. He took a dozen fist-sized rocks and placed them in the jar, pretty much filling it to the top. He asked the class if the jar was full. Some said yes, some said no. He then pulled out a container of sand, and poured a surprisingly large amount of it into the jar. Now, the jar was full.

But what if the teacher filled the jar in the reverse order- sand first, then rocks? Several rocks wouldn't fit and would be left out.

No doubt, you already figured out that the lesson here is not about jars, rocks or sand. It is about priorities. If we can identify and then arrange for our most important priorities, we will have room and time to address them, and may even have the capacity for more. But if we fill up our days with less important concerns, we won't have the time for many of our top priorities.

That's what this section is about- figuring out the sizes and shapes of our big rocks, and making sure we understand what is a rock and what is merely sand.

In this section, we will start by examining our 'Big Picture' priorities in three of the biggest areas of our lives: Family, Career and Money. By critically examining what we want out of life in these three areas, we can then consider where we are relative to where we want to be. Of course, there are trade-offs throughout, and there is no single right answer – especially since priorities can and should change over time.

Once we have a handle on the 'Big Picture,' we can start developing plans and setting goals in each of the areas of our lives.

Ready! Grab your glass jars and turn the page.

CHAPTER 1

———

Identifying Your Work and Family Priorities

I've got a job I don't hate, and I might even like. But it isn't my dream job. Not by a long shot. But I make enough money to support my family on a single income, which is important to me and my wife. We're very lucky and I'm very grateful. The way I look at it, the thing I love most is being a husband and a father. If I have to take a second choice job that doesn't completely light up my days, but allows me to support my family, video tape dance recitals, coach little league, and get home in time for dinner every night — in other words, to be a husband and a father — then I'm lucky. I'll suck it up. It's a means to an end. I'll deal with work stuff and not be completely in love with my job, if it means I get to do something better.

• • • • • • • • • • • • • • • • • • • •

I own my own business and this takes me on the road a lot – sometimes for weeks at a time. When my son was little, he and my wife would come along, and we'd have great family travel adventures. I always swore I'd get off the road after he was in school and in travel basketball, but it is hard to turn down work when the family depends on me- plus I love my job. But now, I fear I'm really missing out. I always wanted to coach basketball, but I make, at best, 1/3 of the games as it is. I know my wife has sacrificed more of her career than we initially bargained for, and this is putting a strain on our relationship. When I'm around, I'm a loving dad, but I think my son feels my absence.

I know things are off, but can't quite figure out how to make a change.

I was on a radio show two years ago, and the host asked me why men today were more interested in work-family balance. I was a little off my game, so I started with the old cliché, "Well, I guess guys are realizing that, on their death bed, no one says they wished they spent more time at work ..."

The host excitedly jumped in and told me that, in fact, his very successful workaholic father, in the hospice at the end of his life, cried with regret that too many times, he chose work over family. He added that his father's expression of regret caused him to think about how he was allocating his time. As a result, he reprioritized family, changed careers and ended up on the radio. I guess even clichés can hold powerful truths.

We continued our on-air discussion and I expressed my hope that more busy men who feel pulled between being good providers and involved dads can figure out what they want out of life, and then allocate their time in better accordance with their priorities. Of course, finances and other considerations constrain, and may even dictate, our choices, but by being clear about priorities, over time, we can work our way to achieving our definitions of success at work and at home. I hope we can begin this process right now. Let's start with a success story.

■ My Brother-in-Law

My brother-in-law, Mike, did everything differently than I did. Yet, Mike is one of the best dads I know.

He and my sister Donna have been successful spouses and co-parents because they share the same values, support each other, figured out their work and family priorities, and, even more importantly, they live their priorities. To use our running analogy, they know their rocks from their sand.

Mike was always an exceedingly hard-working, ambitious guy. If you spent two minutes with the 19-year old Mike whom I first met when he started dating my sister, you'd come away knowing that he was going places (He also bailed me out of a jam or two during my teenage rebellion years, so he's always been aces in my book!). He and my sister share more traditional values. It was important for them that their kids had a full-time parent at home, and that she would be that parent.

Once my nephew was born, my sister put her career as a medical technologist on hold (once the kids were older, Donna got re-certified and jumped back in). Mike pursued a career path which required travel, stress and intense time demands. He frequently changed jobs and employers, seeking better opportunities. He worked his way to a position of status, responsibility and earning power, just as he always wanted – both to fulfill his professional aspirations and to provide a comfortable life for his family. He has provided a beautiful home, two college tuitions, and a life of financial security. No small task.

For several years, he took an early morning flight each Monday from Newark airport to his client and then flew back home on the Thursday red-eye. The Continental flight attendants all knew him by name and the VIP club started making his drink as soon as he walked in. As a side perk, he accumulated so many miles that their family can splurge on a big vacation every year, pretty much paid for with frequent flier miles! Mike explains:

> When I took the job that required me to travel, we discussed what it would mean and how we would handle everything. In some ways, it wasn't that different as my job at the time already had me home quite late most nights.

Donna and I also agreed how we would handle the distance. We committed to daily phone calls with the kids that we had all the way through high school. In fact, we set up a private phone line just for me and the family. Like the Bat-phone, when it rang, I would drop everything else, no matter what I was doing at work or where I was, to take the call.

When traveling, I held my commitments even though, on a few occasions, it meant being in California on Monday and Tuesday, back in New Jersey with the family on Wednesday, and then back in California on Thursday and Friday.

During those red-eye years, you could excuse Mike if he simply crashed out on his days at home, or if he obsessively checked in to work during downtime. But that's not Mike; he has always been, first and foremost, a family man. He comes from a large and very close-knit Italian-American family. He hardly ever missed a family milestone, was at nearly every school event, and was even an assistant coach for his son's travel hockey team. More than many busy dads I know, Mike was present for his family – and when he couldn't be physically present, he made sure his family felt his presence (More on this in Chapter 10).

But, as with any choice of priorities, there are tradeoffs and drawbacks. Mike's career involves long hours and lots of travel. While he was always vigilant to avoid missing out on family time and major events, he couldn't help but miss out on some of the everyday joys of parenting, including at least four family dinners per week during the red-eye years. The demands of Mike's career meant that Donna had to put aside her career path. So much of the hard work of raising two kids fell to my sister.

The fact that their family relied on his sole income for many years meant that Mike probably felt intense pressure for the financial well-being of his family, and they had less of a fallback plan if he were to be unexpectedly laid off. I'm sure there were nights when Mike was in his hotel room exhausted and frustrated he couldn't be with his family, while at the same time my sister was exhausted and frustrated after a hard day caring for two toddlers.

This traditional breadwinner/caretaker arrangement worked well for Mike and Donna because it fit their priorities and Mike's income is sufficient for the family's needs. As a result, my niece and nephew are pretty amazing young adults – hardworking, respectful, with their heads on straight and chock full of promise. Twenty-plus years later, Donna and Mike are as solid as any married couple I know.

Their story is also instructive for us. Specifically, it shows us how important it is to understand your orientation towards career and to family in light of the financial and other trade-offs involved, as well as the importance of being on the same page as your spouse.

▌ Career and Family Identity

Academics who conduct research in work and family often measure how central career and family are to people's personal identities, priorities and senses of self-worth. High scores on career identity do not necessarily mean low scores on family identity, and vice-versa. One can be high (or low) in both.

If I were to assess Mike's career and family centrality, for example, he would end up high on both scales. He might rate 10 out of 10 on career identity and 10 out of 10 on family identity. As described in his story, both career and family are essential to Mike's sense of self.

In contrast, the dad whose quote opened this chapter would receive different scores. His career identity could be something like 5 out of 10, while his family identity is 10. For him, work is a means to allow him to live out his priorities as a present husband

and father and to provide for his family in such a way that his wife can be home with the children. He found a way to live according to his priorities, seems happy with his choice, and seems to understand the trade-offs involved.

Career identity only tells us part of the story. Alost every dad I know would respond that fatherhood is central to their identity and rate it somewhere close to a ten. This makes the follow-up question really important. The next thing researchers ask is how much time and effort they spend on their careers and their family roles. Sometimes, dads are consistent, and they spend their time very much in line with their priorities. Opening-quote-dad is a good illustration; he would choose family time over career trajectory every day and twice on Sundays. Put another way:

	Work Priorities	Work Actions	Family Priorities	Family Actions
Quote 1 Dad	5	5	10	10

It is also instructive to note that it is extremely hard for anyone to score a 10 on both their work and family actions. In fact, a 15 is the maximum that most people have the time and energy to attain. This illustrates just how hard it is to "have it all" with work and family. Very often, something has to give – we need to adjust our priorities or build in support systems to help us make up for a deficit.

A dad like Mike, who strongly prioritizes both work and family, has a tougher path towards living his priorities. After all, there are only so many hours in a day. Please don't look at his small discrepancy between family priorities and actions as a criticism. Instead, think of Mike as an Olympic athlete attempting a gymnastics routine of the highest difficulty level.

	Work Priorities	Work Actions	Family Priorities	Family Actions
Mike	10	10	10	8.5

I think he's pretty amazing – almost none of us have the energy or dedication to score 18.5 when adding up our work and family actions. Among dads with high-powered careers, he's among the best I've seen at walking the talk on his family priorities. Plus, he and my sister smartly arranged things so that she can cover for him at home during his long days of business travel. Well done.

Finally, let's take a look at the dad from the second quote at the top of the chapter:

	Work Priorities	Work Actions	Family Priorities	Family Actions
Quote 2 Dad	10	10	10	5

This dad is struggling to live his priorities. He aspires to be a present father and husband, but he can't quite figure out how to make choices fully in line with that priority. He has not made peace with the financial and career-identity tradeoffs involved. This is why he feels unfulfilled and believes his family is not as happy as they could be. But his scores give him guidance on what he could change. Like Mike, he could increase his hustle, improving his family actions score, or, also like Mike, he could work with his spouse to ensure the family gets what it needs. Alternately, he could lower his work priorities, opening up more time for family.

For all of us, living closer to priorities means understanding and accepting trade-offs. Running a thriving business, or aspiring to top positions like law partner or C-level executive, usually means substantially less family time and requires your spouse to sacrifice her career aspirations. Conversely, being more present at home usually entails a lowered career trajectory and less income. This may require both parents to work, paying for child care, student loan debt for your kids, and missing out on some finer things in life. Either way, these may be difficult trade-offs for you and your spouse. It is vitally important that you talk through the implications of your choices. In the exercises at the end of the chapter, I'll encourage you to analyze your work and family priorities, and what actions you can take to act in closer accordance with them.

As I was hitting the job market while finishing up my dissertation, I was faced with an unbelievably clear career/lifestyle choice between academia and high-stakes management consulting. My friends who chose consulting and corporate paths out of college and grad school probably out-earn me 4 to 1 (unless this book becomes a best-seller!). But I feel I made the right choice for me. I earn enough money for my family to be secure, but my work is very fulfilling, has reasonable demands and has allowed me to be a very present father. Even within academia, I am happy being a professor at my really good, but non-brand-name university. More ambitious academics often relocate multiple times to work in more high-profile positions at more prestigious universities, or climb up the career ladder to Dean and beyond. I made my choices based on my family vs. career orientation and haven't regretted it, even if I can't quite go to a class reunion in the same style as some of my fellow alumni.

	Work Priorities	Work Actions	Family Priorities	Family Actions
Me	7	6.5	10	9.5 There's always room for improvement!

Whatever your career and family orientation, there are upsides and downsides. The only wrong choice is to choose against your priorities and values.

▉ Different Family Structures

One of the most important decisions we can make to achieve balance between our priorities and actions is how we structure our families. Some, like Donna and Mike, as well as opening quote dad and his spouse, illustrate the advantages and disadvantages of a "traditional" sole income approach. My family illustrates the pros and cons of a dual-earner, shared care model.

The "Traditional" Approach - On the upside, this structure allows one parent to be "all in" for their career, which is usually required for the highest levels of financial and career success. This arrangement also means that children are cared for in the home by a parent, as opposed to being brought to day-care and put in the hands of relative strangers.

In many dual-career families, one spouse (almost always the wife, but increasingly the husband) opts out of the workforce for a few years until the kids are off to school, creating a temporary "traditional" arrangement. If this is what both parents want, then this is the best arrangement. However, I've witnessed strained marriages when the at-home spouse is not *really* on board with staying home.[4] To make matters worse, the breadwinner will often miss out on precious family time. (That sounds a lot like second-quote-dad and his family).

Sole providers also often feel intense financial pressure, and may have less latitude to change employment. In some ways, they are more dependent on their jobs and their employers because there is no fallback income in case of layoffs or other contingencies. As a result, many sole providers feel they must and stick it out through soul-sucking jobs, idiot bosses, and being passed over for earned promotions – all in order to keep the family's health insurance and make rent. Maybe he has a great idea for a new business or just needs a few months retraining for a dream career, but can't extricate himself from his job because of his financial responsibilities. Meanwhile, his spouse feels cooped up and overwhelmed while raising the children, watching Team Umizoomi over and over and over, and often feeling cut off from the world of clean clothes and adult conversations.

As a result, marriages in which there is a sole breadwinner get divorced at a rate 14 percent higher than that of dual-earner couples. This is likely due to the fact that these "traditional" family structures are more likely to have lower income, more financial stressors, a more stressed-out provider, and a home-maker who may be frustrated by her restricted role.

Finally, I've been putting the word "traditional" in bunny quotes for a reason. Despite the fact that less than one in four households has a sole provider dad with an at-home wife, this is still what many of us think of as a "traditional family structure." Nostalgia for "Happy Days" can be pretty persistent. Still, this family arrangement can be great – if it fits with the values of those involved and works within financial constraints.

Dual-Earner/Shared Care Families - The 2013 Pew Survey shows that, in 85 percent of two-parent households, both parents work. For the majority of us, a different arrangement is either preferred or necessary.

> Overall, we have a pretty healthy work-family situation. Both my wife and I work but we're both involved parents. She actually has the more demanding career and I know this takes a toll on her. There's lots of pressure to be "supermom," and she's sometimes anxious about having

enough family time. But she makes up for this in so many ways. I have more flexibility in my job, so I do most of the pickups and shuttling the kids to activities. Overall, our workload is never 50/50, but we work well together. Our girls feel close to both of us. It's not easy, but the juggle can sometimes work.

When Amy and I got engaged, my well-meaning-but-from-a-different-generation relatives all met her for the first time. Several asked Amy, "Are you still going to be an actress now that you're getting married?" At first, this question puzzled Amy. She smiled and responded with grace and humor that "Yes, and Scott is still going to be a professor." To us, of course our lives as a married couple and future parents would include both of our careers. To our older, more traditional relatives, of course Amy's career would be secondary to mine, and to future motherhood.

Part of the reason Amy and I have been a successful married couple/co-parents is that we fully discussed and are on the same page about how our lives together would include commitments to our family and each other's careers.

My career as a college professor, while demanding, allows for flexibility in terms of where and when work gets done, and my supervisors have been very supportive of my need for flexibility. This has allowed me to better accommodate Amy's career; if I had a different job and a less-enlightened employer, our lives would be much harder.

The importance of getting on the same page was especially true when we had Nick. Amy emphasized that, after the baby, she was not going to interrupt her career for long. She was back on stage four months after Nick was born, and in the years since, her already successful career has taken off with Broadway shows, a long-running off-Broadway hit, some high profile short-term work, and even a few small TV gigs. As Nick has gotten older, she's been able to take some short-term out-of-town work, but she only takes these jobs if, after we talk it over, she's convinced it works for the family. Amy has turned down some good job offers because they did not fit with my work constraints or Nick's need to be with his Mom.

On a more day-to-day basis, when Amy's called for an audition, it is often scheduled for *tomorrow* and it cannot be rescheduled to fit her preferences. When she's rehearsing, it's usually 10-6, six days a week, plus a driving commute to/from NYC. When she's in a long-running show, she works at night and on weekends. In general, entertainers work when others don't, and the world is not set up to help parents with non-traditional work hours.

Because of Amy's career commitments, there were times in which I did most of the day-to-day parenting. Sometimes it was hard, but, looking back, my stretches of being the primary parent gave me an amazing opportunity to bond with Nick in a way that many dads' work schedules may not allow for. Amy holds the fort when I have work commitments. Between her gigs, I have been able to devote huge chunks of time and energy to my career, and she takes over the majority of work at home. In fact, this book would not exist if she didn't have my back these past several months.

Because Amy and I worked to get on the same page about our priorities, we are able to strike an ever-changing but workable balance. However, it is almost certainly true that, had either Amy or I gone "all in" for our career, that person would have probably advanced further – but at the cost of the other's career, and on shared family time.

Challenges of Dual-Earner Couples - Dual-earner couples like mine face several challenges. Obviously, when family roles are less clear, there are more opportunities to disagree over what needs to be done and who needs to do it. Many feel torn that their decision to work may entail professional day care, even when kids are quite young. When dads don't pull their weight, working moms are forced into a "second shift" in which they work all day at an employer and then come home having to still do most of the work of the family – an enormous predictor of divorce.

The biggest problem facing shared-care parents is, unfortunately, the workplace. Getting ahead often requires jobs that mean long hours, travel, and "on call" expectations. Without a spouse taking care of the kids, shuttling them to band practice, preparing meals and cleaning the house, it is exceedingly hard to put in long uninterrupted hours at work. Further, odd, haphazard, or shifting schedules, last minute-work demands, or even a school snow day can torpedo even the most carefully constructed family schedules, leaving us scrambling for child-care. As a result, it often seems like we are constantly on the go, shuttling out kids back and forth, eating on the run, and never seeming to slow down.

I've often mused that a fantastic, yet unrealistic, solution would entail each parent having two-thirds of a job – I think most families could make this arrangement work. However, if anything, most of us are in jobs that require more than 100 percent of "9 to 5" work hours. Juggling upwardly mobile careers with all the work that still needs to be done for a thriving family sometimes seems impossible. Flexible work and understanding employers are critical for managing dual careers. (We'll discuss the underlying workplace dynamics in Part 2 of the book).

All that said, if you can work your way through the difficulties, shared-care parenting can be very rewarding. Even when Nick was a baby, Amy didn't feel the need to hover over me, and has never made me feel like anything but an equal parent. Our ability to share the load has served us well as Nick has gotten older. Now, if Amy has to work late or I have to travel to a conference, we don't worry if Nick will be ok. We know that the other has it totally covered, and Nick does too.

There are other emotional and material benefits to a dual-earner shared care arrangement. It is likely that, if both spouses work at least some outside the home, they have more common experiences, have more to talk about, and can better relate to each other's problems and emotions (as opposed to *"my wife doesn't understand the pressure I'm under and my need to relax some when I get home"* and *"my husband doesn't recognize all the work I do all day and that I need a break when he gets home."*)

This second job doesn't have to be equally lucrative or demanding to bring these benefits. A 20-hour a week part-time job brings extra income and psychic benefits to both partners. In fact, balancing one high-income, demanding career job, with a second job that is more family- and lifestyle-friendly, seems to be the best match, especially if the secondary income has health insurance. (Perhaps this is the closest we'll get to my idealized notion of a two-thirds job!) In fact, research shows that couples who have a roughly 62/38 split on income, and roughly the opposite proportion of housework/child care, exhibit divorce rates 51 percent lower than other types of financial arrangements.

Relieving Financial Pressure - Remember the intense financial pressures sole providers face? In a dual-earner households, the secondary income means that dads are freer to change jobs and careers, weather layoffs, or even start businesses. Most dads in my social circle are in dual-career families. I've seen the benefits of two incomes play out in several of their lives:

- One left his OK job and went into business for himself, thanks to the fact that his wife is a state employee with a good enough income and great family benefits that allowed him to make the leap.

- One was able to leave his job and enter a training program in a different field, and now he is working at a job he loves (and with higher income upside potential), because his wife is a federal employee with great benefits.
- One was unexpectedly laid off. He found work relatively quickly, but having the financial buffer of his wife's career meant they stayed afloat.
- One became a stay-at-home-dad and started a home-based business after their daughter was born. His wife had the more stable job/income, allowing this to happen.
- One was able to leave a pressurized full-time job for a dream 18-month consulting opportunity because his wife took a job with benefits.

From where I sit (and you never really know about people's marriages from the outside), these families seem happier than they did before the career switches. In many ways, happier people make better, more involved parents, and everyone, especially the kids, gain from this.

So, Mike and I took very different paths to balancing work and family. Fundamentally, however, we actually did the exact same thing – followed our priorities, chose arrangements that fit both our and our wives' values, and worked hard to stay on the same page. Our rocks were different, but we were both able to locate them.

Divorced Families - Finally, not every family is intact, and getting and staying on the same page with your ex-spouse can be really difficult. However, over time, if you and your ex have the same priorities, a lot of the time, and through many of the same kinds of conversations, you can find a way to make it work.

> My ex-wife and I are becoming really great co-parents. We've seen it through the worst and most warlike of times, but now that the animosity has faded, we now

keep everything productive and amicable- and focused on what is best for our son.

Our son lives with her, but I live right around the corner and I'm with him almost every day. We both acknowledge that we are both really good parents and we want our son to have both of us truly present in his life. We found our way through the worst to get to this point, so, no matter how awful divorces can be, it is possible to get to a better place.

Ultimately, when we consciously think about our actions and how we spend our time, we tend to make decisions that are consistent with our priorities. When we set our life to auto-pilot, we drift from our priorities and towards whatever happens to be most urgent at the moment. The need for periodic reconsideration is especially important as family situations can constantly change. I hope this chapter helps you be more intentional about your priorities.

In the exercises at the end of this chapter, I'll try to help you separate the rocks from the sand for the "big picture issues" of work and family. In the next chapter, we'll look at our finances. In chapter 3, we'll discuss the importance of breaking down work and family priorities into a set of shorter-term goals.

Chapter 1 Exercises

1. Articulating Priorities

First, place a number between 1 and 10 to indicate the degree to which work and family are central to your identity. Then, rate the time and energy you put into work and family on the same 10 point scale.

Work Priorities	Work Actions	Family Priorities	Family Actions

Looking at your results should lead to the following questions;
- Where are your actions consistent with your priorities?
- Where are you not aligned?
- How can you get back to the balance you want?

Further, this is a good opportunity to reassess priorities. Take some time to think about your over-arching priorities for work and family, and how these priorities inform the choices you can make in your life. After some reflection, here are mine:
- Being a present husband and father is my first priority. As long as we can still afford the basics, family time comes first
- Amy's career is as important as mine
- I want a career in which I can pursue a variety of interests, have control over my schedule, and feel like I'm having an impact. I'll make a financial trade-off to do so

- Provide for my family to the level to which we are secure and comfortable, but I do not need to be rich, and am not prepared to make the sacrifices need to do so

Now, please take some time on your own to consider these issues. When you are ready, write them down here. Please remember to look at this list a few times a year, to see if anything needs to be reassessed and as a reminder to make choices that are aligned with your priorities.

Priorities:

2. Detailed Work and Family Analysis

Relatedly, we should take time to identify what helps bring us closer to the work-family balance we want, what gets in the way of achieving that balance, and what can be reasonably changed to help make the situation better.

By reasonable, I mean what things could realistically change. So, please no wish-casting. Yes, winning a big lottery would solve a lot of problems, but how realistic is that? Similarly, your wife agreeing to quit work and staying home with the kids may help you feel less conflicted about your frequent business travel. However, if her career is important to her and it is unlikely she would ever agree to do quit, don't list it.

On the other hand, if we think flexibly, I bet we could come up with a lot of realistic changes we can make, even in the short term, that would help get us closer to a workable balance. For example, maybe negotiating for a one-day-per-week work-from-home arrangement would really help. Maybe throwing money at the problem and hiring a two-times-a-month lawn service or house cleaning service would free up time for family while helping you and your wife avoid tasks you dislike (and fight about).

Finally, under each category is space for a long-term fix that would make life easier, but would require significant forethought and planning, and may even prove disruptive in the short-to-medium term. Things to include in this category are changing employers or career paths, moving to an area closer to extended family who could help you out with childcare, or significant financial simplification. For example:

> I had what most people would call a great job- I made a great living and got to work and interesting, cutting-edge projects. But, the hours were just killer, and even after 5 years, I finally had it, as I knew I wasn't spending enough time with my girls or living the life I wanted.
>
> So, my wife and I sat down and we came up with a two-year plan to manage our finances and build up our rolodexes, so that we could, a few years down the road, start up our family business. Years later, we're so glad we did, even if the two years were financially difficult. We're living a lifestyle we want and have never looked back to my days in the corporate world.

Obviously, for long-term fixes, you would need to discuss these with the important people in your life and decide whether such disruptive changes are worth it. But, at this point, it is helpful to explore all possibilities. You can probably start right away with some of the short-term fixes.

As an example, I'll give my answers and some commentary about my choices. Then, there is a blank assessment form for you, and additional blank forms can be found at http://WorkingDadsSurvivalGuide.com, so you can regularly re-assess your priorities and goals.

Category- Work	
Gets Me Closer to Balance	Gets in the Way of Balance
Flexible work. Can do ½ of work from home or other places Supervisor tries to accommodate my schedule requests Freedom to choose projects	Lack of structure sometimes means I work in "boom or bust" cycles I juggle many work, family and side-projects
Short-Term Fixes	Long-Term Fixes
Be more disciplined in managing my time, creating more differentiation between work and personal time Set up no-smartphone time each day	Developing online classes would open up more work from home, freeing up time for family and side-projects Create criteria for selecting among available projects, so saying 'yes' or 'no' to opportunities is easier

To-Do List (things I can start doing this week)

1. Use iPhone calendar function to schedule work hours during days/times Nick is in school or at activities, creating more structure.

2. Buy a good six-pack of beer. Reward myself with a bottle or two on Friday- only if I adhere to weekly work hours

3. Stop carrying phone around with me in the house- Leave my phone next to the key bowl in the entryway. This way, I'll be less tempted by it

4. In next two weeks, set up a meeting with department chair about possibly shifting one or more of my classes into an "blended"(part in class, part online) format

Category- Family	
Gets Me Closer to Balance	Gets in the Way of Balance
• Amy is understanding and supportive of my career • We are financially ok • Just one kid, who is now in school, plus everyone is healthy • Have a good set of neighbors and friends who can help with watching Nick	• Her career has weird hours and she is often "on call"- I need to flex around her • In-laws and other family live 2-4 hours away • Nick's gymnastics getting to be a bigger time commitment- Little league, school plays and computer classes mean his schedule is becoming a big juggle • Lack of child-care options on evenings and weekends or those with odd schedules
Short-Term Fixes	Longer-Term Fixes
• Establish family calendar to better coordinate with Amy's work and Nick's activities • Talk with Nick about prioritizing activities when baseball season begins and may conflict with gymnastics	• See work fixes

To-Do List (things I can start doing this week)

1. Sync iPhone calendars with Amy so planning around each other becomes easier

2. Ask parents at Nick's activities about carpooling

3. Schedule a visit from my mom

Now it's your turn. What aspects help you in balancing work and family? What do you struggle with? How can you get started improving your situation?

Category- Work	
Gets Me Closer to Balance	Gets in the Way of Balance
Short-Term Fixes	Long-Term Fixes

To-Do List (things I can start doing this week)

Category- Work	
Gets Me Closer to Balance	Gets in the Way of Balance
Short-Term Fixes	Long-Term Fixes

To-Do List (things I can start doing this week)

CHAPTER 2

———

Financial Prioritization

I went from having a house, cars, a Jacuzzi – To buying oatmeal in bulk and eating just that three times a day. After being laid off and getting divorced, it almost wiped me out. Fast-forward a few years, and I have a great job making more money than I ever did before. My priorities are my special-needs-son's education and medical bills, and everything else comes after. I still treat myself from time to time, but I'm smarter about it. I've been poor, like, really poor. I realize that material items aren't the things that bring happiness.

· ·

I really don't care if I get to buy a fancy new car or live in a super deluxe house. What I do care about is having time to play with my kids, spending a relaxing evening with my wife, and enjoying a good book. Yet everything is a balancing act — would I be as content if I worked in a job that paid me half as much? Not likely. Finding that "sweet spot" is challenging and probably unique to each person. Ultimately, it's a question of priorities.

Poet David Whyte wrote a great book, *The Heart Aroused: Poetry and the Preservation of the Soul in Corporate America*, aimed at helping people find meaning and balance in their careers (and here I thought poets just lived in their mom's basements while pulling a few shifts at a hipster coffee shop). There is a one-line poem in his book that, 18 years ago, led me to reassess my professional goals:

Ten years ago, I turned my head for a moment and it became my life.

Today, this poem makes me think about our roles as fathers and providers, and the needs of those who depend on us- not what they want, but what they need. Here's my stab at a priority list:

1. Baseline providing- e.g., food, a decent house/apartment, safe neighborhood, schools, basic stuff, basic fun stuff, too

2. Time with you

3. Better stuff- e.g., fancier clothes, new toys, video games, new bike

4. Extra stuff for you- e.g., new cars, a big house, fancy vacations

How much of No. 2 do we sacrifice for No. 3 and No. 4, without even realizing it? I contend that, when we pursue priorities 3 and 4, we sometimes fail to think through the opportunity costs – the economic concept that basically means that the time, money or other resources you spend on one goal can no longer be used to pursue another goal. If we thought about this more, many of us might reconsider how we spend our time.

Another great book, *Why Men Earn More* by Warren Farrell, looks at factors that cause certain careers, industries and jobs to pay more than others. Farrell explains that, among other things, jobs that require or strongly encourage extensive travel, long commutes, long work weeks, bringing work and/or performance-related stress home, and being on call when away from the office earn significantly more than jobs that are more stable, have more regular and reasonable hours, and do not make such time-based or psychological demands.

In contrast, jobs with lower earning potential may not make us "richer" financially, but often have other non-financial benefits – more satisfying work, better work-life balance, less stress and more free time. In short, jobs that give us lots of 2 usually represent a tradeoff on priorities 3 and 4, and jobs that provide us the means to pursue 3 and 4 usually represent a tradeoff on priority 2.

If you have a demanding career, it is extremely hard to scale back or downshift without jeopardizing all you've worked and sacrificed for. Partner tracks and corporate ladders are not exactly forgiving if you try to revise the deal. Big-time income also often means financial commitments to such expenditures as private schools or jumbo mortgages on houses requiring upkeep and landscaping. It is seductively easy to get stuck on auto-pilot and continue on a fast track, even if it is no longer what is best for us or our families.

There is nothing wrong with working hard and earning a lucrative paycheck. I'm not saying we shouldn't have nice things if we can afford to. After all, providing our children the financial resources to make their lives easier is part of our very important fatherly role.

What I am suggesting is that we first think through the tradeoffs involved, and then choose what's best for us and for our families. And if we do that, I think more of us may realize that priority 2 should come before priorities 3 and 4. As much as our families appreciate having really nice things, they need YOU far more.

I hope that none of my friends and readers look back and say, "Ten years ago I turned my head for a moment and it became my life".

In this chapter, we'll cover the last of the "Big 3 Priorities" – our finances. First, let me be clear that I am not a financial planner[5]. There's no investment advice in this book. As a business school professor and a fellow busy dad, however, I can share some general perspectives that can help us think through our priorities. In this way, we can better determine whether our financial commitments are enabling or getting in the way of our career and family goals.

Finances and Freedom

My over-arching philosophy when it comes to finances, work and family, is that the key to success is **the freedom to act in accordance with our priorities**. Pursuing career goals, family goals or both require freedom of choice of how to spend your time and money. We have to be careful with our financial commitments because they can, subtly and over time, restrict this freedom. Sometimes, this is inevitable and necessary – many of us feel that paying college tuition for our kids is a moral obligation, so that financial commitment is a priority. But this large obligation constrains you in other ways.

> Between tuition at my kids' school and my student loans from law school, we don't have much discretionary income. But it's really important to us and our values that our kids go to Catholic school, and, to us, that's worth the sacrifices.

Unlike tuition, other obligations are not quite so, well, obligatory. Leasing a brand new car, instead of buying a gently used one and keeping it for eight years represents a questionably necessary financial obligation. Are you sacrificing family time to be sure to earn a big end-of-year bonus to get ahead on car payments? If you are, perhaps you are working for your possessions instead of having them work for you. Now, of course, if you are fortunate enough to be able to comfortably afford a luxury item like that car, then go for it man. Cars are awesome. But if the car payment is causing you stress and dictating how you allocate your time, it is time to rethink your choices.

Bad Advice

For most of us, our biggest financial commitment is our house. When we sign 8,000 pieces of paper, cut far too many checks, and then finally shake hands and get the keys, we've signed ourselves up for 30 years of significant monthly payments, plus property taxes and upkeep expenses. Even though a house is both a place to live and a financial investment, if the past 10 years have taught us anything, this investment is far from a sure thing.

The financial gurus suggest we buy as much house as we can afford, because they assume our incomes will continue to rise while our house payments stay constant. I think that's really bad advice. This dad also agrees:

> It is easy to get caught up in keeping up with the Joneses and living for your Jumbo mortgage. Unless we own our homes outright, we are probably sitting on at least a 3:1 levered position. Any blip in the housing market may wipe away our down payment and leave us on a pile of debt... This makes the corporate trap even the more frightening. The need to work every day of your life just to keep up with the housing costs is far from a dream.
>
> The thought of a layoff or a bad performance review are really frightening. What will I do? Where will we go? Do we need to move? Do my kids need to change schools? And then the other questions, What will we tell our friends? How could this happen to us after all our work? Quality of life is fragile when egos are attached to careers.

Following their advice means you sweat out initial house payments and then are reliant on your employer for continued employment and rising salaries – neither of which are assured. Best-case scenario, you have a wonderful house and extremely constrained choices in career and family. Worst case scenario, things don't go according to plan and you sink into debt, putting a strain not only on your other financial commitments but also your mental well-being, and maybe even your marriage.

85 Percent of My Dream House

The best piece of advice I received when Amy and I bought our house was to make a list of what would make up our dream house, and then try to find the "85 percent" house of our dreams. After having grown up in a lovely suburb of Boston, Amy lived in the big cities of Chicago, Los Angeles and Manhattan, and wanted to get back to a beautiful place to live. She fell in love with the Lower Hudson Valley just north of NYC. I'd been a suburban New Yorker my while life and also loved that area.

We settled on the Village of Nyack, NY, which is about a half-hour's drive to my Northern New Jersey campus and a somewhat reasonable commute for Amy to get to Midtown Manhattan. Nyack is also a very walkable town, with several blocks of dense suburban houses around a cute town center full of shops and restaurants, all within a few minutes' walk to a beautiful park on the Hudson River. Exactly the kind of neighborhood we both wanted.

We bought our house before we had Nick, and our dream house would have had four bedrooms – for us and the two children we were planning on, along with room for guests. But four bedroom houses are super-expensive; we settled on three. As it turned out, we only had the one kid, so the fourth bedroom would have been less necessary.

I always wanted a nice back yard for playing Wiffle ball, grilling burgers and making snow angels. Our yard's a bit smaller than I envisioned (the Wiffle ball goes over the fence a lot), but it fits the bill, and its size means I don't need to spend all my spare time mowing, landscaping, raking or shoveling.

I always wanted a fireplace, garage, big Jacuzzi tub and eat-in kitchen, and, well, I still want those. But our house, while smaller than we'd originally envisioned, is nice and we have awesome neighbors. Our basement was unfinished but finishable and once we renovated, we had a great space for Nick and his friends to play; Amy and I have since reclaimed the living room.

The best thing is, while the house and its property taxes are indeed too expensive, they are expenses that fit into the family budget – a budget we set based only on my university salary. Amy's income is inconsistent, depending on the frequency and profile of her yearly gigs. My sidelines also come and go. But, even if Amy's work dried up, or I chose not to pursue very many consulting opportunities, we can make the monthly payments.

In fact, this peace of mind meant that, over time, I no longer picked up summer classes or for the extra money – more time for being a husband and father. I can pick and choose side-projects and focus on the few that feed my soul (like writing this book) or I can work around the time I set aside to coach little league and share lazy family weekends. Similarly, Amy can be more choosey in selecting her roles, sometimes trading off short-term income for roles with higher artistic merit or ones that set her up for long-term career success.

Having more time freedom was especially important during Nick's pre-school years as we didn't want to use more than part-time day care. We were both able to temporarily cut back on work without opting out in order to live closer to our priorities. I don't want to toot my own horn here. I was lucky enough to get and follow good advice. But the fact that Amy and I do not sweat our mortgage payments means that we have more freedom to choose how to allocate our time.

▌Financial Anchors

If you ever heard yourself saying "I need to sacrifice family time to provide for the family" or "I'm stuck at my job because of the bills," it is probably because you are being a responsible working dad, and providing for the family is often job No. 1. However, it is also possible that we have made things harder for ourselves with our large financial commitments.

Maybe instead of working harder and sacrificing family time, you can free up time by examining and reducing these large regular expenses. It's not so easy to sell your house and buy a smaller one, but there are many other ways, large and small, we can free ourselves of financial anchors. The big ones will take time, but the payoffs, both financially and family-wise may well be worth it. Here's what one dad had to say:

> When I was 29, the Dean of my business school heard a business idea I had and told me to quit my job and do it full-time. I thought he was so flippant, "just quit your job and go for it...No big deal". I told him I had bills, I had a mortgage, I had school loans. He just laughed at me. Now I know why he was laughing. It just took me 11 years to figure it out, dig out from under and give myself the financial freedom to pursue that business idea. I'm so glad I did.

Getting out from under our big financial commitments is not easy, and may take years. Planning can start right away. More on this in the exercises at the end of this chapter.

Financial Habits

So far, we've been looking at our big financial commitments – the rocks in the glass jar, using the analogy from earlier in the book. As the rocks are the most important, it was good we started there – but the sand is important, too. It is deceptively easy for our finances to get out of whack because of the smaller stuff.

A few months ago, a financial planner gave a guest lecture to students at my university about the importance of smart financial management right out of college. He talked about his own spending habits when he got his first job. As he drove to work for his first day, he stopped along the way for a Starbucks – after all, he had money now, and he deserved a treat. Later that day, his new colleagues took him out to lunch at a local café. What started as one-off decisions quickly became habits.

Eventually, on his way to work, his brain went on autopilot and so he stopped at Starbucks each morning. He never got into the habit of packing a lunch, so most days he went back to the café with a few coworkers, or even by himself. A few months later, it dawned on him that his paycheck didn't go as far as he'd thought – because he was spending $15 a day due to his unconscious spending habits (quick math: $15/day x 5 days/week x 50 weeks/year = $3,750). This was more than two months' rent!

I'm not saying you should never treat yourself, and I recognize the incredible awesomeness and indispensability of large amounts of morning caffeine. However, making his own coffee and lunch at home four days a week and splashing out for Friday Starbucks would have saved him over $3000 a year. That's enough for a weekend getaway, a gym membership or a host of other purchases that are enjoyable and/or create time for family (more on spending money on family time instead of "stuff" in Chapter 10).

Alternately, he could invest or save that money, and then use the accumulated interest to start his own financial consultancy. In fact, this is what he did. This book is not just about family time, after all. The range of our career choices can be enabled or constrained by everyday financial decisions.

I bet a lot of us, myself definitely included, spend little bits of money unwisely. Like a small drip in a pipe, over time, little things can add up to big problems. I never started smoking, but I often say I was too cheap to start. A half-pack a day at $10 a pack (about what it costs in New York State) equals $1,825 over the course of a year. Plus it makes you smell bad and hurts your health. No, thank you.

I know I spend too much on my cable bill and cellphone plans. There are lots of places to economize. Here are some tips from fellow working dads:

- *Back when I was a poor grad student, one way I saved money was to never order anything but water to drink when at a restaurant- whether it was McDonalds or Chili's (which was the upper end of what I could afford then). Three dollar Cokes and five dollar beers add up.*

- *I have always been -- and will always be, I fear – an idiot when it comes to economizing and saving money. But one really smart thing we've done as a couple, my wife and I, was to set up the my state's prepaid college tuition program for both our kids- a little bit from every paycheck goes into it, before I have the chance to waste the money, like an idiot.*

- *We are constantly on the lookout for good family deals- things like "kids eat free" or free drink refills. Groupon has become a friend, as we often organize entertainment around the very good deals you can find on Groupon.*

- *We just bought a new car, but we drove the last one into the ground over 12 years. The new one will be a 12-year car as well.*

- *Although I often feel cash-poor, I know we are doing the right thing by making almost all our bills get automatically paid out the day after my paycheck gets direct deposited. It reduces the temptation to spend too much.*

- *My son and I are sports nuts, but it's really expensive to go see the Rangers or Mavs. Instead, we go to our minor-league stadium, or better yet our local high school football and basketball games. $5 for me, the kid is free, and $1 sodas and popcorn.*

- *Our family vacations are mostly spent camping. After the one-time cost of a tent, it's like 15 bucks a night for a campsite. You could camp a whole week for the price of one night at a hotel.*

- *I used to buy the latest gadget, phone or game system as soon as it came out. But a used PS3 nine months later is like half the cost. I just had to get over the mental habit of being an early adopter.*

- *Things aren't always cheaper at Costco, but certain things, like dog food, diapers and formula, really are. Also, once we got a second freezer for the basement, we could buy our meat in bulk and really save.*

I bet if we all went through our regular expenses, we could come up with lots of ways, large and small to reduce our expenses to the point where we'll have more freedom to choose what to do with our time. Then, we can pour that time into career, family or other life goals. Money is a tool we should use wisely, or else it starts to control us.

▌ Budgets and Discipline

Pat Katepoo, a financial professional who specializes in helping working parents negotiate for higher pay and greater workplace flexibility, once wrote a guest post for *Fathers, Work and Family*. In it she advises:

> Forging a different path, spending less than you make, takes courage and discipline. But when life's realities take an unexpected shift, you'll have a financial cushion that gives you the flexibility for dealing with them. Whatever the reasons for wanting more control of your time, with prudent budget practices in place, you'll have more liberty to make self-directed decisions about your work-life choices, instead of being forced into them.

The best way to keep track of expenses is to work out a family budget. Most of us HATE doing this (I know I do), but we've got to do what's necessary. After all, we need to know what our current situation is before we can make positive changes.

At my university, we use a two-cycle budgeting process, which I think is really smart. Our first budget is set in August, and is based on projections of the coming academic year's revenue. However, at that point, we still don't know our exact enrollment numbers and financial aid commitments. So, the August budget is always very conservative- not quite a worst-case-scenario, but a bad-case-scenario. This forces our academic units to prioritize our expenses so that we can stay within this conservative budget. Because of this, we are rarely caught with expenses above budget, and the academic units are forced to identify and plan for our rocks first. The sand can be poured in in October.

Then, students officially enroll and classes begin. Our second budget is set in late October, when we have a much better handle on our financial picture. It is almost always better than what was projected in August. Academic units are now allowed to spend money on "nice to have" items – extra marketing, a few more Bloomberg terminals, stipends for travel and special projects, etc.

I think this is also a great model for families. Our family budgets should be based on bad-case-scenarios. Amy and I set our budget on my very reliable university salary. We do not budget for her inconsistent income, or for my side-projects to bear fruit. If this book becomes a best-seller, we'll have more money, but the mortgage and Nick's gymnastics lessons don't depend on it. (But please tell your friends how much you like this book!)

My situation's a bit unique, but we can all probably come up with ways to do bad-case-scenario planning. What if your annual bonus is cut in half? What if a financial downturn means $20,000 less in sales commission? What if a third of your regular freelance gigs dry up? What if your new venture only breaks even instead of generating income?

If you can see your way to making all your regular expenses fit into your bad-case-scenario income, you have now opened up lots of freedom. By reducing the size of your rocks (large expenses and necessities), you now have more room to pour lots of sand into your jar. You will now probably have the money for a nice vacation or to splurge out on a backyard swing-set or whatever other extras would bring more joy and family togetherness into your life. You may now have extra money to put aside for a new business, career re-training, or to invest in an IRA or 529 college savings plan.

Lots of my MBA students tell me they had to economize a few years to save up to enroll in our program. An MBA degree accelerates careers and earning potential, but it is expensive both in terms of time and money. Gotta budget for these career investments.

Financial freedom also insulates you from unpredictable events. God forbid, what would happen is someone got terribly sick? At least you have more slack in your budget for medical expenses. What if woodpeckers nested in your house's wooden shingles, requiring a $15,000 repair? (no, really – this happened to a friend of mine.) Or if you unexpectedly need new gutters or a new hot water heater? Stuff like this is aggravating, but at least you'd have some financial slack to deal with them.

If your regular income and regular expenses simply equal each other out, your finances can be compared to a rope already pulled taut. With no slack, the rope has no more capacity to be stretched further without fraying. But if we do 85 percent budgeting, we have more slack in our finances to accommodate unexpected expenses.

▍Talk it Through

Depending on your situation, you may want to speak with a professional. Beyond that, since it is a family budget, you have to include others. If you are married, you need to enroll at least your spouse, and maybe your kids (if they are old enough) or other relatives into your conversations. If you are divorced and share custody of your children, your ex-wife need to be consulted – and I know this may not be a pleasant experience.

This complicates matters, because we all have different orientations towards money. Some people are risk-takers and others are financially conservative. Some may want to spend surplus money right now, others may want to save for a retirement that could be 40 years away. And, of course, even in the best of circumstances, discussing finances is never easy.

But, you and your spouse are partners, and your family is a team. Ultimately, we need to push through these difficult conversations, listen and adjust to others' needs. If you've already discussed career and family priorities, financial conversations become easier. I know this is hard work, but it is worth it.

> My wife and I talked about my transition from a long-hours, good-paying job with good benefits to going out on a limb and starting my own consultancy. We had many conversations over a period of a few months before I felt fully comfortable to make the plunge. We have some financial cushion, but it is scary. But now I can have a much more family kind of lifestyle, and we can share the load more easily at home.
>
> The fact that my wife and I talked all the implications through – what does this mean for our mortgage, for college savings, for health insurance, for her work? – made the transition so much better. My wife was unbelievably supportive and we really connected in figuring out all the details.

Well done. A fitting end to this chapter.

Wouldn't you like to have significantly more freedom three years from now? The conversation you have tomorrow can be the second step that gets you there. The first could be the exercises on the pages that follow.

Chapter 2 Exercises

1. Big Things

Let's take stock of our major financial commitments by filling out this chart.

Financial Commitment	How much does this cost per month?	How easily does this fit into the monthly budget? (scale of 1 to 5)	How much stress does this cause me? (scale of 1 to 5)	If magically, you no longer had that commitment, how much new-found freedom would you have? (scale of 1 to 5)
Housing				
Car				
Child-Care				
Tuition				
Others:				

Looking down the final column, list what you could do with the extra time that the increased financial freedom would bring you (in terms of career, family, or "me" time). Would you take a yearly family vacation, save up for an MBA, join a gym? Brainstorm here:

1. _____

2. _____

3. _____

4. _____

5. _____

6. _____

7. _____

2. Little Things

Now, let's focus on our smaller, day-to-day purchases and where we can economize. What could we do with that extra money?

Regular or semi-regular smaller expenses	How much does this cost per month?	How could I cut down on this expense?	How much would this save me per month? per year	What could I do with this extra money (including buying time)
Cable				
Cellphone				
Eating Out				
Coffee				
Others:				

3. Bad-Case Scenario Budgeting

Could you get by on only 85 percent of your stable income? If so, you have tons of financial freedom. It can be really hard to get to this point, and the first step is knowing what that number is.

1.   What was your total household income last year?

_____

(If this varies year to year, use an average of the past 3-5 instead)

2.   How much of this yearly income can be totally relied upon (e.g., salary from a very secure job)?

_____

3.   Multiply this number by .85:

_____

4.   How realistic is it to pay for all your big, regular financial commitments (that we identified in Exercise 1) with the number on line 3? What can you do to get there? How can you start?

CHAPTER 3

———

Goals for a Well-Balanced Life

When my son was born, I left my career as a teacher to stay at home and be the primary caregiver. If I was going to give up my career for fatherhood, I determined that I was going to do everything 110% and be the 'best damn dad in the whole world'- change every diaper, be there for every moment, make all his baby food from scratch with organic vegetables from the farmer's market- the whole nine yards. After a while, I realized I had lost myself somewhere along the way. I wasn't me – I was "Danny's Dad." I had lost my former connections and never saw my friends. It was a very isolating experience.

Hands-on fatherhood is awesome, but it is much better since I learned to keep a foot in the larger world. I now have fulfilling part-time work, see friends regularly, take time with my wife and keep up with my hobbies. It took me a while, but I now feel like I have a well-balanced life.

• •

We had our first baby a few months ago, and my wife is staying home, at least for now. I'm a lawyer at a big firm. But I don't want to be "that" dad who leaves his wife to do it all. So, I'm getting up half the time to change diapers and give bottles. I spend my non-work time helping her out. Doing this and working long hours is really hard. Sometimes it feels like I will never sleep again or get to the gym, let alone have a night out or some downtime. Please tell me things get better!

Whether we're carrying the load at home or juggling the demands of career, family and other commitments, it can often feel like we're stuck running on a giant hamster wheel. The two dads quoted above are in very different situations, but they both feel this pressure. Sometimes I feel it, too. It is hard to jump off the hamster wheel, sit in the pile of cedar chips, shove some nuts into our cheeks, and take time to look at the bigger picture. But, in the long run, we'd be better off slowing down and attending not just to work and family, but also to all of the aspects that make up a full life. Life is not a marathon, and it is especially not a series of sprints. It's more like a decathlon with lots of different events leading to an over-arching goal – and each component requires a slightly different skillset. Work and family come first, but we need to pace ourselves and spend some time thinking about how we can be more effective in all aspects of our lives.

▌ A Balanced Diet Approach

So far in this book, I've been making frequent use of the term "work-family balance." A lot of people don't like this term. Some prefer "work-life balance." I don't. After all, work is an important part of life and the two are not opposites or enemies. Also, there's lots in life that is neither work nor family. Others take exception to the term balance, and prefer terms like integration, fit, blend or success.

But I like the word balance, as long as we have the right visual in mind. When some see "work-family balance," they think of balance as in a scale, seesaw, tightrope or balance beam in which there is a single, hard-to-find, precarious equilibrium point between two opposing forces. Thinking about balance that way leads us (and, unfortunately, managers and employers) to think about work and family solely as trade-offs. I think this is the wrong way to think about it.

We need to stop seeing work and family as "either-or." Time for work and time for family are both very important components of a full, meaningful life, and there's more to life, too. If we don't reflexively see them as opposing forces, we may come to understand that both can enhance the other in helping to build a balanced life.

Therefore, when I think about a balanced life, I find it helpful to visualize a "balanced diet" rather than a tightrope. A balanced diet means eating enough of different types of food without eating too much from certain categories. Similarly, a full life means that we must tend to various parts of our lives (family, work, health, relationships, friends, hobbies, exercise, etc.), all of which are important parts of a whole.

Sometimes we need to prioritize one aspect of life over others and temporarily slip out of balance. There are inevitable ebbs and flows in both home and work. Some work weeks require intense hours and/or travel. Some weeks, home requires our full attention. The use of a tightrope metaphor frames temporary imbalance as a failure; anything less than 50/50 means a perilous fall. If, instead, we think about a balanced diet, eating too many carbs one day can be balanced out by extra salad the next. And it also helps us recognize that we need many food groups to be healthy.

My friend and neighbor Joe is an amazing example of a dad who embraces and feeds all the different aspects of his life.

Joe works really hard, and has built a thriving small business. Through this business, he is providing for his family, doing work he loves, and building something to be proud of. Joe is also a great hands-on dad. When I look out my front window, I often see him and his son skateboarding in their driveway. I chat with Joe at the bus stop each morning and see him at lots of school and town events. His wife also has a demanding career, and, from my vantage point, they seem like really supportive partners.

Joe also addresses his needs for social time, flow, and exercise through his love of extreme sports. He's an avid snowboarder and skateboarder, and will go with his adult friends to skate parks to show the kids how it's done. In the winter, he and his family take lots of daytrips to ski in the Adirondacks; in the summer, lots of time at Jones Beach.

Joe is also active in our community. He was one of the leaders of a group that raised the money and developed plans so that our town now has a shiny new skate park. He volunteers to run the lights and sound for town outdoor concerts and events, and is a regular attendee and participant at his church.

And, oh yeah, he is always working on some home improvement project and he and his wife have an awesome vegetable garden (and they give us a nice batch of tomatoes every year).

Whew! I'm exhausted just listing all the things Joe does. I'm not quite sure how he does it, and I know I can't match his energy level. (However, I do know he watches a lot less TV than I do, and wastes less time on Facebook, more on this in Chapter 9) I'm not sure we all can be expected to be quite as active as Joe, but we can learn from his example. Joe shows us that there is, in fact, time to address all the things that make up a well-balanced life.

A well-rounded life isn't just work and family. We need to take care of our financial, health, social, and relaxation needs. For those of us who are religious or spiritual, we must tend to these needs, as well. But these things don't happen unless we set goals and put in the time and effort to address all the different aspects of our lives.

▌ Better Goal-Setting

For the past few years, my New Year's Resolution has been "To get in better shape." Which, like most New Year's resolutions, is a lousy, vague, "do your best"-style goal. No wonder these are largely ineffective. In fact, research shows that we are more likely to stick to and reach our goals when they are specific and measurable, when they are difficult enough to require sustained effort but are still realistically attainable, and when they have a deadline[6].

In a humor piece at the *Good Men Project*, I once wrote that exercising in my twenties "meant three days a week at the gym, plus racquetball, volleyball and pick-up hoops," and now that I'm in my forties, it "means parking at the far end of my work's parking lot and making sure to use the stairs instead of the elevator." Sadly, sometimes this is true. There have been too many days that my pulse rate did not go above rest. I would go a week or two using the elliptical and rowing machines in my basement after Nick is in bed, but, after a while, being done with the day too often meant a glass of wine, Netflix and/or a compulsive 19th edit of my next blog piece. Sadly, my exercise equipment too often gathered dust and laundry.

I had been struggling with vague fitness goals for quite a while, but my habits started to change when Amy bought me one of those exercise-tracking watches/apps for my last birthday. I wear it all the time, and it automatically tracks the number of steps I take per day, the number of active minutes (activity which elevates my pulse rate above rest) and the number of staircases I climb. It can also be programmed to track calories in and out, as well as monitor my sleeping patterns. The app comes pre-programed with a goal of 10,000 steps and 60 active minutes per day.

While I don't get to 10,000 steps (about 5 miles) every day, I get far closer than I normally would. Seeing that I'm only at 2,500 steps by mid-afternoon motivates me to walk the halls at work, take a walk around the neighborhood once I get home, or dust off the elliptical machine. The fitness app motivates me because the goals are specific, constantly measured, well balanced between ambition and realism, and can be tracked over time.

There are two other things we can do to maximize the chances that we persist in our goals. First, we need to tell others about them. This way, we'll feel accountable to others, feel dumb if we don't reach our goals, and, most importantly, we can get moral support and encouragement. For instance, I now write down the number of steps I took each day on the family calendar, and Amy and Nick use that to cheer me on. Second, attaching a reward when we reach our goals also helps. In fact, I can now only have a late-night treat (*mmmm, Ghirardelli chocolate caramel squares!*) if I have burned more calories that day than I consumed.

Ok, this book isn't about fitness, but I've been thinking about how effective this fitness app has been in changing my behavior, and how the same principles can be applied to better work-family balance. Similar to "get in better shape," most of us also have vague aspirations to "spend more time with our wives and kids," "be more efficient at work," or "lead a more balanced life." Noble goals, but I bet we'd be more likely to consistently act toward them if we made them more specific and measureable.

So instead of "have more couple time with Amy," I recently set specific goals of seeing one adult movie a month (well, not *that* kind of adult movie, I just mean anything but the latest from Pixar or Dreamworks for once!), and eating out as a couple at least once every two weeks. That's not too much to ask, but it means I have to plan ahead. We mark these down on the family calendar and keep track, and of course, I'm accountable to Amy for this, so she's likely to give me subtle (or not-so-subtle) reminders to come up for air during long days spent writing or grading to spend some valuable couple time.

My specific fatherhood goal is to set aside one additional hour per week for fun, one-on-one time with Nick. To do this, I have to track my daily time use, and I've already taken a specific action: Nick and I agreed to at least two father-son *Wii Just Dance* challenges a week. We also agreed to read the next few books in *The Warriors* series together before bedtime over the next month or so. Specific goals lead to specific actions.

Similarly, for work, I have set up goals for the number of words per day I have to average in order to complete my next book by the deadline, and I have arranged for a "second set of eyes/ accountability partner" who has agreed to read early drafts of each chapter before they go off to the editor. Not only will I get his feedback, it keeps the pressure on me to not slack off. I will also be measuring my time use during Nick's two-hour gymnastics practices to be sure I spend at least 90 minutes on work tasks, as opposed to just killing time surfing the web. For my day job, I set learning goals for the classes I teach this semester, including trying something new each class. I also have goals for the committee I'm a part of and the campus project I'm leading.

These are just a few ideas, and I encourage you to develop your own. We'll explore ways to do this in the exercises at the end of the chapter. The final step in the process is to build short-term "to do" lists that help us reach our medium-term goals.

■ Better "To Do" Lists

Have you ever been to one of those corporate strategic planning retreats? Yeah, I hate them too. The only part I find useful generally happens right at the end (no, not the happy hour afterwards). After far too many speakers and breakout groups and eager beavers showing off their corporate jargon to impress the bosses, the facilitator will often list the different themes that emerged during the retreat on various sections of the conference room walls. Then, folks are given a stack of Post-its and asked to write down "to-do" items and then stick them on the appropriate part of the wall. Finally, after all that talk, we're doing something productive!

I really like "to do" lists because they are oriented to action. But they only are effective when they are attached to longer term goals. That's why sticking the Post-its to the goals already on the wall is really effective. Without an attachment to goals, to-do lists become random collections of unrelated tasks that stressfully hang over our heads. Even worse, they give us no guidance as to what is most important, what needs to be done first, and why.

▌ Let's Do This!

OK, now we are ready to start. Specifically, for each section of our wall – Work, Family and Finances – we'll brainstorm a few six-month goals. Then, we'll list several items for us "to do" in the next three weeks to support those goals. We'll also identify a "stop doing" item for each section, so we can work on eliminating bad habits and other "time sucks" (see Chapter 9 for more). I'll describe each section and also provide my own example on the first two.

Chapter 3 Exercises

1. Family and Life Goals:

Fatherhood goals - For most of us, out top life priority (and the reason you are reading this book) is that we aspire to be involved dads and to build close, warm relationships with our children. Here are my current goals and my to-do list, there's a blank one for you directly afterwards (also, there are blank templates available for you to download at http://WorkingDadsSurvivalGuide.com, so you can revisit your goals every 6 months).

Fatherhood goals
<u>6 month goals</u> • Build one additional hour per week of unstructured fun time for me and Nick • Improve Nick's skills and confidence in time for next baseball season • See three Rockland Boulders (our local minor-league team) baseball games together
3-Week "To-Dos" • Spend ½ hour twice a week with Nick to doing a few songs from Wii *Just Dance* together • Pick up book 5 in "The Warriors" series from the library • Investigate the upcoming Boulders schedule and, if possible, but some tickets now • Have a catch and/or take Nick to the indoor batting cage every Saturday
<u>1 Thing to Stop Doing</u> • Checking out the fitness app on my phone when I'm spending time with Nick

Your turn

Fatherhood goals
6 month goals
3-Week "To-Dos"
1 Thing to Stop Doing

Relationship goals - In their excellent article, Danielle and Astro Teller write that,

> Couples who live entirely child-centric lives can lose touch with one another to the point where they have nothing left to say to one another when the kids leave home.... Is it surprising that divorce rates are rising fastest for new empty nesters?

As the above quote suggests, we also need to tend to our other most important relationship- the one we have with our spouse. (For those who are not married, you can substitute your ex or any other important relationship.)

Relationship goals
<u>6 month goals</u>
• See one movie a month together • On Fridays in which I don't have to be at the office, steal two hours for a quick lunch date • Arrange for a couples night with a few of our local friends
3-Week "To-Dos"
• Be more efficient working during the day so I have more time to spend with Amy in the evening • Shave more often so Amy will enjoy kissing me more
<u>1 Thing to Stop Doing</u>
• Stop "screen-sucking" at night by checking out the latest on ESPN and sports blogs

Your turn:

Relationship goals
<u>6 month goals</u>
<u>3-Week "To-Dos"</u>
<u>1 Thing to Stop Doing</u>

Friendship/social goals - As we will discuss in more detail in Chapter 12, many dads struggle to make new friends and stay in close touch with those we have. While we are all busy, it is also important to have a wide set of relationships that are not based on either family or work.

I confess this is an issue I struggle with, but I am starting to make some progress. Luckily, a friend and neighbor of mine is good about organizing neighborhood get-togethers. Also, I try to get together with my high-school friends and my college friends four times a year. I figure if I get a guy's night out with one of these three sets of friends once a month, that's a pretty good start.

Friendship/social goals
6 month goals
3-Week "To-Dos"
1 Thing to Stop Doing

Extended family goals - While we have been focusing on our nuclear families in this book, it is also important to recognize the importance of relationships with our extended families. Some, like my brother-in-law, are lucky enough to have been born into large, sprawling close-knit families who get together often. Others of us don't have much local family, and it is harder to get and stay in touch. And, frankly, I think we all need a reminder to "call our mothers!"

Extended family goals
6 month goals
3-Week "To-Dos"
1 Thing to Stop Doing

Health/exercise goals - I think I covered this topic to death a few pages ago. But let me just add that, if we don't take care of our bodies, we won't have as much energy to be more effective at work and as fathers. Also, if we don't exercise and eat mostly well, we are less likely to be around for our families down the road. It is easy to feel as if we are too busy to exercise, but we all have 168 hours every week, and I bet we could easily cut out two hours of TV/Internet and convert that into exercise time (more on this topic in Chapters 9 and 11).

Health/exercise goals
6 month goals
3-Week "To-Dos"
1 Thing to Stop Doing

Religious/spiritual goals - I'm not a particularly religious person, but I see the benefits of religion and spirituality in the lives of my friends and family. Proper practice of religion reminds us of what is most important in life, helps guide our decision making, and can bring peace and calm. If religion is not your thing, you should be sure to make space in your life for contemplation or renewal.

Religious/spiritual goals
6 month goals
3-Week "To-Dos"
1 Thing to Stop Doing

Hobbies/interests/relaxation goals - While exercise and religion are vital, it is also important to feed our hobbies and outside interests, and find activities that help us feel flow and relaxation. If we don't rest and replenish our physical, mental and psychic energy from time to time, we get burned out and lose our effectiveness. If we are constantly chugging away on the giant hamster wheel, our legs get too tired. Short renewal breaks on the cedar chips do us a lot of good.

In my life, my volleyball league helps me both with exercise and renewal. I'm also an avid reader and love doing crosswords and other word puzzles. These are good ways for me to shut down the noisy parts of my brain for a while and unwind.

Hobbies/interests/relaxation and renewal goals
6 month goals
3-Week "To-Dos"
1 Thing to Stop Doing

2. Work Goals:

About a decade ago, Tony Schwartz and Jim Loehr introduced the concept of the "Corporate Athlete" – using the mindset and training techniques of elite athletes to help us be more successful at work. One of their key insights is that the bulk of an athlete's time is not spent on actual performance. Rather, they spend far more time on development, practice and training, as well as building in time for recovery and rest. In contrast, at work, we are often so laser-focused on performance that we lose opportunities to develop and pursue other work-related goals that can pay off in the long run.

In their classic *Harvard Business Review* article, Schwartz and Loehr tell the story of how an executive they worked with came to embrace a more well-rounded approach to work:

> Connor had imposed on himself the stricture that he be the first person to arrive at the office each day and the last to leave. In reality, he acknowledged, no one would object if he arrived a little later or left a little earlier a couple of days a week. He realized it also made sense for him to spend one or two days a week working at a satellite plant 45 minutes nearer to his home than his main office. Doing so could boost morale at the second plant while cutting 90 minutes from his commute.
>
> Immediately after working with us, Connor arranged to have an office cleared out at the satellite factory. He now spends at least one full day a week there, prompting a number of people at that office to comment to him about his increased availability. He began taking a golf lesson one morning a week, which also allowed for a more relaxed drive to his main office, since he commutes there after rush hour on golf days. In addition, he instituted a monthly getaway routine with his wife. In the evenings, he often leaves his office earlier in order to spend more time with his family.
>
> Connor has also meticulously built recovery into his workdays. "What a difference these fruit and water breaks make," he says. "I set my alarm watch for 90 minutes to

prevent relapses, but I'm instinctively incorporating this routine into my life and love it. I'm far more productive as a result, and the quality of my thought process is measurably improved. I'm also doing more on the big things at work and not getting bogged down in detail. I'm pausing more to think and to take time out."

In this spirit, let's take some time to think not only about our goals for performance at work, but about other important aspects of our careers: our development, advancement, networking, and flexibility goals. We'll take a deeper dive into these topics in Part 2 of this book, so it is great to have some of your goals in mind before continuing on.

Performance goals - Ultimately, our success at the workplace does come down to job performance, so it is very important that we have clear performance goals. Further, so many of our other work and family goals are dependent upon our doing well at our jobs. If we perform well, over time, we get paid more, and this money can pay for family trips and things that open up family time. Similarly, if we perform well, we have more leverage to ask for accommodations like part-time telecommuting or getting sent to training seminars and conferences. Finally, you may want to check in with your supervisor about his/her expectations for you in the next six months. This could be an opportunity to get valuable direction, guidance and feedback.

Performance goals
<u>6 month goals</u>
<u>3-Week "To-Dos"</u>
<u>1 Thing to Stop Doing</u>

Development/advancement goals - There's a saying that we shouldn't dress for the job we have, but rather we should dress for the job we want. That's a bit silly. I don't recall many power suits walking their way through the mailroom. But I think the larger point is a good one. We can't just be focused on doing well in our current job, we need to have an eye out for our next job.

This means setting aside some time for our own professional development. Some of this, we can do on our own: Pick up a book, take a night class, attend Toastmasters. Sometimes, though, it is better to reach out and share our intentions with others at work, especially our bosses. There may be training or mentoring programs you can get access to, or the company can send you to seminars or conferences. Many large companies host their own suite of on-line courses, and some partner up with local universities. It is a good idea to think about where we'd like to be in our career a few years down the road – this could be climbing the ladder or changing our careers entirely. Setting a course of action should help.

Development/advancement goals
6 month goals
3-Week "To-Dos"
1 Thing to Stop Doing

Networking goals - A couple of hours a month focusing on making and maintaining a wide set of mutually beneficial connections is very important. It is one thing to be on LinkedIn. It is another to use it as a tool to comment in discussion groups, read about the latest developments in your field, and share information that can be useful to others. By staying on others' radars as a good professional and a generous person, you'd be surprised how many opportunities can come your way.

Beyond the Internet, we should train ourselves to get better at following up with people we meet at work or in other professional settings. We should also take the very good advice to "never eat alone" at work. Lunch and break times are great opportunities to develop professional friendships and share information.

I confess, these things don't always come naturally to me, and eating at my desk is far too common, and frankly no fun. But, I've been doing better. Over the course of the past few years, with my blog, social media, and now this book, I have had the occasion to meet so many people and greatly expand my network. So many people have taken the time to help me, and I try to reciprocate. For a partial list, check out the acknowledgement section at the end of the book.

Networking goals
6 month goals
3-Week "To-Dos"
1 Thing to Stop Doing

Flexibility goals - One of the themes we'll explore in the next part of the book is how we can add more flexibility to how, where and when we get our work done. For many, this is the key to being able to succeed at work and still be there for important family time.

If you feel like you are stuck in the office too much, perhaps we can use this exercise to think about how you would like our situation to change six months from now and what you can do to make it happen. Alternately, if you struggle with workplace flexibility because you find yourself tethered to work 24/7 through email and smartphones, we can use this section to start thinking about how to change that.

Flexibility goals
<u>6 month goals</u>
<u>3-Week "To-Dos"</u>
<u>1 Thing to Stop Doing</u>

Financial goals - Finally, we'd be remiss if we didn't discuss finances. We've already done some financial planning in the previous chapter, but this is another opportunity to drill down deeper and translate our budgets and spending habits into intentional goals.

Financial goals
<u>6 month goals</u>
<u>3-Week "To-Dos"</u>
<u>1 Thing to Stop Doing</u>

PART 2

Success at Work

At the end of most of the undergraduate business classes I teach, I spend some time discussing careers. I encourage my students, wherever they are in their academic journeys, to think about what they can do to ensure open doors in the future.

But first, I have to shock them to attention. The fact is, in our adult lives, we spend about one third of our time sleeping, about one third of our time working, and only one third of our time doing everything else. For most of us, this means 50-60 hours a week on work or work-related tasks (commuting, travel, getting prepared, etc.), for about 45 years post-college. When I tell them this, the look in their eyes reflects exactly what they are thinking:

"Are you crazy! 45 years, 50 weeks a year, 55 hours a week!!!"

Those of us who have been working for a while know this is true. But it doesn't have to be as bad as my students believe.

In fact, the third of our lives we spend at work can be very rewarding. Yes, of course, work is work and we're mostly in it to provide for ourselves and our families. But if we're lucky, if we understand workplace dynamics, if we negotiate for what we need, and if we, over time, make smart decisions about our careers, we can have a work that adds meaning to our lives, provides us the time and flexibility we need to lead a full life outside of work, and gives us work for which we can be proud.

Work doesn't have to be a drudgery, and we can succeed in even demanding careers while also creating enough time to be the involved, loving dads we always wanted to be.

In this part of the book, I'll run through the most common forms of workplace flexibility and help you think about how you may or may not be able to access them. Next, we'll discuss how to negotiate for more workplace flexibility (or for more work hour stability), even with "old school" bosses. We'll discuss time management and other techniques to be more efficient and adaptable at work. We'll cover the ins and outs of taking paternity leave. Finally, we'll explore how integrating work and life can be part of your ongoing career planning.

CHAPTER 4

The Ins and Outs of Workplace Flexibility

When we had our first son, we decided my wife would stay home. But I didn't make enough in my job to make that work. I took a different job with better pay, but it required a two hour daily commute. This quickly became too much for me, but I kept at it for the sake of the family. After a while, I went to my boss and worked out an arrangement so I can work from home three days a week. She was super-supportive of the idea, and it's worked well for the office. It's worked great for my family too, and my performance at work, if anything, has gotten better, since I'm not as stressed and am not wasting so much time on the road.

· · · · · · · · · · · · · · · · · · · ·

I asked my boss if I could take a half day off so I can be home with my daughters for the afternoon – and even offered to log in from home if needed. But, even though there was no particular work emergency, I got the managerial middle finger! What does it say when an employer denies your request for time you have to use before the end of the year and you offer to LOG INTO WORK ON YOUR VACATION TIME if needed? I think I need to spruce up my resume.

In the modern workplace, most jobs don't need to be performed exclusively, or even mostly, at the office. But most of us still have to be at the office most of the time during traditional working hours.

Sometimes, all we need to make our work-family juggles work better is just a little help from our employers. Just compare the quotes from the two dads at the start of this chapter. One was able to co-create a great solution with his boss – a real win-win. The other has a bad boss standing in his way, leading to a lose-lose situation.

The engrained workplace tradition of chair-time is hard to overcome. "All in" work cultures are pretty well entrenched, and this leads even well-meaning supervisors to hold onto control instead of seeing the possible benefits of more flexible work. And sometimes, we internalize these concerns and wind up trapping ourselves.

Lots of working dads have benefitted from working alternative work schedules, but, for the most part, companies will not come to us to ask us about our needs for flexibility. We have to take the first step. This can be difficult, but most good things in life are.

In this chapter, we'll examine some of the most common forms of workplace flexibility, and examine how applicable each solution could be to our work-family juggle. We'll explore some ways to analyze the family-friendliness of our workplaces. We'll also consider that we all have different orientations to balance – some prefer to separate work and family, others thrive on integration. Of course, we'll have several exercises and assessments at the end of the chapter.

To start us off, here are a few factors to consider that might limit or enhance the options at our disposal for balancing work and family.

■ Control over Work Schedule

Many time-intensive jobs, such as finance, consulting and the law, are dictated by a client's schedule. Especially when clients pay a premium for services, there is pressure to be constantly available, day or night, whenever they have a question or a problem. Remember my brother-in-law from Chapter 1 or this dad from the Introduction:

> I have a pretty high-octane career in international finance. I confess I work very long hours, travel a lot and have a killer commute. My job pays really well, but it's stressful because so much depends on my yearly performance bonus- I have to be "on" for work all the time. One Sunday, I remember bringing my son to his friend's birthday party. I was exhausted from a more than full workweek and looking forward to relaxing. Then I got calls on both my Blackberries about a client emergency, and had to leave and go into the office. I think I'm a great dad when I'm around, but my kids and wife sometimes don't get enough of me.

I'm at the other end of the scale. While my career as a college professor is demanding, I have a lot of control over my time throughout the week, and very few emergencies. Aside from classes, office hours and a few meetings, I can shift my work around Amy's work and Nick's activities. I know that my life would be much harder without this autonomy.

But, for me, workplace flexibility also has a downside. I sometimes find it hard to separate work and family time; the two sometimes bleed into each other. Organization and time management are not my strong suits, and I often it hard to shut off my mental to-do list when I should be more focused on Amy and Nick.

Most dads are somewhere between these two extremes. We are often asked to work more than full-time hours and have some discretion over our time. We have some tasks we can take care of on our own and in our own way, and other tasks that require collaboration and time with coworkers. Sometimes technology enables communication, other times only face to face will do. Some days we are in wall to wall meetings, some days we are out with your clients, others are spent in quiet, steady concentration behind a closed office door.

Take a look at these items used in surveys of workplace flexibility by the Families and Work Institute:

1. I have the freedom to decide what I do on my job
2. It is basically my own responsibility to decide how my job gets done
3. I have a lot of say about what happens on my job
4. How easy is it for you to take time off during your workday to take care of personal or family matters

If you agree with these statements, you probably have a stronger hand in negotiating for flextime, telecommuting or work from home. You may be relatively free to adjust your schedule without it damaging your job performance or career prospects. If you largely disagree with these items, your quest for more flexibility will be more difficult. (I'll include these and other survey items in the exercises at the end of this chapter).

Workplace culture for work family and supervisory support

A few years ago, I was at the Academy of Management conference and attended a mid-career faculty consortium – a full-day workshop for professors who recently earned tenure to think about what was next for our careers. In one breakout group, I was extolling the virtues of professors' time flexibility and how it gives us the freedom to pursue such a wide range of options and have life balance, when another attendee jumped in:

> I don't feel that way at all. A few years ago, I was leaving the office after accomplishing a lot that day, and my senior colleagues were horrified I was leaving so early. It was 6pm. I think it's crazy, but that's what gets rewarded and punished at my university- our culture requires us to spend long hours in the office, even if we can get work done elsewhere.

Even though that professor and I had the same job, the workplace cultures at our two universities were quite different. Mine enables me to balance work and family while valuing my performance over "face time." As long as I teach my classes well, am accessible for my students, produce enough research papers, and volunteer for enough committees, I am given the freedom to work where and when I want. I cherish this and am very grateful to my employer, my department chair and Dean. I can't imagine a more supportive workplace and career, and, as a result, I'm not looking for another place to work.

My unfortunate colleague seemed to be evaluated primarily on how long he stayed at work, and only secondarily on productivity. I'm sure, as a management professor, the extremely poor management exhibited by his colleagues was not lost on him. It wasn't his job demands, but rather his workplace culture that prevented him from using his time more flexibly.

As this example shows, along with the particular demands of our jobs – even ones that should be conducive to life balance – workplace cultures and the attitudes of supervisors can either help us with family balance or create quite a hindrance. These effects can be even more acute in more traditional, and especially in more intense, work settings, as expressed by this commenter on an article I wrote for the *Harvard Business Review* Blog Network last year:

> When the boss needs something and you know the desired timeline is 'Right Bloody Now,' even if it was your fondest desire to be home in time for dinner, or bedtime, just once this month/year, the reality is that you do what your boss wants. In this economic environment, there will be someone else to replace you once you've established that you are not entirely the property of the company. Of course the precious few years with your kids as they grow up, or with your spouse before you grow too old, are irreplaceable. But these days, a job is irreplaceable too, and houses, food, college, etc., are not free.

Even if he is exaggerating for effect, I get his point and sympathize. However, I think that we can, with conscious career planning, escape the treadmill-style workplaces he describes. Poor guy, I hope he reads this book.

Here are the items the Families and Work Institute uses in their surveys in terms of workplace culture and support for work-family balance. This may help you think through and assess how your workplace stacks up, and what barriers or supports you may face in your workplace.

Career Concerns

1. There is an unwritten rule at my place of employment that you can't take care of family needs on company time

2. At my place of employment, employees who put their family or personal needs ahead of their jobs are not looked on favorably

3. If you have problems managing your work and family responsibilities, the attitude at my place of employment is: "you made your bed, now lie in it!"

4. At my place of employment, employees have to choose

between advancing in their jobs or devoting attention to their family or personal lives

Supervisory Support

5. My supervisor is fair and doesn't show favoritism in responding to employees' personal or family needs

6. My supervisor accommodates me when I have family or personal business to take care of- for example, medical appointments, meeting with child's teacher, etc.

7. My supervisor really cares about the effects that work demands have on my personal and family life

8. My supervisor has expectations of my performance on the job that are realistic

9. My supervisor is understanding when I talk about personal or family issues that affect my work

10.I feel comfortable bringing up my personal or family issues with my supervisor

Again, the degree to which you agree or disagree with these statements indicates how possible it is for you to adjust your schedule to your life. Once you assess your situation, you can consider what this means for your ability to balance work and family.

- Perhaps you are more able to deal with family concerns than you originally thought?
- Maybe you need to polish off your resume to find a better situation? (In fact, that's what my conference colleague did the very next year)
- Maybe your answers to these questions influence how you negotiate for alternate work arrangements.
- Maybe your organization is unsupportive, but you can work something out unofficially with your supervisor

- Maybe you have to stay under the radar, and act to balance work and family through informal and ad-hoc arrangements and other "holes in the system."

▍ Working Dad's Blues

Dads face an additional cultural hurdle when it comes to work-family balance. Men who put family first are often seen as violating *both* "all-in" work cultures and traditional gender expectations, and, as a result, fear being seen as uncommitted and "unmanly." We wish to avoid negative career consequences, so many of us lay low. According to the Workplace Flexibility Stigma studies which I referenced in the Introduction, dads who use workplace flexibility face even more resistance than women who do the same. Among their research findings:

- Fathers who engage in higher than average levels of childcare are subject to more workplace harassment (e.g., picked on for "not being man enough") and more general mistreatment (e.g., garden variety workplace aggression) as compared to their low-caregiving or childless counterparts.

- Men requesting family leave are perceived as uncommitted to work and less masculine; these perceptions are linked to lower performance evaluations, increased risks of being demoted or downsized, and reduced pay and rewards.

- Men who interrupt their employment for family reasons earn significantly less after returning to work.

While many workplaces are becoming more amenable to work-family concerns, some are still stuck with the notion that work and family is a working mother's issue. Throughout the course of the next few chapters, I'll specifically discuss how we working dads need to be especially smart when pursuing workplace flexibility. We need to negotiate carefully, use informal and ad-hoc accommodations, seek employers who are more father-friendly, and, when we can, take a stand both for ourselves and our fellow dads. Now that we have looked at some of the workplace factors that either facilitate or inhibit our ability to balance work and family, let's explore our options.

▌ Flextime

With flextime, you still work the same amount of hours, but can shift your work times earlier or later than the typical "9 to 5." For example, you may wish to work "7 to 3" so you can be home to see your kids after school, or it may work out better for you to on a later "10:30-6:30" schedule. Further, some flextimers work longer hours two days a week, and shorter hours on other days. Most companies that allow flextime mandate that there be some core hours in which all employees must be at the workplace, such as Mondays through Thursdays from 10am to 2pm.

Flextime can be particularly useful for managing the work-family juggle in dual-career and single-parent households. Employees can benefit from flextime by arranging their work schedules around their family or other life demands and make up the work when they are more able to do so. From the employer point of view, flextime is advantageous because it still requires full-time hours at work, and, along with core hours, allows for sufficient coworker interaction and accessibility to clients. For this reason, many employers are more amenable to flextime arrangements than telecommuting.

▌ Telecommuting

Here's more from the dad whose quote opened the chapter:
Working from home has its challenges- it is sometimes hard to separate work time when my youngest son starts crying or needs to take a nap, and, frankly, it can be

isolating to never leave the house or be in the world of adult conversations. Plus, I don't have enough space for a home office; I'm usually working from the kitchen. My son's at that age he wants attention all the time, even if this means I have to let him pound on my keyboard every now and then.

This is why three days of telecommuting is perfect for me. Some days, I can see my kids a lot, and it is nice to be the last thing my older son sees before getting on the school bus and the first thing he sees when he gets off.

But Tuesdays and Thursdays, I must confess, are sometimes really nice. I've been listening to the podcast of "Serial" during my commute, and, during the day, I'm out in the wider world. It also means I'm still connected at the office- bouncing ideas of off people, making sure my boss knows I'm around. All this has its advantages.

Telecommuting involves working from somewhere other than the traditional workplace. Most often, this means working from home using computers, smartphones and internet connections. Some companies are completely distributed, with employees rarely working in the same physical location. Others, like the dad from the quote, prefer to use of part-time telecommuting. In a typical part-time arrangement, one-quarter to one-third of an employee's work hours is performed at home. Others rely on telecommuting in ad-hoc situations, such as when a key employee must be home for family reasons or in the aftermath of severe weather.

The obvious benefits of telecommuting for employees include:

- the reduction or elimination of commutes
- increased work autonomy
- increased ability to integrate work and family demands on customized schedule

Many employers also see telecommuting as advantageous. Telecommuting:

- allows companies to manage distributed teams and attract talent from beyond the local labor market
- reduces office space requirements
- allows them to retain talent who may need telecommuting solutions for their work-family demands

On the other hand, many employers are leery of telecommuting because they fear that:

- Employees may abuse the privilege and slack off
- A lack of coworker interaction may harm cohesiveness, the generation of new ideas and collective performance
- They will lose the ability to evaluate and manage employee performance without "face time."

While many of these fears are unfounded, they make it difficult to negotiate for anything more than part-time or ad-hoc telecommuting options. We'll discuss how to negotiate for such arrangements in the next chapter.

▌ Work from Home

Work from home is kind of like telecommuting on steroids – no need to come in at all. Depending on the work, your personality, your family demands and the employer, this can work out great. As one dad explains:

> I'm in my dream job. I can work from absolutely wherever and whenever – as long as have my laptop and gadgets, I can get things done. When I need time for family, I take it. There's no need for me to take sick time or personal days. As long as I get everything done – and they do hold me accountable – they keep giving me this freedom. I can be at the PTA, my son's occupational therapy, bring him to his tutor, be at his school, and supervise playdates during the day. We had a snow day last week, and I didn't have to take a day off. I was with my son, and did my work from home around him. I wish more dads could work that way.

In some organizations and for some jobs, there is little to no requirement that one does their work on site. For example, the dad quoted above writes computer code for a relatively small tech company. While work-from home can be useful to many, it can also pose several challenges.

At work, the separation from the workplace can mean you get lost in the shuffle when it comes to promotions and career advancement – out of sight, out of mind. Working at a distance form coworkers could inhibit communication, collaboration and creative ideas. Some dads I know who work from home feel isolated and cut off from the world of adult conversation. Some find it hard to resist the temptation to both parent and work at the same time.

John Pearce, who writes the blog, *14 Step Commute*, expresses the pros and cons this way:

> Imagine it, no more racing home to walk the dog who's been left alone for 10 hours. You can just walk Fido anytime you need to because you're home, right? The problem is that these thoughts, and the activities that result from them, can absolutely kill your productivity. In fact, one of the hardest aspects of telecommuting is blocking out the temptation to cut the grass, run to the store, and even walk the dog. While in most cases, you can get away with sneaking out to do one here and there, be careful. Don't make it a habit.

Some suggestions for managing yourself as a full-time telecommuter include:

- Setting designated work hours, even if this means hiring a sitter
- Designating a specific work area
- Resisting the temptation to schedule things like dentist appointments during your peak work hours
- Get up and move- telecommuters are often susceptible to a sedentary lifestyle

- Schedule frequent phone calls with your office-based colleagues
- Document and regularly report your activities and accomplishments to your boss and others at work

■ Compressed Work Weeks

> I love my schedule. I work a little longer each day, but then get every other Friday off. We usually take advantage of this by driving up to my in-laws on Thursday night. Then, the kids get grandparent time and my wife and I can sleep in, relax and have some time together. If we don't drive up to the in-laws, we sometimes use that Friday to see a movie or go to the children's museum when these things aren't so crowded.

Compressed work weeks (CWW) involve working longer hours each work day, but then earning extra days off. The most common CWW approaches include four 10-hour days per week with a three-day weekend or, more commonly, nine 9-hour days with every other Friday off. In essence, you bank extra hours and then spend them for long weekends.

A CWW benefits employees by allowing them long weekends for travel or family commitments and the ability to have time off during normal working days and times. Having weekday time off for errands or family opens up weekends for more free time and relaxation. CWWs can reduce the need for paid childcare – four days a week instead of five represents a cost savings and more dad and kid time.

Employers often prefer CWW to other flexible workplace arrangements because they can be assured that employees are indeed putting in full time at work, and because employee time off is more predictable, making it easier to plan meetings and other work activities. As such, it is often easier to negotiate with your employer for a CWW than other alternative work schedules.

Free Time During Work Time!

I really love alternative work schedules that allow for people to have time off work during regular business hours, so please indulge me in this tangent. Think about all the things that daytime time off makes easier:

- Errands- You can actually get someone at Home Depot to help you without hunting 20 minutes for an employee. You can take your time in the power tool aisle without your kids whining and begging you to leave.
- Christmas shopping- The mall is far less packed at 11am on a Tuesday. Parking spaces are plentiful! Lines are short! Crowds are non-existent!
- Movies- You have the theater to yourself during matinees. No one spilling popcorn or texting their way through the movie while crushed in the seat next to you.
- Skiing- Weekends at most ski areas are super-crowded. On a Thursday, all that powder's just for you.
- Kid's activities- Playgrounds, children's museums, aquariums, zoos and the like are far less crowded, making it easier to enjoy your time instead of enduring it
- Your kid's school- time off during the day means you can volunteer at school or visit your kid's classroom

What activities would be easier for you to accomplish if you could do them during normal business hours?

Schedule Certainty

Most of us in white-collar jobs put in more than a full-time work week; having more control and flexibility over where and when we work is the important workplace accommodation that allows for work-family balance. However, for others, more stability and structure around when and where work gets done is the way to better work-family balance.

> I have a set weekly schedule – nine to five on Mondays, Thursdays and Fridays, and twelve to eight on Tuesdays and Wednesdays. The days I work late, I'm home only for the bedtime routine, which is a bummer. But, because we can plan around my late nights, things aren't so bad. My mother-in-law picks up my daughters from school the days I work late and keeps them through dinner until my wife gets them. Also, I have the place to myself on Tuesday and Wednesday mornings, which allows me to sleep in, put in longer workouts, do chores around the house – and it gives us a consistent window so we can schedule the plumber or cable guy or whatever.

> Also, while I work hard when I'm at work, there's no call for me to be available afterwards. So, when I'm home, I can really be home. Lots of folks talk about flexibility and integration as the key. But for me, I like that there's a wall of separation between work and family.

For some dads, and depending on the job, work flexibility is not the best solution. Rather, having certainty over work hours can allow you to know when you will be working, so you can plan family time around it, and make day-care and other arrangements.

In fact, for most hourly employees, schedule certainty is the key workplace factor that allows for better work-family balance. When a waiter or a retail employee only gets a few days' notice whether they are working day or night shifts, it can wreak havoc over their family's schedule. How can you make or keep a doctor's appointment, or know you can pick up your kids from day care? Without the help of grandparents or other extended family, it can be virtually impossible to schedule time for life.

In fact, when I was at the White House Summit for Working Families, this distinction between the need for more flexibility for white-collar employees and for more schedule certainty for blue-collar and hourly employees was very clear. At that event, Macy's employee Kay Thompson gave a moving address in which she reported that the collective bargaining agreement between Macy's and her union guaranteed that employees must be given their work schedules at least three weeks in advance, that they can choose days off up to six months in advance, and they can designate, ahead of time, the particular days they cannot be asked to come in early or stay late. "This assured stability in scheduling allows me to prepare my children for school every day.... While I am grateful for my work situation, I want all retail workers to experience a sustainable working environment where family friendly workplace scheduling is a priority for all companies."

▌ Integrators and Segmenters

It is not just the demands of the job that makes flexibility or stability the preferred option. Some, like the dad quoted above, enjoy the wall of separation between work time and family time. To him, this means his weekends are devoted to family without being clouded by thoughts of work or the worry that he'll receive a panicked email from a client while out at the ball field. I suspect that, to many of you, this sounds like heaven.

If so, you are probably a segmenter by nature, which means you prefer to, and tend to be able to, draw a psychological line between work and the rest of your life. Segmenters prefer to put in their time at work, and then come home and shut off the "work parts" of their brains. As Lazlo Bock puts it in his *HBR* article, "They tend not to dwell on looming deadlines and floods of emails, and can fall gently asleep each night."

Gosh, I envy segmenters.

In contrast, many of us are integrators. We either prefer to blend our work and non-work time and activities, or simply have a hard time separating work from the rest of our lives. Sometimes this integration is good, as "life stuff" can be taken care of during work hours, even if "work stuff" creeps in around the edges of family time. But, smartphones and late-night emails and blurred boundaries are killers for integrators.

> To me, using flexibility is both good and bad. I can do it, but then pay the price for it by working late from home. There's no clear line between work and home and no 'exhale time' when I can feel fully done with work and just relax.

While I have always felt energized at juggling multiple work and non-work activities and thrive on flexibility, I am also a victim of the incessant "to do" list constantly running in my brain. Plus, the lack of structure in my schedule means that I need to be very disciplined and organized to prevent work time to spill into family time. Frankly, I'm not great at this, and sometimes I find that I'm not mentally present with Amy and Nick when I am physically with them.

Following on the work of Ellen Kossek and her colleagues, Google has been surveying its employees to decipher their preferred work-family styles and then customize work-family solutions for each type of employee. Google found that about 30% of their employees are segmenters and about 70% are integrators – although 70% of integrators wish they could segment. You can use the exercise at the end of the chapter to determine your preferred style for work-family balance.

Both approaches to work-family balance have their pros and cons, and each group would benefit from different types of workplace changes to help them lead more balanced lives. Segmenters need solutions that reduce chronic overwork, such as reasonable time demands and the ability to be fully unplugged from work during non-work hours. They need sufficient time at home in order to, well, have sufficient time at home. Their non-work time needs to be respected by their employers.

So, if you are a segmenter, you should strive, over time, to find a way to create clear separation between work time and family time, even if your work hours are long. This could be done through a formal arrangement (as we'll discuss in the next chapter) or by being ultra-disciplined in protecting family time from the creeping demands of work (as we'll discuss in Chapter 9). One segmenter dad I know went so far as to get rid of his iPhone and go back to the world of cellphones that are just phones.

For us integrators, the trick is to find ways to create more work flexibility so we can actively manage the integrative nature of our lives. Integrators need solutions that open up possibilities for autonomy and flexibility over where, when and how work gets done, such as ad-hoc or part-time telecommuting. We need the freedom and tools to customize our work schedules around family (and vice-versa), being held accountable for performance but freed to work in the way that matches our idiosyncratic styles and the day's life demands.

Bock concludes that,

> If indeed, some employees show a preference for, or seem to work best when segmenting- making clear delineations between work and non-work, while others either thrive on, or work best when the lines between work and life are blurred, then it is clear that some workplace interventions will work better for some and not for others.

In other words, one-size-fits-all solutions aren't all that great for work-family concerns, as every person and every family has different, and often frequently-changing, needs and priorities.

▍Turning of the Tide?

While many workplaces are not particularly supportive of work and family issues, especially for their male employees, the tide is beginning to turn in our favor. There is hope for more supportive work conditions for dads. Here's just a little bit of evidence.

Many pioneering companies now offer generous paid parental leave to new dads, for example, Facebook (16 weeks), Bank of America (12 weeks) and Patagonia (eight weeks). Deloitte and other leading companies support dads with informational resources and parenting groups. Other companies are paying much more attention to men's issues in their diversity and work-life programs, even if they haven't yet fully articulated robust policies for dads. These companies are not addressing our concerns out of the goodness of their hearts. They understand that a balanced approach to employee management and workplace flexibility are important ways to attract and retain key talent while avoiding the performance declines associated with chronic overwork.

Three CEOs recently demonstrated the importance of work-family balance for fathers through their words and public actions. PIMCO's Mohamed El-Erian and MongoDB's Max Schireson stepped down from corner offices in order to be more involved dads. They have both found other lucrative employment, but have chosen roles that limit their travel and reduce their hours, opening time for being everyday participants in the lives of their families. They made a point to publicly explain their actions in the hope that it would further the cause for working fathers.

Even better, Ernst & Young's CEO, Mark Weinberger, has not stepped down. Rather, he makes work-life balance a personal priority, talks about this commitment publicly, and, as a result, EY has taken many steps, both large and small, to be a more family-supportive employer for both moms and dads (more on EY and other forward-thinking employers in Chapter 7). He was one of several male CEOs, including the CEOs of Johnson and Johnson, PriceWaterhouseCooper and Goldman Sachs, who spoke about their personal work-family challenges and their commitment to work and family at their own firms at the White House Summit for Working Families in June 2014.

The next generation of corporate leadership will consist of men and women for whom work-family juggles have been real and constant challenges in their lives. Their experiences should lead them to embrace more flexible work arrangements that do not force parents to choose between being "all in" for work or consigned to "mommy" or "daddy tracks." Progress will be uneven, but I think it is inevitable.

> Bryan Dyson, during his stint as CEO of Coca-Cola, said:
>
> Imagine life as a game in which you are juggling some five balls in the air. You name them – Work, Family, Health, Friends and Spirit and you're keeping all of these in the air.
>
> You will soon understand that work is a rubber ball. If you drop it, it will bounce back. But the other four balls – Family, Health, Friends and Spirit – are made of glass. If you drop one of these; they will be irrevocably scuffed, marked, nicked, damaged or even shattered. They will never be the same. You must understand that and strive for it.
>
> Work efficiently during office hours and leave on time. Give the required time to your family, friends and have proper rest. Value has a value only if its value is valued.

I can't imagine too many CEOs said things like this a generation ago.

Our challenges are real, and it is often a struggle to get the flexibility and support we need to succeed at work and at home. However, please know that, however slowly, the business world is catching on.

With this thought in mind, let's transition to our exercises for this chapter. These exercises will help us as we progress to the next chapter on how to advocate for ourselves and for the workplace changes we need.

Chapter 4 Exercises

1. Assess Your Workplace

For each of these questions, indicate how much you agree or disagree with the statement (1 = strongly disagree, 2 = disagree, 3 = neither agree nor disagree, 4 = agree, 5 = strongly agree)

Schedule Autonomy

_____ 1. I have the freedom to decide what I do on my job

_____ 2. It is basically my own responsibility to decide how my job gets done

_____ 3. I have a lot of say about what happens on my job

_____ 4. How easy is it for you to take time off during your workday to take care of personal or family matters

Career Consequences

_____ 5. There is an unwritten rule at my place of employment that you can't take care of family needs on company time

_____ 6. At my place of employment, employees who put their family or personal needs ahead of their jobs are not looked on favorably

_____ 7. If you have problems managing your work and family responsibilities, the attitude at my place of employment is: "you made your bed, now lie in it!"

_____ 8. At my place of employment, employees have to choose between advancing in their jobs or devoting attention to their family or personal lives

Supervisory Support

_____ 9. My supervisor is fair and doesn't show favoritism in responding to employees' personal or family needs

_____ 10. My supervisor accommodates me when I have family or personal business to take care of- for example, medical appointments, meeting with child's teacher, etc.

_____ 11. My supervisor really cares about the effects that work demands have on my personal and family life

_____ 12. My supervisor has expectations of my performance on the job that are realistic

_____ 13. My supervisor is understanding when I talk about personal or family issues that affect my work

_____ 14. I feel comfortable bringing up my personal or family issues with my supervisor

Follow-up questions:

Based on your responses, think about the following:
- How much control do you have over your work schedule?
- How happy are you with your level of control?
- Brainstorm three things you can do to expand the control you have over your work schedule?
- How supportive is my workplace of employees' family concerns?
- How supportive is my workplace of dads and their concerns?
- Considering this level of workplace support, does this give

you more or less freedom to act in ways to balance work and family?

- How supportive is your supervisor in general?
- How supportive is your supervisor of your work-family concerns?
- How could you work with your supervisor or persuade him/her to be more accommodating?

2. Are you a Segmenter or an Integrator?

These items were developed by Kossek and Lautch, for their great book, *CEO of Me: Creating a Life That Works in the Flexible Job Age*, Financial Times Press, 2008. I found them listed in an article on the *Financial Times* website

For each of these questions, indicate how much you agree or disagree with the statement (1 = strongly disagree, 2 = disagree, 3 = neither agree nor disagree, 4 = agree, 5 = strongly agree)

_____ 1. All in all, I try to keep work and personal life separated most of the time.

_____ 2. Except in an emergency, I generally try to take care of personal or family needs at work only when I'm on break or during my lunch hour.

_____ 3. During my workday, there is very little blurring of boundaries between time spent on work and time spent on personal activities.

_____ 4. It is clear where my work life ends and my family or personal life begins.

_____ 5. I rarely attend to personal or family issues during the workday.

_____ 6. I almost never do extra work after normal work hours.

_____ 7. In general, I don't take work-related phone calls or e-mails during evenings, weekends, holidays, or vacations.

_____ 8. In general, I talk as little as possible about my family or personal issues with most people I work with.

_____ 9. I usually handle e-mails related to my family or personal life separately from e-mails related to my work.

_____ 10. When I'm at home, I rarely think about work, so I can fully get away from my job.

_____ 11. If I work or ever were to work from home, I would work in a space that is designated for that purpose only.

_____ 12. I do not think about my family, friends, and personal interests when at work, so I can focus.

Integrators tend to mark 1 or 2 to most items. Segmenters tend to select 4 or 5 to most items.

What implications do your results have for your preferred working style? For your strategy to improve your work-family balance?

CHAPTER 5

———

Negotiating for Work Flexibility

I work at a global company in which long hours are expected for those trying to move up and get ahead- and I've always been a workhorse. As my daughter started growing up, I felt I was missing too much that I'd never be able to get back. So, I bit the bullet and approached my boss about making a few changes. He was surprisingly open to my idea of "daddy-daughter Wednesdays" in which I could be home with my daughter and would come in to the office at 12:30. We also reallocated some job duties requiring travel.

A few years later, my career has kept on keeping on – plus I feel so much more connected with my daughter, and she with me. Sometimes our own anxiety keeps us from asking for what we need- I'm really glad I did.

This dad stood up for what he and his family needed. Yes, his requested workplace accommodation isn't earth-shattering, but for his very competitive employer with its "all-in" work culture, his actions were very brave. He took a chance and was relieved to find his supervisor and colleagues to be supportive. As a result, he was able to spend time building his lifetime bond with his daughter, and to be more present throughout her one and only (and all-too-fleeting) childhood.

Years later, he's still at his firm, and now holds a very high position. He repaid the favor of a small, informal, family-related accommodation many times over by the value he adds to his employer. He shows that work-family balance and high performance can be complementary rather than contradictory forces.

Not all of us are so lucky to have supportive supervisors or jobs that lend themselves to flexibility. But wherever we work, it is brave to stand out and make a case for a time and place flexibility for your work. Depending on your situation, it may be well worth it despite the risks.

In this chapter, we'll think through how we can be more successful in negotiating for flexibility and cover key points that should be included in any request. The chapter will end with a template you can use for structuring that request. With this mindset, we can usually succeed in advocating for ourselves and getting at least some of the flexibility we need.

▋ Getting to Yes

Like any request or negotiation, the key is to see the situation from the other person's side. You can then focus your communications so that you dispel most of their concerns and show them how they will also benefit from the arrangement. This is the essence of *Getting to Yes*, the classic book on successful negotiation by Fisher and Ury.

As Henry Ford once said, "If there is any one secret of success, it lies in the ability to get the other person's point of view and see things from that person's angle as well as your own." Here are some ideas to keep in mind as you plan your request for more formal or informal flexibility:

1. Be valuable
2. Negotiate well. This includes:
   - Understand the reasons (even the dumb ones) why supervisors may be reluctant
   - See it from their point of view and figure out what you could offer them
   - Make it a business case, not just a personal one
   - Propose a set of rules that will make it easier for them to keep track of your performance
   - Take the initiative to arrange for the resources you will need to work remotely
3. Use this template

The overarching principle is to make it easy for them to say yes. This means minimizing the risk to your supervisor and doing everything to anticipate and address potential concerns, even before your supervisor can think them up. In the words of Dale Carnegie, "Before you ask, pause and ask yourself, 'How can I make this person want to do it?'" If you take away every reason for them to say no, they are more likely to say yes.

Step #1- Be Valuable (and Sell Yourself Gracefully)

My wife has an inspirational plaque on our dresser that reads "Be so good they can't ignore you." This is great advice for standing out among dozens of other fantastic actresses vying for the same part. In Amy's case, this mindset is one component of her success.

But let me twist this the other way. If, over time at your workplace, you prove to be great, you can earn more latitude in how you succeed at work and at home. Because your employer knows how valuable and reliable you are, she can ignore you, leaving you alone to succeed your own way.

Further, most employers will tell you that good employees are hard to come by, and they don't want to lose employees of value. The best way to protect yourself in uncertain economic times and/or gain leverage for work requests is to become as valuable as possible. This means you need to be good at your job – and that you need to make sure people know you are good at your job (without being a jerk about it). Learn a skill that few others have. Get access to important information and clients. Prove yourself over time. That's what the dad in the quote that opened the chapter did.

Not long ago, I read an interesting *ESPN.com* article about how pro football players transition back into family life after the season ends. Players work such incredibly long hours during training camp, pre-season and the season, often living apart from their families, and then suddenly find themselves home at season's end. Encouragingly, most rededicate themselves to being involved fathers as a way to make up for lost time. But one anecdote stuck out to me:

> Hall of Fame defensive back Darrell Green treated his job with the Washington Redskins as just that — a job. It was 9-to-5 to him. He left early during the season and was home in time for dinner. "I was already dealing with the kids [during the season]," said Green, who played for the Redskins from 1983 to 2002. "I couldn't take them to school all the time, but I was still getting to the evening events. I was still going to the recitals in the evening. I was still home for dinner. I was just living a normal life.
>
> "Maybe I'm the crazy one. I just lived a normal life. I didn't see it as something that it wasn't."

How did Green get away with working "normal" hours when the rest of his peers spent far more time working out and preparing for the next game? Well, he was just that good.

Green played at a high level for 20 years, holds 11 NFL records, was a four-time All-Pro selection, was a seven-time Pro Bowler, is a member of the Pro Football and College Football Halls of Fame, was a key contributor to two Super Bowl winning teams, is considered one of the 100 greatest players of all time, and was even named NFL Man of the Year for his charity work.

Maybe at one point some coach or teammate resented that Green only worked "normal hours" to be with his family. But what were they going to do about it? Considering how great he was, I bet most didn't care very much and, after a while, stopped thinking about it.

So, what's the lesson for us? Once you prove your value, you can use your built-up credibility to act more in accordance with your personal priorities. I know this is easier said than done, depending on our jobs, financial situation and employers. After all, we all can't be the NFL's fastest man. Still, in almost any walk of life, being really good earns you perks others may not have access to. Be sure to earn credibility, and then be sure to use it to support your priorities!

In my own life, I find that when I perform the core parts of my job at an "A" level, I am often afforded the space and freedom to pursue the rest of my work more flexibly. Over the past several years, I maintained an active academic research record, earned a reputation as a very good teacher and spearheaded a major campus initiative. As a result, my chair is usually happy to work with me on arranging a teaching schedule that avoids evenings and weekends, which is when Amy works. Similarly, my Dean and others exempted me from other FDU projects and encouraged me to pursue my professional interests. It is fair to say that developing and writing this book would have been much harder without the latitude they gave me. But first I had to earn that latitude by proving, over time, that I would continue to perform at an "A" level, and not abuse the privilege of flexibility.

For Darrell Green, earning the trust and respect of his bosses meant that he could maintain a family-friendly lifestyle, even during peak football season. For you and me, it may mean being able to work from home once a week, or to carve out the time to take a night class.

Building a track record of excellent performance is the best way to enable ourselves to work more flexibly and to confidently negotiate with bosses over work arrangements. High performance also gives you credibility with clients and coworkers. If you do all this, you will build up a well of credibility that you can draw from in order to make a request. And, please, do not make a request if you are not perceived as valuable by your supervisor – you'll ruin it for the rest of us!

Step #2- Negotiating Well By Understanding Your Boss' Concerns

Concern #1- They Won't Be Able To Monitor Your Work

Perhaps the most important reason that managers are reluctant to allow for flexible work arrangements is that they are concerned that they will no longer be able to monitor your performance. For some managers, this belief is an offshoot of their assumption that most workers are lazy and will try to get away with slacking off if they are not closely supervised. But for most managers, their concern is less about assuming you'll goof off, and more that it will expose them as a mediocre judge of performance.

It's a bit like that classic Dilbert cartoon in which the Pointy-headed Boss tells Dilbert that "I can't let you telecommute because then I won't be able to manage you." To which Dilbert replies,

"You're managing me right now and all it is doing is preventing me from working!"

The fact is most supervisors are very bad at evaluating performance, and they know it. As a result, they rely on visible indicators of performance like "face time" or "chair time." This, of course, is silly; "face time" is easily gamed – productive people finish and go home, political opportunists stay late while being less productive (and probably spending time on Facebook or fantasy football). In fact, when financial firm Ryan LLC[7] converted to a system in which they allowed employee autonomy on work hours and expanded work from home options, they found that the employees who spent the most time at the office were, very often, below average performers.

The best way to address this managerial concern is what some people call "Managing Up" – the subtle art of making your supervisor a better manager. If I was to make a request for the ability to work about 1/3 of my hours from home, and I knew my boss was wary about being unable to measure my performance, I'd lay out an entire performance evaluation system for him. It would look something like this:

- We will set performance goals, and the objective measures we'll use to determine whether I am meeting or exceeding those goals
- We will meet formally every three months to discuss my performance against those goals
- I will provide bi-weekly progress reports on how I am meeting those goals
- I will provide a weekly time log for the hours I work outside the office
- I would also assure my boss that I would arrange for the things I would need to work remotely and stay effective. I'd take the initiative to set up Skype, Google chat, scheduling software, Citrix online meetings, Free Conference Call, and other free or low-cost tools myself.

This way, you address one of your supervisor's major concerns right off the bat. You've just given them the tools to actually do a far better job at monitoring your performance than they ever did before. And it requires little to no extra work on their part.

Concern #2- Risk Aversion

Remember that TV game show *Who Wants to be a Millionaire?* It's a fun show – I always enjoy watching dumb people losing by whiffing on easy questions or smart people winning by answering difficult ones. Plus, Regis and Meredith are really great at selling the drama. But "Millionaire" is also an interesting study into the psychology of risk aversion. Once someone starts earning a fair amount of money, they start to get very conservative. Imagine you are at $250,000 and facing the $500,000 question. If you get it right, you are up to $500,000; you get it wrong, you fall to $125,000 and leave the game. Imagine you use your last lifeline to narrow the choices to two, but are still totally stumped. What would you do?

In this case, a fully rational decision to maximize your payout would be to guess. The upside is higher than the downside. But what do most contestants do in this situation? They decline to answer, keep their $250,000 and walk off screen.

While it is not fully rational, this decision is quite understandable. The thought of losing $125,000 horrifies people more than gaining an additional $250,000 elates them. As a result, they minimize risk.

Most managers are like this, too. They just want their department to do a good job and they don't want to risk the ire of higher-ups by trying something different or something that goes against the prevailing corporate culture. As a result, many see their most important task as eliminating problems and potential problems, as opposed to seeking opportunities and taking risks. It's why football coaches almost always punt on fourth and one, when a more rational analysis would suggest going for it. And when you are asking to work from home or try something new, you are injecting some risk and reward into their calculus.

It is your job to help your boss understand that what you propose is all upside and no downside. One way to do this is to educate them on the benefits of telecommuting. The most definitive study on the effects of telecommuting[8], which included 12,500 employees in 46 companies, found that part-time telecommuting results in:

- Higher employee job satisfaction and organizational commitment
- Slightly higher levels of employee performance
  - o All the accumulated evidence shows that, for appropriate jobs, partial telecommuting is at worst performance-neutral, and many studies demonstrate moderate performance gains
- Lowered employee turnover intentions, employee stress and work-family conflict
- No evidence on harming workplace relationships and the ability to collaborate for those who telecommute fewer than 2.5 days a week.

Additionally, others have found:
- Reducing turnover can be a major cost savings. HR professionals estimate that replacing a quality professional costs up to two times their annual salary. This means that, if part-time telecommuting prevents just one $80,000 employee from quitting, the company has saved up to $160,000.
- Telecommuters are less likely to be absent from work as they can work from home while sick, juggling a family-related matter, or during dangerous weather.

- Significant cost savings to employees in terms of lowering driving, tolls, and commuting costs (not to mention reduced greenhouse gas emissions)
- Potential cost savings to employers in terms of office space utilization and lowered utility bills.
- Telecommuting can help attract better employees – It is an important consideration for high-quality job seekers choosing among employment options, especially for Generations X and Y.
- Telecommuting can help retain better employees – It has been called the best non-financial perk for doing so. One website estimates that 36% would choose partial work from home over a pay raise.
- Today, telecommuting has virtually no costs for the employer. Almost everyone has a home computer/laptop and smartphone.

A recent report from the Working Mother Research Institute shows that, among men who use formal or informal workplace flexibility:

- 85 percent state that it enhances their performance at work
- 84 percent state that it increases their morale, satisfaction and motivation
- 82 percent state that it enhances their loyalty and commitment
- 77 percent state that it enhances their relationships with coworkers
- 81 percent states it helps their communication with coworkers
- 80 percent state that it reduces their stress level
- 87 percent state that it helps them manage home responsibilities

In short, telecommuting costs an employer virtually nothing – except for a leap of faith. It can result in significant benefits for employers and employees. In fact, according to Herb Greenberg, founder and CEO of the talent management consultancy, Caliper, the best day of sales in their company's history was the day a huge snowstorm pounded the Northeast US (Caliper is headquartered in Princeton, NJ). Their employees had long been encouraged to telecommute and work flexibly as needed. As a result, they were able to keep working from home while all their competitors were shut down.

Many managers may be unaware of these benefits or may perceive that telecommuting is disruptive and risky. Our job is to convince them that the benefits far outweigh any concerns they may have. This way, faith will not be necessary. One dad who worked out part-time telecommuting with his boss embodies the win-win nature of such arrangements:

> I am trusted to work independently and am not micromanaged. It's funny to say, but I LOVE my boss personally and professionally. Where I work is what a company can be if it is open, flexible and deals honestly with employees and their situations.
>
> For all they've done for me, I would never do this company wrong. Corporations have to understand that if they work with their employees to help them with their family needs, employees will go above and beyond, and will never leave. Companies will benefit from loosening the reins.

Until more employers understand this, we need to advocate for ourselves.

Further, risk-averse managers are often reluctant to try new things for fear they will expose themselves to criticism. We also need to show our managers that telecommuting is increasingly common, and they are not really sticking their necks out very far, if at all, by approving your request. Some statistics to back this up:

- 84 of Fortune 100 companies allow extensive use of telecommuting. More than 20 percent of employees at such companies as SC Johnson, Qualcomm, Booz Allen, Fidelity, Cisco and Goldman Sachs telecommute. If managers in these companies can allow for telecommuting, why can't they?

Finally, you need to give your manager an out. As part of any agreement with them I would volunteer the following:

- I will provide all my contact information to you, my coworkers, and my clients, so they can always reach me.
- I agree that emergency situations (e.g., ramping up for a new client, deadlines during tax season, a coworker unexpectedly quitting) may mean a temporary pause in the flexible work arrangement.
- I agree that, after the first three-month trial period, we will meet to re-assess the situation. At this time, if you are not happy with the arrangement, we can adjust accordingly.

Remember, many managers are risk-averse and dislike change. You have to make it easier for them to say yes.

Concern #3- The Wrong Kind of Fairness

There are many ways to define fairness:

- Everyone is treated the same
- Everyone gets outcomes depending on their contributions
- Decision-making processes are fair, even if outcomes for employees differ

For many supervisors, being fair means treating all employees the same. It's easy for the manager and easy for employees to understand. However, this is probably not the best way for managers to be fair. A better approach combines the second and third bullet points above- all employees are treated with equal respect and an unbiased decision-making process, but then get individualized treatment based on their contributions, needs, and built-up trustworthiness.

Hall of Fame football coach Bill Parcells embraced the third definition on his way to winning two Super Bowls and transforming three franchises. He explained his view of fairness in an interview before his Hall of Fame induction:

> I never believed in treating everyone the same... I don't believe in consistency as it relates to handling players. I believe in being right for each guy. I tried to do my best to understand what a particular player needed to be pushed to do his best. I felt an obligatory responsibility to give the players what they needed for the best chance to win.

Parcells was famously hard on Phil Simms, because he believed that's how he would get the best out of him. He coddled Lawrence Taylor, treating him with kindness and fatherly love, despite Taylor's off-field problems. He felt it was the best way to get the most out of him. You can't argue with the results.

More enlightened managers should view flexible work as a standard benefit[9]. However, many will view your request of an alternate work arrangement as an appeal for individualized consideration. So how can we nudge our supervisors away from the first definition of fairness to something more nuanced and flexible?

- Be indispensable, and make sure your supervisor knows how indispensable you are, before you ask for "special treatment"
- Suggest something in return for your individualized arrangement. You could volunteer for extra assignments, or find other ways to make your supervisor's job easier.
- Remember to offer the performance-management system, performance goals and measures, time-logs, and commitments to certain availability that I suggested earlier.
- Assure your boss that you are requesting a temporary, trial arrangement, and that continuation depends on continued top performance.

A related fairness concern of supervisors is that they fear if they give a special arrangement for you, then soon everyone will make similar requests. However, since you have already documented both how great an employee you are and the strings you attached to the deal, you have given your supervisor:

- A process to make decisions regarding flexible work arrangements that upholds their ideas of fairness
- Information to help your supervisor advise employees how they can qualify for an arrangement
- A way to explain their decision when potentially accepting or denying other requests

You also need to make it clear that you are not asking for a favor, or for them to act on your behalf only out of personal consideration or sympathy. You need to reassure your boss that his decision to give you individualized consideration if fair. One way to do this is by framing your conversation as a business request, not a personal one. This means you have to address your supervisor's needs as well as your own. Making a request like:

It would help me if I could work at home on Thursdays so I can coach my daughter's soccer team.

- isn't likely to be effective. In this request, you get all the upside, and the supervisor gets none. Instead, I'd suggest phrasing your request like:
- If I could work from home two days a week, it would save me four hours of commuting time that I could better spend helping clients. Also, considering the nature of my work, I need long stretches of uninterrupted time, so working some days outside of our busy office would help me be more productive.

In this second request, there is upside for both you and your supervisor. You are assuring him/her that you are focused on fulfilling the needs of your workplace. Also, this request is framed as a business proposition, and is not focused on family concerns. While I don't believe you need to hide your family issues, neither do I think you should highlight them as the central reason for your request. After all, some bosses still see family as a women's concern.

Concern #4- "Old-School" & Paying Dues

> I've been with three major companies since the late nineties. I've been fortunate in that they are all ranked as top employers, but unfortunate in that I worked for some really bad managers. Not only did this impact my job satisfaction, but it also impacted my ability to spend time with my family.

Unlike this dad, in my experience, most managers, even those of earlier generations, really want to do right by their employees. Now, they may have the wrong idea about what is right or they may be unable to figure out how address employee concerns, but I've found most managers are well-meaning people doing their best.

That being said, there is a significant minority who are completely self-centered and actively disdain employees. Some are aggressively "old school" in their approach. Some really believe family concerns are for women only and look down on involved fathers. Some feel as if they paid their dues by going "all in" for work even if it prevented them from being the father and husband they wanted to be. And they'll be damned if their subordinates won't have to pay their dues as well.

> About 10 years ago, I was aiming for partner at my law firm. I was divorced and my ex and the kids lived in London – I flew out on a Thursday night red-eye to see them every other weekend. After two monster weeks of work, I was leaving the office to get to JFK when a senior partner started yelling at me, "Where are you going?"

> I tried to calmly explain that I bulked up the past two weeks and my client was satisfied, so there's no reason for me not to fly to Heathrow and see my kids. He angrily responded, "Bullshit. You see your kids more than I do, and I live with mine. Besides I need you here tonight — and over the weekend." During his rant, he actually called me a "family man" as if that was an insult.

Frankly, I'm not sure how to deal with managers like this. If you found yourself nodding along to this last anecdote, you may just be out of luck. My best advice is to keep your head down for now, continue to do good work, actively network, and brush up your resume. Take the first available chance to escape an aggressively unpleasant boss. They'll ruin the one-third of your life that you spend at work, and they'll contaminate the rest with stress. In fact, getting away from that boss is exactly what that dad wound up doing:

> I simply turned and left and caught my flight, but that was it for me at this firm. I left not long afterwards, actually left the law altogether, and never looked back. Life is just too short.

▌ Putting It Together

> My company is pretty family-friendly, but so much of it varies from department to department based on the manager and the personalities involved. Some are great, and others, well, are not. During my career, I've had to know how to navigate my different bosses. There was always a learning curve.

I've covered the most common reasons managers are reluctant to embrace workplace flexibility. But, as this dad points out, I'm sure there are others specific to your work situation and your current boss.

No matter the particulars of your situation, if you plan ahead and think through possible sources of resistance, you will have a much stronger hand to play when making your request. To sum up, any formal request for a flexible work arrangement should include the following elements:

- A brief description of the alternative work arrangement, being sure to describe it (both in-person and in a memo) in terms of:

  o How your work performance will be maintained and enhanced

  o How it is not very different from how you are productively working now

  o How it may affect your clients and coworkers, and what you will do to minimize any disruptions (having set meeting hours, sharing cellphone numbers, etc.)

  o How it costs the company very little, since you already have a home computer, internet access, a skype account and a smartphone. (there may be some minimal costs, such as a gotomyPC.com subscription, be up front about these)

- A proposed 3 month trial period at which you and your supervisor will assess how well the arrangement is working out and adjust accordingly

- A proposed set of performance goals and the measures to evaluate your work by the end of the trial period

- Bi-weekly progress reports on your time use, activities and progress towards goals

- A promise that the arrangement can be put on hold, no questions asked, for any urgent situation, as determined by the supervisor (ramping up for a new client proposal, increase in work demand during tax season, etc.)

By being proactive in making this request, you are assuring your supervisor that your performance will continue to be rock-solid, and that you have pre-addressed their concerns. Remember that many managers are risk-averse and dislike change. You have to make it easier for them to say yes.

I'll provide a template for you as a guide in the exercises at the end of the chapter. The template is perfect for a formal request. However, if you'd rather handle things more conversationally and over time, the template will help you organize your thoughts and develop your strategy.

▌ If negotiating for flexibility is not right for you

Based on your financial situation, job security or the barriers posed by an unsupportive boss and intense work culture, it may not be wise to visibly announce your intentions to work more flexibly. You may need to keep your family concerns under the radar. There are still things you can do informally and on an ad-hoc basis to add more flexibility to your work. And there are ways we can maximize our time at work so we can reduce our work hours and also protect our family time from work demands. We'll explore these in the next chapter.

Chapter 5 Exercises

1. Flexible Work Arrangement Proposal

Proposed by:

For:

Date:

Description of desired flexible work arrangement:
For a trial period beginning _____ and ending _____ . Please note that the arrangement may be put on hold during work emergencies.
How my time spent on work and work performance will be maintained and enhanced:
Ways in which my work will not be altered:

How I will ensure access to coworkers and clients:

Needed tools and resources, including those supplied by me, and those supplied by the firm:

Performance goals for trail period:

Measures we should use to evaluate our performance against proposed goals;

Format for bi-weekly progress reports on my time use, activities and progress:

Other concerns and arrangements

Signatures:

_____

_____

Date: _____

CHAPTER 6

Other Ways to Work More Flexibly and More Effectively

I work for a major consultancy and the ethic here is to put in really long hours. If I want to stay on partner-track, I have to keep up the pace. My co-workers are, and they'd leave me in the dust.

. . . .

I don't like my job or my boss, but what can I do? Money doesn't grow on trees and providing for a family of five isn't cheap. It would be great if I could flex my hours or work from home sometimes, but that's not going to happen here.

Based on your financial situation, career aspirations, or lack of job security, you may not be able to visibly announce your intentions to work more flexibly. Because of the barriers posed by an unsupportive boss or intense work culture, you may be unable to use formal flextime or telecommuting, and negotiating with your boss about flexibility may seem like career suicide.

Many dads, including the ones quoted above, need to keep family concerns under the radar. But take heart: There are still things we can do informally and on an ad-hoc basis to add more flexibility to our work. There are ways we can maximize our work efficiency so at least we can focus on our families once we get home. In this chapter, we'll take a problem-focused coping approach to navigating the workplace and think through strategies we can use when we're stuck in an unsupportive situation. Specifically, we'll cover:

- Informally and invisibly addressing family responsibilities when we are unable to do so openly
- Maximizing our effectiveness through time management, careful planning and smart use of technology
- Understanding and combatting the effects of chronic overwork
- Knowing when and how to take a stand

█ Problem-Focused Coping

> You promised your family you'd get home early to get to the school recital. But your boss just pushed back the department meeting to the end of the day. You can't be in two places at once. What do you do? How do you feel? STRESSED.

Stress occurs when the demands you face seem to exceed your capacity for handling them. You can't be at the meeting and the recital. Can you miss the meeting without consequences? How will your family react?

In the 1970s and 1980s, pioneering psychologist Richard Lazarus and his colleagues studied how people respond to stress and identified two major categories: Emotion-Focused Coping and Problem-Focused Coping. With emotion-focused coping, we don't do anything to actively change our situations. Instead we focus on how to deal with or re-interpret the stress we feel. Examples of emotion-focused coping thoughts and behaviors include reframing, denial and wishful thinking. Some examples:

- I should look on the bright side, at least I have a job
- Well, things can be worse!

- I'm not going to let it get me down
- I'll take some deep breaths and try to keep my composure
- I hope I can make the next recital

If there is really nothing we can do to alter our situations, at least emotion-focused coping can make us feel better about the hole we're in. However, I'd like to think there's almost always something we can do, especially in the medium to long-term. That's where problem-focused coping comes in.

Problem-focused coping involves taking active steps to change the situation that is causing stress, including proactively seeking out information, changing our behavior, or attempting to change our circumstances. Some problem-focused coping behaviors include:

- Talking to my boss to see if we can work on a solution together
- Asking for advice from someone who faced a similar situation
- Brainstorming ways to tackle this head-on
- Dusting off my resume

When facing a dilemma like the situation described above, problem-focused coping may mean talking to your boss asking him to reschedule the meeting, arranging to call into the meeting on your Bluetooth while driving home, asking for help from your mentor, or telling coworkers you feel a migraine coming on and you may have to go home soon (generally not a good long-term strategy, but the temptation to do so is often a sign that your situation is becoming untenable and action is needed).

Maybe you are out of luck today, but setting up a time to talk to your boss to prevent future last-minute scheduling changes or taking a personal day for the next recital can help avoid future dilemmas. Some tactics may work, some may not, but at least you are doing something.

▮ Flying Under the Radar

My dissertation research years ago focused on coping strategies that were specific to work-family conflicts and allowed employees to address their situations while avoiding scrutiny at work. As discussed earlier in the book, very few dads raise their hands for formal flextime or telecommuting as they fear brushback from their supervisors or coworkers. I saw a need to discover how working parents coped and whether these strategies were effective.

I identified a set of work-family-specific coping tactics, broken into three categories, and through a series of studies found:

- Virtually every working parent faced work-family conflict
- Those who faced work-family conflict but used the tactics I identified felt less stressed out than those who did not
- Employees who felt less stress were more satisfied with both work and family, more committed to their employer and expressed a stronger desire to stay at their employer
- Workplaces with more positive work-family cultures_gave people more freedom to engage in these tactics

Here are the three categories I uncovered:

Tackling Small Stuff During Work Time - Most people with white-collar jobs and some discretion over their work are allowed to use small bits of time and resources (e.g., a little bit of company emailing[10]) to take care of small errands or to coordinate with family. Clearing away some smaller family items during work hours can allow family time to be more focused on family. Unless abused, most companies and supervisors don't have much problem with allowing such small morsels of flexibility. Here are two examples:

> My daughter gets home from high school, and the first thing she has to do is call me at work. We talk for a few

minutes and plan our evening. No one at works minds my 10 minute daily phone call. And why should they?

I fly a lot for work, but I use the time at the airport or while taxiing at the gate to tackle lots of small family-related things. I'll do my taxes on a flight, make the soccer team lineup while waiting for a connection, do Christmas shopping at the airport – with a little planning, you can really maximize your time. The more I get done on the road, the more I can be focused on my family once I get home.

Time-Shifting - As opposed to formal flexible work arrangements, the following actions may help us informally shift some of their work time to accommodate family needs. By working ahead or making up the work later, these actions have no negative effect on performance. The work still gets done, and you are freed up to handle family concerns. The optimal way to time-shift is to speak with your supervisor, using the techniques discussed in Chapter 5. However, if this is not a good option for you, you can probably do some of this under the radar.

I coach most of my kids' teams. With my long commute, I have to leave work by about three to get there in time. I plan ahead at work accordingly, and check in with my coworkers. But then I go – I don't flaunt it, but I don't ask for permission, either. My coworkers know I make up the work time either at night or over the weekend. Sometimes, I even trade off some tasks with my friend at work so we can cover for each other if any last minute things come up.

Using "Time Holes" - Most work days have short periods of time for breaks or lunch. Using this time to accomplish work or family-related tasks frees up time later on. The downside is that you may not get to use this downtime to relax or recharge. Eating lunch while working at your desk is not always ideal, but it could get us home faster.

Part of my job involves visiting local vendors. I use the dry cleaner and bank near this one vendor right after my weekly visit. I can kill two birds with one stone, take care of a few errands while I'm out, and not have to hustle doing these things later on with kids in tow.

None of these tactics is a magic bullet for dealing with work-family conflict. But, taken together, they can be part of a problem-focused coping solution.

■ Managing Your Time

There are many great apps, guides and ideas out there on time management (see Sources and Resources section of this book for a few). This section is by no means an exhaustive list, but I want to share a few ways we can think about how we use our time at work.

I often tell my MBA students that, "if you can't measure something, it's awful hard to manage it." One reason many of us find it hard to manage our time is that we don't keep good track. In the first exercise at the end of the chapter, I'll ask you to keep a diary of your time use at work. This will serve as a guide for planning our future workweeks. When we construct our new and improved weekly schedules, we should keep the following ideas in mind:

- Switching between tasks really slows you down
- Some work tasks can be done quickly and others require large chunks of uninterrupted time
- We need to protect time for the most important items on our to-do lists, or else urgent but less important items get in our way
- We have to fight procrastination whenever we can
- We can save a lot of time with smart use of technology

Let's elaborate just a little further on each.

Avoiding the Off-Ramp - When you drive on a highway, you can go at good speed and get where you need to go quickly. When you are on an on-ramp or off-ramp, however, you have to slow down, and then it takes lots of energy to get back to highway speed. Similarly, when you are focused on a task and in a good flow, you can work effectively and efficiently. However, when you switch from one task to another, your brain off-ramps from your first task and then on-ramps to the second, slowing your progress.

I learned this the hard way in the early days of writing this book. I would be on the computer and a notification would pop up in the corner of the screen, with a little whoosh, whenever I received a new email. So, I would, of course, go to my email folder to see what was sent. This popped me out of my writing flow, slowing my momentum. Even though it was just a minute, that time represented an off-ramp and on-ramp that cost me many more minutes to re-collect my thoughts and get back on task.

I learned quickly, however, to close the email folder and stop notifications. Now I only check emails when it does not interrupt other work. Similarly, I shut off the dings and beeps on my phone that tell me there is a new text, email or Facebook message. The temptation to check them is just too great. At my office, I silence my phone when in head-down grading papers or prepping class. If I have a student in at office hours, I close up the laptop so I'm not distracted from our discussion. I'm trying to stay on highway speed and avoid detours.

Time Chunks- Especially when you have big tasks that require concentration, we need to allocate and protect long stretches of time to that task. In her amazing book, *Overwhelmed*, Brigid Schulte describes the importance of time chunks both at the workplace and at home (more on this in Part 3 of this book). Usually, we can get more done and feel less pressed if we can devote hours to a single task instead of piecing together multiple fifteen-minute windows of time.

For example, three hours with the office door closed is conducive to creating a killer sales presentation. You can concentrate, get on highway speed, work efficiently, and finish without having loose ends causing you residual stress. You may even have time for a break or to tackle secondary responsibilities. However, spending your afternoon split between prepping that presentation and taking phone calls and filling out expense reports and making plans for racquetball is not as conducive to efficiency. At the end of the day, the presentation may not be finished or as good as you'd like. We've felt rushed and scattered all day and now we'll carry the stress of uncompleted work home with us. This stress, of course, can contaminate our family time.

One way to free up larger chunks of time is identify the little things that need to get done, and keep them separate from our needed time chunks. You have twenty minutes before the staff meeting? This is a terrible time to start the budget report, but a great time to plow through some emails, get one expense report done, organize your desk drawer, or some other task that can be done quickly or without much thought. Setting aside separate times for big things and little things can be really helpful.

Even Better To-Do Lists- In Chapter 3, we discussed the need for the items on a to-do list to be tied to larger goals and priorities. I'd like to add two more considerations for even better to-do-lists: deadlines and time estimates for each task.

Before I became more disciplined about my to-do lists, my typical list was a hodgepodge of big things and little things, urgent matters and far-off deadlines. I'm not sure how helpful they were, and the unfinished tasks stressed me out. To illustrate, I dug out a to-do list from an old document in the deep recesses of my hard drive. Here's a piece:

- Call Steve
- Finish grading MGMT 3361 exams
- Get final version of results section to Suzanne
- Pick up Nick after school
- Update teaching portfolio for faculty review
- Email Gwen
- Schedule student club meeting, find guest speaker

What a mess! Updating my portfolio will take a few hours. So will grading. The results section might take a whole day. Emails take two minutes. School pick-up is today. The portfolio's not due for two weeks. What does Steve need to talk about? In short, this list gives me no guidance on what to do now, what can be saved for later, what can be done quickly and what needs a time chunk.

The to-do lists I make now are better. First, I try to group things together under headings. For me, these include teaching, research, book stuff, blog stuff, FDU stuff and family stuff. Also, items now come with a deadline and an approximate amount of time the task will take. For example, part of my to-do list from late January 2015:

- Book stuff:
  - Edit chapter 7 (3 hours, by Thursday)
  - Write first draft of chapter 8 (two days, by Sunday)
  - Study cover art options, set up phone meeting (2 hours, by Friday)
- Teaching:
  - Finalize MGMT 3700 syllabus (2 hours, by Saturday)
  - Review and update MGMT 4730 PowerPoints for weeks 1-5 (4 hours, by Sunday)
  - Get classroom changed for MGMT 4730 (10 minutes, by Friday)

This is so much more helpful for planning Wednesday through Sunday. I need big time chunks for writing and editing the book.

I'll edit on Wednesday evening, start Chapter 8 Friday morning and save all day Saturday to write. I'll find a play-date for Nick to free up time, and make it up to him with an epic Bananagrams session Saturday night. I can squeeze in the room change request whenever, and can even split up my PowerPoint work into five smaller time periods and tackle one a day. I take Nick to his two-hour Friday afternoon gymnastics session, and can finalize my syllabus while he's swinging on the high bar. This new system really works well for me, and I bet it could for you.

Overcoming Procrastination - There are competing lines of thought on this issue. Some say you should start each day by taking on the hardest task, the one you least look forward to doing (for me, that's grading papers). By "eating the frog," you conquer this task early, and then have the rest of the day for more pleasant tasks. Conversely, others say you should start with some small successes to build up momentum for bigger tasks. Others say you should figure out when in the day you typically have the most energy and save the big tasks for then – even if this means pulling all-nighters. Others say to do the most important things first. In *Overwhelmed*, Schulte recommends identifying "one big thing" each day that you must do and do well, and suggests we can give ourselves some slack if other to-do's don't all get done (this is in line with our rocks and sand analogy).

I think there is wisdom to all these approaches, and think we should each identify the method that works best for us. Maybe give a few of them a shot to see which best fits your style. These days, I'm leaning towards Schulte's "one big thing" approach. The goal is to combat procrastination and dead time; it doesn't matter exactly how we accomplish that.

Wise Use of Technology - Technology is a double-edged sword. I can work from anywhere – I'm free! Or I can work from anywhere – I'm trapped! We'll talk more about separating yourself from constant accessibility to work in Chapter 9. For now, let's concentrate on the positives that come from smart use of technology. For instance, teleconferencing can reduce our need for travel:

> For each trip, I ask, "will my physically being there bring significant value?" For things like presentations and sales calls, the answer is almost always yes. But for other meetings, sometimes a call or a video conference can be enough. Or maybe it's a live meeting THIS time and a virtual meeting NEXT time. But if you are caught up in travel and don't ask the question, you will default to getting on that plane, and that takes you out of the office and away from family probably more than you'd like.

Technology can help us be more efficient on our commutes:

> I'm so glad I got the wifi plan for my iPad. Now, when I'm on the train to work, I can take care of emails and get a jump on the day. I have my decks cleared stepping into the office, meaning I can usually get things done more quickly and get home.

And, as we covered in the previous chapters, technology can allow us to shift where and when we get work done. Remember this happy dad from Chapter 4:

> I can work from absolutely wherever and whenever – as long as have my laptop and gadgets, I can get things done. When I need time for family, I take it. There's no need for me to take sick time or personal days. As long as I get everything done – and they do hold me accountable – they keep giving me this freedom.

■ Combating Chronic Overwork

In high school, I was on the cross-country track team. I was only a decent athlete, and midway through the season, my coach demoted me to the "B team." I wanted to prove to him I deserved to be back on the "A team," so I launched into my first "B race" at a far faster pace than normal.

I was leading the pack almost the entire way, and, even though my legs were burning, I thought that I could win, get a shiny medal, and more importantly, get my deserved promotion higher up the team pecking order. My coach was thrilled by my "all in" performance. Coming down the last ½ mile of the 3 mile race, however, my legs turned to jelly and I fell from the lead all the way to the back. I even threw up! Afterwards, my coach asked what happened.

I think he knew the answer, and most of us who work in competitive fields know it too. I hadn't paced myself. I lost my race because I treated a three-mile run like a 100-meter dash. As a result, I had no energy in reserve for the last, most important stretch.

I bet you understand what it is like, both at work and at home, to work so hard for so long under so much pressure that we run out of energy. This takes a toll on our mental and physical health, but also diminishes our long-term job performance. We are not alone. According to a recent Families and Work Institute study, one third of employees report chronic overwork. Those reporting chronic overwork cite:

- Extreme job demands, in that they are given more work than can be reasonably accomplished even in 50-60 hour workweeks
- Expectations that they stay connected to work remotely after work hours
- The inability to avoid "low value-added" tasks such as paperwork or unnecessary meetings
- Having too many projects to work on at one time, diminishing their ability to focus and prioritize among projects and creating too many interruptions and distractions.

This being said, occasional overwork is often the cost of getting ahead in our careers – think accountants during tax season, the week leading up to a big client meeting, or prep work for a big trial. If we use the "balanced diet" approach to life balance, occasional overwork is the equivalent of carbo-loading or having a few too many desserts over the holidays. It may not be ideal, but we can even ourselves out over time.

I try to make the case at the companies I work with that "all in" and "work before all" cultures and expectations are actually enemies of sustained high performance. It doesn't always sink in[11]. Specifically because many bosses and workplaces encourage chronic rather than occasional overwork, we have to be smart and protect ourselves. This not only protects our sanity and family balance, it prevents burnout and diminished performance over time. Combatting chronic overwork helps us win the long race.

Have You Bought Into the "Culture of Overwork?"

Here's a quick checklist from my friend, Greg Marcus' book, *Busting Your Corporate Idol* that can tell you if you are exhibiting signs of chronic overwork and have internalized corporate "work before all" priorities.

1. You find yourself doing "what is best for the company" instead of "what is best"

2. You joke that you are 'married to the company"

3. You are getting persistent feedback from a loved one that you are working too many hours

4. You are experiencing health-related illnesses, such as insomnia, headaches, high blood pressure, weight gain

5. You work more than 60 hours a week

6. You don't care how you treat others at work as long as the work gets done

7. You are considered successful in your career, yet unfulfilled in ways you cannot define

8. Someone has stated that "you are drinking the Kool-Aid"

9. You feel indispensable to the company and fear that if you work less or say "no", the company will suffer

If you said yes to more than one or two of these items, it may be time to consider whether work is getting in the way of a full life.

How do we fight back?

Scheduling in Unstructured Time - Imagine a glass that is filled to the brim. Now, you need to add in an ice cube. But, if you do, what happens? The water spills over because the glass has no more capacity. Similarly, if we are always booked solid and working 60 hour weeks, we have no bandwidth for a last-minute client demand, a family emergency, or an opportunity to attend a useful training seminar. We are at capacity and the only way to do it all is to work longer and longer high-pressure hours.

Once we get a handle on our schedules, we need to allocate chunks of unstructured time into our workweeks. If our glass isn't filled to the brim, we can handle that unexpected ice cube. We have capacity for a last-minute client demand, an "all-hands" meeting, or an unplanned networking opportunity. If no emergencies pop up, this time can be used for the other non-performance work goals – development, advancement, networking, flexibility – that we identified in Chapter 3.

Detach from Technology - As stated earlier, technology is a double-edged sword in that it can blur the lines between work and family and between the workplace and the rest of the world. We'll discuss this further in Chapter 9, but there are several things we can do to ensure that our non-work time does not needlessly get interrupted by work. For example, a dad I know lets his coworkers know that he will only check work email once, at 9:30pm every evening after work. Employers are even starting to catch on. For instance, a few years ago, Volkswagen decided to shut down its email servers after hours to force their managerial employees to stay unplugged.

Use Time Off Wisely - Perhaps the best way to combat chronic overwork is to take breaks every now and then.

> In many companies, vacation days are "use it or lose it." Many dads I know use their vacation days only for full blown family vacations. I realized that I was leaving days on the table, so I decided to make a change. Every winter, I take at least 3-4 individual days off to go skiing with my buddies. It's a just a day trip, I don't miss time with the family (kids are in school, wife is at work), and it refreshes me for the rest of the week. I do similar days in the summer for golf. This really works well for me.

We'll discuss paternity leave in more detail in Chapter 8, but I always thought a good model for parental leave is a few weeks home with the newborn, and then the use of unpaid Family and Medical Leave to take a day or two off each week for the next few months. In this way, you stay connected to the workplace, but take the time to pace yourself in the face of amplified family demands.

▌ Taking a Stand

Finally, most of the advice in this chapter has been to help us navigate work-family issues as if our workplaces are intolerant of family concerns and that workplaces can never change. To some degree, this is good advice. Many workplaces are not open to discussion of family, and work schedules and demands are still structured around an "all-in single-breadwinner with at-home spouse" approach that is a relic of another time.

But employers will never change if dads assume that employer hostility towards family demands are set in stone, and that dads must only resort to working through holes in the system, through informal arrangements or "invisible" accommodations.

We need to live in the world as it is, but we should not give up trying to make things better. If our generation of busy involved dads doesn't start making change happen, more dads will struggle seemingly alone. Change is possible, and, as we will discuss in the next chapter, there are many examples of workplace cultures that are supportive of work-family.

So how can we start? I have a few ideas, but first a note of caution. These actions require courage, and some degree of respect and security at your workplace. You may encounter some short-term pushback. But, you might not. Sometimes by assuming the worst, we contribute to building our barriers ourselves.

> In my second year working at a huge multinational company, I had gotten a reputation as being a workhorse: long hours, plenty of overtime – I was the guy that would work until he dropped to get the job done. After my son was born, I wanted to spend more time at home and be an active part of family life. So, I decided I would leave the office at 5:30 two days a week, spend time with my son (dinner, bath, bedtime stories), and then log back in at 8pm to finish my work day. My total hours remained the same, but I DID feel a little sheepish about leaving

the office at 5:30. What would other people think? Did they know that I would be logging in later to finish my 12 hour day? Was my "workhorse" reputation going to suffer? I found myself yearning to justify and explain myself, despite the fact that no one had said one word to me about my new schedule.

If you have the security, flexibility, courage and inclination, we can make it easier for fellow dads to discuss and address work-family demands. We can do this by talking about our families and asking other men about theirs, and by making sure other men in our workplaces see us use work flexibility for family reasons. This dad makes sure to discuss family right up front:

> I'm a training instructor and run new employee orientation at my company. When I introduce myself to a new class I have a picture of me and my family on the power point projector. This helps new employees relax and I get to brag a bit about my kids. It's a good ice breaker.

There are lots of small actions we can take. For example, you can keep pictures of your family not just in a small frame facing you on the desk, but in a prominent place at your workstation where anyone coming by can see it. During "water cooler" chit-chat with other men, you can change the subject from *Monday Night Football* to what you did with your kids last weekend, making sure to ask what they did with their families.

Similarly, the next time you have to leave work early for family reasons, don't just mumble something or sneak out. Be brave, and matter-of-factly tell your coworkers why you are leaving. And don't feel guilty about it. If your work remains great, eventually very few people will care that you sometimes have to accommodate work to family. And, more importantly, more men at your workplace will see your example and feel more secure in following it.

These actions are even more powerful if you are a supervisor and can generate conversations with men who report to you.

The goal is to make it more normal for men in our workplaces to discuss family issues, and to bring our full selves to work. This lays the groundwork for more supportive workplace cultures. Here's one dad's experience:

> I always made sure to discuss my family at work, and people saw that I adjusted my schedule without apology. After a while, more than a few people who worked for me or with me said that, as a manager, I set a good example about family time. They told me it made them feel more comfortable and shaped how they approached work and life.

As Mahatma Gandhi said, "Be the change that you wish to see in the world." If you are in a position to start shaping your workplace culture, please do.

In the next chapter, we'll explore how we can make work-family balance considerations part of our job search and ongoing career management. For now, in the following exercises, let's focus on better short-term time management.

CHAPTER 6 - **Exercises**

1. Assessing your weekly time use at work

Use this first calendar to record your work activities each hour at work. Take special care to note all the different tasks you've worked on, especially if you quickly shifted from one to the next.

Week of [Dates]

	Monday	Tuesday	Wednesday	Thursday	Friday
7					
8					
9					
10					
11					
12					
1					
2					
3					
4					
5					
6					
7					

At the end of the week, evaluate your time use. When were you most efficient? Did you use time chunks? When did you feel rushed or frenzied? When weren't you as efficient?

Based on these questions, think ahead and try to set up a schedule for next week. Remember the principles in the chapter about:

- Time chunks
- The problems with constant shifting between tasks
- Scheduling in unstructured time
- Keeping yourself from feeling chronically overworked

Also, remember to make time for your various work goals from chapter 3:

- Performance
- Development
- Advancement
- Networking
- Flexibility

	Monday	Tuesday	Wednesday	Thursday	Friday
7					
8					
9					
10					
11					
12					
1					
2					
3					
4					
5					
6					
7					

2. Even Better To-Do Lists

Find a recent to-do list. Now re-write it making sure to:

- Place items into categories
- Add an approximate amount of time the task will take
- Add a deadline (real or self-imposed) for each task

CHAPTER 7

An Integrated Approach to Career Management

When I turned 40, I looked at my life and how it would fit with being the kind of father I wanted to be. After lots of thought and discussion with my wife, I left my career in the pharmaceutical industry to go back and get my doctorate. We didn't have kids yet, but I always wanted to be a hands-on dad and be there in ways many dads aren't able to do. Ten years later, I am that dad I always wanted to be with my two girls- picking them up at school and taking them to tennis lessons, fixing dinner, reading to them. So, I guess my experience shows you can make mid-career changes, even if they are scary and difficult and involve risk and luck.

· ·

As a baseball beat writer for a newspaper, you are on the road for more than 100 days a year. Even when you're home, the job's hours keep you out of the house from early afternoon until the wee, small hours of the morning. Essentially, except for mornings before school and rare days off, a beat writer with kids is an absentee parent. So, I asked off the beat. I suppose I'll never really know whether I would've kept my job in 2008 if I had not asked off the baseball beat in 2005, but that doesn't matter. I needed to be off the beat in order to be the father that I want to be. That my sons need me to be.

Like these dads, most of us in mid-career are challenged by the need to balance our work with family responsibilities. There's more to our jobs than how much money we can earn. Now, career success and time for life are both paramount. At this stage, job stability, quality health insurance, and time with family may become as or even more important than maximizing work hours and earnings. Finding employers who are willing to be flexible in terms of where and when work gets done becomes an important consideration.

It is easy to feel trapped. After all, you can no longer up and move without disrupting the lives of your family. Kids are in school and activities. They have their own friends and the beginnings of their own lives. Our wives have their own careers and can't just drop everything to follow us. You belong to a church and a community, and may have lots of local extended family. Plus, we have financial commitments. Mortgages, 401k's and college savings mean that altering our careers can be fraught with financial risk. As we discussed in Chapter 2, good financial planning can give us more freedom to pursue a more balanced path.

In this chapter, we will examine what a balanced approached to ongoing career management looks like, and highlight things we should consider during job searches and ask during interviews. We'll also explore some alternative career paths. Finally, I encourage you to spend an hour or two every six months to take stock of your career and how it enhances or strains the rest of your life. The exercises at the end of the chapter are designed to help you do this.

■ What We Can Learn From College Kids

I gave a speech last year as part of Sacred Heart University's sociology speaker series. Before my talk, I was chatting with my host about how I could possibly get a room of a few hundred young sociology undergraduates fired up to hear about fathers and work-family balance. My host took care of that during her introduction.

She asked the audience, "How many of you would like to have a career after college?" 95 percent raised their hands (I think the other 5 percent were texting). Young men and young women in equal numbers. She then asked, "How many of you would like to be parents someday?" Again, another 95 percent. Again, young men and young women in equal numbers.

This was a really simple and clever way to draw their attention to a future that contained both career and family. In my experience, too many young adults make career decisions during or right after college that have huge implications for their long-term quality of life. But they hardly ever consider how their chosen careers will fit their full range of priorities and life goals.

Actually, let me amend that statement. Many of my female undergraduate business students have made their plans for a family a component of their career plans. Most who do so end up with good jobs, but, as famously noted by Sheryl Sandberg, they run the risk of "leaning out" prematurely and closing themselves off to their full range of career trajectories.

However, it is even clearer to me that many of my male undergrads hadn't spent five minutes thinking about their future families when deciding on majors and careers. The majority were looking at financial success and advancement potential as their only considerations.

There's nothing wrong with choosing a lucrative path, but I wondered if these young men were setting themselves up for work-family conflict and other challenges later in their lives. It seems to me that it is just as important that young men learn to appreciate the truth that so many women spot early: that, once you commit to excelling in a demanding career, it becomes hard to scale back without jeopardizing all you've worked for. Partner tracks and corporate ladders are not known for accommodating those who try to revise the deal. Big-time income also often means big-time financial commitments. It is deceptively easy to get stuck on auto-pilot and continue pursuing a track, even after our lives and priorities change.

As I realized that my students would benefit from a more thoughtful approach to initial career planning, I also recognized that the need wasn't limited to them. The rest of us, wherever we are in our careers, would benefit from a balanced approach to the ongoing management of our careers. Whether it's our first major step on the career path or our tenth, we should think about the implications for all the factors that have to balance out for a successful life, and whether those need recalibrating.

■ The Father-Friendly Workplace

Making a move in light of the full range of considerations would mean thinking about what aspects of work would be particularly father-friendly. There's no male equivalent to Working Mother magazine's guide for supportive workplaces. It's about time someone changed that. So, here's my first attempt of outlining what a "Father-Friendly" workplace would look like.

Boston College's New Dads survey of 1000 professional working dads can give us a starting point. Here are the nine top priorities working dads identified; all were rated as important or very important by a majority of respondents. I broke them into three categories.

- Job Security
- Advancement Opportunities
- High Income

- Sense of Accomplishment
- Interesting Work
- Beneficial to Society

- Allows Flexible Work
- Can Work Independently
- Allows for Leisure Time

Job security came out as the top priority, which is not surprising considering the uncertain job market (the other eight job considerations were all tightly bunched together in terms of importance). Income and advancement potential are also not so surprising. Even highly involved dads are usually the sole or primary income earners for their families, and providing for the family is, for most of us, job one. Stable, well-paying jobs also come with benefits like health insurance and retirement investment.

Dads also rated psychological factors, such as interesting and meaningful work that provides a sense of accomplishment, as highly important. Of course, we can't eat fulfillment, and financial considerations are essential. But many of us would be happier, perform better, attain more career success, and have a more well-balanced life if we persued a career that we felt passionately about.

Most books on careers would end here. But, as you've already surmised, this is not your typical book on career development. I believe in an integrated approach to career management in which work and family priorities are both considered.

I see too many dads who let the sheer force of momentum keep them on a path that no longer fits their lives. Remember this dad from Chapter 1:

> I always swore I'd get off the road after he was in school and in travel basketball, but it is hard to turn down work when the family depends on me- plus I love my job. But now, I fear I'm really missing out. I always wanted to coach basketball, but I make, at best, 1/3 of the games as it is. I know my wife has sacrificed more of her career than we initially bargained for, and this is putting a strain on our relationship. When I'm around, I'm a loving dad, but I think my son feels my absence. I know things are off, but can't quite figure out how to make a change.

He's stuck on a treadmill and can't see a way off. To avoid the same pitfalls, we need to make conscious choices about our careers. I think more dads are starting to understand this, even if we haven't quite figured out how to get there. One piece of evidence, the respondents in BC's study rated flexible work, independent work and time for life as top priorities – every bit as important as financial and psychological concerns. But how do we find a career that matches all of our priorities?

■ Job Search Considerations

When you buy a house, you often look intently at certain aspects more than others, and sometimes even get fixated on one or two smaller details. But there's more to spending the next twenty years of your life in a house than doorknobs and light fixtures. In fact, I've come to appreciate that the most important aspects aren't even about the house at all – it is how living in the house fits with your life.

I've seen too many people buy a great house, but since it is so far away from work, they consign themselves to a commute that detracts from family time. Or a great house tucked far away from neighbors, with no local friends for their kids to play with, and with nowhere to get to within an easy walking distance. Or a great house that strains the budget so much that rooms are left unfurnished. In these cases, the dream house may not fit with living a dream life.

I think all these same points about house/life fit also apply to jobs and careers. I suggest that we expand the criteria we use for our job searches. Specifically, here are a few considerations that often fly under the radar, but can be as important as the more obvious aspects of a job.

Commuting Time

I switched from a job that was 90 minutes each way to 15 each way. This has opened up so much time, and, frankly, has made me healthier. I no longer get up at 5 to scarf down a donut and coffee in the car on the way to work. I have the morning and breakfast routine with my family again.

Imagine you are considering a job opportunity that is a slight step up, but is 25 minutes farther away from home than your current job. A lot of us may overlook that taking this new job would represent 50 more minutes a day commuting. If you tally that up, this is more than four more commuting hours a week. Over the course of a year, this represents more than one entire week of your life, just going to and from work (50 minutes x 5 days x 50 weeks = 208 hours, which is greater than the 168 hours in a single week). That's 2 percent of your year!

The new job may pay a bit more, but taking this job may be the difference between catching the back half of little league games versus missing them entirely. Or the extra hour could be better spent back at the current job, pouring in the extra time and effort to earn a better bonus or out-compete others for a promotion. An additional hour of hustle per day at work, coming at the expense of commuting time and not from family time, may be what you need to get to the next level.

You may even end up saving money with a shorter commute. Mass transit is increasingly expensive, and the price of gas and tolls is always on the rise. As we've been discussing, lowered expenses could give you more freedom in other parts of your life. Shorter commutes also reduce the need for before or after-school child care and may allow you to run errands or attend to home duties in emergency situations. Even if your current job pays less, you may make up for it in lowered expenses, added convenience, and extra time for family. The new job may be worth it, but we should ask these questions before we make this decision.

Ability to Flex - Sometimes we overlook the importance of subtle forms of flexibility. Perhaps taking this new job with the longer commute overall makes sense. But if this new employer is also open to your working from home one day a week, or flexing your hours from nine to five to seven-thirty to three-thirty, you can reclaim some of those hours lost to commuting. As we discussed in the previous chapters, workplace culture and supervisory attitudes can mean the difference between creating and using flexibility and feeling trapped. Be sure to ask about flexible work options at the end of a job interview or if they take you out to lunch with current employees. One smart way to do that is to ask to speak with someone there who works flexibly.

Sector and Organization - Similar jobs in different industries, sectors and type of employers can come with very different work cultures and time demands. It may be worthwhile to explore similar positions at various types of employers. Having more time may be worth more to you than higher pay, or vice-versa. For instance, publically traded companies are beholden to the short-term whims of stockholders, sometimes leading to high-pressure, "all in" work environments and less job security. Partnerships and privately-held firms often take a longer-term view when it comes to employee matters. The public and not-for-profit sectors generally cannot match the pay offered by for-profit firms, but try to make up for this with greater flexibility.

For example, an auditing position at a Big Four accounting firm probably has more intensive time demands than an auditing position for a state government agency. State auditors lose out on the opportunities to get very rich or to make partner at a prestigious firm, but they do have more regular hours. If money and prestige are important to you, then, by all means, go for the brass ring. For others, the financial tradeoffs may be worth the added job security, health benefits and more reasonable time demands.

More than ever, job seekers can get inside information about employers online. Websites such as Glassdoor.com provide anonymous information about employers from current and former employees. On the social media side, LinkedIn can be particularly helpful in finding information. Finally, especially for large employers, Fortune, Fast Company and other trade and business publications often rank and have information about employers with good reputations. More specific to work-family concerns, Working Mother, World at Work, the Families & Work Institute, the Telework Resource Center and 1 Million for Work Flexibility can provide good information. By paying attention to these under-the-radar factors, you will be more likely to find work at an employer that supports your work-family balance.

▌ Ask for What You Need

Remember the dad from Chapter 4 who was so happy in his work-from-home job:

> I'm in my dream job. I can work from absolutely wherever and whenever – as long as have my laptop and gadgets, I can get things done. When I need time for family, I take it. There's no need for me to take sick time or personal days. As long as I get everything done – and they do hold me accountable – they keep giving me this freedom.

Here he is explaining how he got the job:

I was laid-off and going broke. I cashed out my 401k and was in the process of selling my house, when this great job opportunity came my way. When I interviewed for the job, I looked the manager right in the eyes and told him everything, my divorce, everything. I told him how much I needed this job, how I was super-qualified for it, and that I'd knock it out of the park for him. I also told him I'd need to be able to work a lot from home, to care for my son during this tough time. I did everything you are not supposed to do in an interview. It got so personal, so real.

He's right in that we don't normally want to get so personal in a job interview or to air all the drama in our lives. We usually don't want to show how much we *need this job*, giving away all our leverage. But what we all should do is ask for what we need from potential employers. If we get it, we know the company is a great fit for us and the job will help us balance our lives. If we don't, the employer may not be the right one.

■ A View of What is Possible

In this section, I want to share information on a handful of employers who have made a commitment to doing right by their employees. None of them became father-friendly just to be nice; they all recognized that, by being more supportive of employees and helping them with their life demands, they reduce turnover, get better performance, and earn more financial success. It is encouraging to know that there are employers like this out there. Especially for those who feel stuck in a difficult situation, this can give us hope that if we keep on the lookout, we can work at a supportive employer.

I became familiar with these companies' commitment to working parents through our work together on the White House Summit for Working Families during the summer of 2014. Please note that I am not specifically endorsing any of these firms and this is by no means a comprehensive list. Information is based on publically-available sources as well as my understanding of their workplace and conversations I've had with managers at each. I don't have all the answers or insider information.

Ryan LLC - Ryan LLC is a Texas-based tax services firm. Throughout the 1990s, it was a successful company, but had developed an intense "face time" culture – extremely long hours were the seen as the way to succeed and advance. Over the past decade, Ryan completely transformed the way they manage employees, and have seen significant increases in revenue, profitability and employee engagement.

In 2005, they started an eight-year transformation into what is commonly known as a "Results-Focused Work Environment." In these workplaces, as long as high performance standards are maintained, employees can work how, where, and whenever they need to satisfy clients and bring value to the firm. At Ryan, managers, employees and teams co-create clear performance measures and track them continuously. As long as employees and teams meet their standards, they are accorded almost unlimited workplace flexibility. Employee autonomy has become part of the accepted work culture

Remember the section in Chapter 5 on how managers are often reluctant to allow flexibility because they fear they can no longer monitor performance and keep employees accountable? Ryan shows that, with the right approach to management, accountability and performance can go hand in hand.

Thanks to their efforts, collectively known as "MyRyan," Ryan was ranked as the #6 medium-sized company in *Fortune Magazine's* 2012 list of the "100 Best Companies to Work For," and has received over 200 awards for its workplace innovation and commitment to employees. Consider this – in 2005 only 42 percent of Ryan employees agreed with this item on their employee survey, "People are encouraged to balance their work life and their personal life." In 2015, an amazing 91 percent did.

State Street - In most cases, employees have to stick their necks out to requesting flexibility from their supervisors. State Street, a Boston-based financial service firm, recognized that this represented a major roadblock, as many employees are fearful of stigma and, as a result, do not make requests for the flexible work arrangements they need. In contrast, State Street turned this on its head and implemented "Manager Initiated Flex."

With this system, managers are responsible (and held responsible) for examining the jobs they supervise across a set of criteria that reveal the parts of work that can be done more flexibly. The manager then goes to the employee to discuss and present the range of available options, including flextime, telework, compressed schedules and job sharing. As a result, internal surveys showed that the expanded work options led to greater employee engagement and effort, as well as reduced turnover. It has also been a boon for employee recruitment. A real win-win approach. State Street has won numerous awards for their progressive and innovative approach to employee flexibility and internal measures show that increased flexibility has led to significant financial success.

Caliper - Caliper, a talent management firm headquartered in Princeton, New Jersey, has long been recognized for embracing telework, work from home, paternity leave and compressed work weeks. In 2014, Caliper received its second consecutive When Work Works Award from the Families and Work Institute and The Society for Human Resource Management. As I mentioned earlier, Caliper had its most profitable day ever during a major snow storm that shut down much of the Northeast. Because Caliper employees had been enabled and supported in working from home, they were able to stay on task when all their competitors were shut down. Caliper reports a voluntary turnover rate of less than 2 percent, less than a quarter of the industry average.

Ernst & Young - Ernst & Young is one of the Big Four global accounting firms. In this and many other competitive industries, high turnover among valuable employees in their "prime parenting years" has been a persistent problem. These firms also employ lots of millennials, who are often more assertive in their desire for flexible work. EY and other progressive employers have, for several years now, made strides in supporting their employees' work-family juggles.

At the recent White House Summit on Working Families, EY's CEO Mark Weinberger told an anecdote that, to me, represents our best hope that corporate leadership is finally recognizing the importance of work-family balance and will begin to sincerely address this issue. Before Weinberger became CEO, he discussed the opportunity with his wife and four children. His family agreed that he could take the job only if he remained a highly-involved dad.

Shortly after becoming CEO, he was in China giving his first big speech to EY partners. He was nervous about the speech and wanted it to be memorable. There was to be a big dinner reception afterwards.

Weinberger gave his speech, but ended it with an apology – he would have to skip the reception to get right on a plane back home so he could take his daughter to her driver's test. He had promised a year ago that he'd be there, and needed to keep his commitment to his family. "Everyone remembered that. No one remembered my speech."

Although he was just trying to be a good dad, it turned out that his flight back to his daughter's driving test became a story repeated many times throughout EY. The lesson, I think, is that if the CEO acts on his family priorities, then other employees can, too.

Such visible leadership from the CEO of a leading financial firm gives me hope that corporate America is finally recognizing the importance of work-family balance, not just in theory, but in practice. In fact, at the White House Summit, the CEOs of PriceWaterhouseCoopers, Deloitte, Johnson & Johnson and Goldman Sachs, among others, all spoke about their dedication to this issue and how it was a business "no-brainer" for them as corporate leaders. As always, the devil is in the details and the execution.

In EY's case, Weinberger recognizes that flexibility "can't just be an initiative, it has to be a culture." To that end, EY has implemented a set of metrics around flexibility and family support, and they hold managers accountable for these results. They track employee engagement in their annual employee surveys, and have found that working parents report high levels of engagement thanks to the availability of formal and informal flex options.

Perhaps the best evidence of their commitment to the notion that family and career success can complement each other is that many of the individuals promoted to senior leadership positions in 2014 had utilized flexible work options, telecommuting and even temporary part-time status during their careers.

EY was an early adopter of paternity leave, and over 500 US employees take paternity leave annually. Finally, EY partners with Bright Horizons to provide back-up day care services for times in which employees' regular child care arrangements fall through. This gives employees peace of mind while also reducing absenteeism. Like most major employers in competitive industries, they are not there yet, but are making significant progress. Take heart, even major global financial firms are capable of being family-supportive.

Shake Shack - The other employers I've profiled have been in professional services, with mostly well-educated, white-collar, salaried workforces. In contrast, Shake Shack employs mostly hourly workers, and, amazingly, there is hope for employee-oriented workplaces even in food service.

Shake Shack offers new hourly employees at its NYC locations almost two dollars more than the state minimum wage. They also include all hourly employees in profit sharing, adding, on average, seventy cents per hour to each paycheck. Finally, unlike many similar employers, Shake Shack provides health, dental, vision, retirement, and disability benefits, as well as paid time off, to full-time employees. This is among the most generous benefits packages in its industry, perhaps only rivaled by Starbucks. Shake Shack also has impressive record of employee development and an internal promotion policy, so that those starting as burger-flippers can, over time, rise into management.

Shake Shack CEO Randy Garutti is on the record as saying that these employee policies easily pay for themselves in terms of being able to be more selective when hiring, reducing turnover, and providing better customer service. One hopes that Shake Shack will retain its policies after its 2015 Initial Public Offering.

In all, these and many other progressive employers demonstrate that you can find family-supportive workplaces. Further, the range of their offerings of flexibility and family support can give you an idea of what to look for, and ask for, when conducting your own job search.

Job Search Specifically for Remote and Flexible Work

In addition to the more traditional employers listed above, many employers are looking to fill telework and work-from-home positions. There are several major job search sites and portals that connect applicants looking for remote and telecommuting-based work with these employers.

One of these search sites, Flexjobs.com, releases an annual list of the Top 100 Companies to Watch for telecommuting and remote jobs. On their 2015 list, they note a 26 percent increase in the number of telecommuting and work-from-home positions listed with them. Encouragingly, their list features a range of small to large-sized companies and a variety of career categories. They broke down their list into seven main industries, and here's a quick list, including some employer examples:

- **Medical and health**: UnitedHealth Group, Aetna, Humana
- **Customer service:** Amazon, Teletech, Convergys, Language Line Solutions
- **Sales:** Appen, VMWare, Overland Solutions
- **Computer & IT:** Xerox, Apple, Salesforce, SAP
- **Administrative:** FlexProfessionals, Healthfirst, McKesson
- **Education and training:** K12, Kaplan
- **Marketing:** ADP, HD Supply, Teradata

For many job seekers, the ability to work largely from home would allow for better life balance. Remote and telework jobs could also offer you the opportunity to find great companies to work for outside of your local area. Finally, dads transitioning from staying at home could use telework options as a way to transition back to more typical employment.

▌ Life in the Slightly Slower Lane?

Lily Tomlin once quipped, "The problem with winning the rat race is... you're still a rat"

"Downshifters" are those who choose alternative career paths that open up more time for family or other pursuits. For many, the trade-off is more than worth it. In this section, we'll examine five common types of downshifting, and discuss whether this strategy may be best for our lives.

When we think about career paths, we often think about climbing the ladder – stepping up our career one rung at a time to positions of greater status, demands, responsibilities and financial rewards. Career advancement is great, but it often comes at a cost to mental and physical health and especially to time spent with family. From the dad whose quote opened the chapter:

> It is so hard to get off a particular track once you are on it. If you want to be a C-level executive, which is the path I was on, you have to be prepared to put in huge hours for many years. It's a demanding lifestyle. It may be worth it to you, but don't fool yourself, you won't be taking your kids to tennis lessons at 3:30.

Several writers and researchers have identified "downshifting" as an increasingly common choice of people in high-powered careers who changed gears to better accommodate family needs or pursue other life goals. In her fantastic book, *Downshifting: Reinventing Success on a Slower Track*, Amy Salzman identified five common downshifting patterns.

1. Back-Trackers

2. Plateauers

3. Career Shifters

4. Self-Employers

5. Urban Escapees

Back-Trackers - actively choose self-demotion in order to pursue other goals or open more time for family. For example, this dad:

> When my husband and I were getting ready to adopt, I had to decide what to do with my business. So much of the parenting was going to fall on my shoulders, as his high-power career was not going to change. Do I want to try to make more money and go with day care from start? Or do work from home and only take on the work that will fit with the baby? For a while, between this and the adoption process, I felt paralyzed by the weight of the decision.
>
> Now I run my business around being a parent. We get some part-time care. There are job opportunities I miss out on, and sometimes that's tough for the ego, but, all in all, this was a good decision for our family.

My mother would also be considered a back-tracker. Years ago, she stepped down from a 30-year career as an elementary school teacher and became the most overqualified teacher's aide in the Albany, NY school district. This decision allows her to continue working with children, which she is amazing at and loves doing. It also allowed her to avoid the stress associated with the responsibilities of running the classroom, bringing work home every day, and dealing with parents and administrators.

Plateauers - don't self-demote, but rather choose to stay in place by turning down promotions and opportunities for advancement. In some ways, I'd be considered a plateauer. I was department chair several years ago and filled in during my chair's sabbatical leave last year. Both times, I was happy to leave this position of more responsibility, prestige and money to return to faculty status. I did this despite the fact that many, including those in upper leadership, encouraged me to stay on and even consider higher positions in the future.

I love teaching and writing, but never liked administrative work. If I were a full-time academic administrator, I'd be a constant ball of stress. Being a faculty member gives me the time and place flexibility to spend more time with my family, work my schedule around Amy's, and pursue other professional goals (like this book!).

Career Shifters - make a seemingly small change to their career trajectory or employer that often makes a huge difference in lifestyle – as opposed to moving to an entirely different career (so lawyer-turned-novelist John Grisham doesn't count, but a lawyer-turned-mediator would).

Shifting careers is more common than you'd think. Many management consultants escape their intense work pressures and time demands by taking internal positions at client companies. These positions are still financially rewarding and prestigious, but tend to have more regular hours. I know a lawyer who, for family reasons, left a prestigious clerkship to become in-house counsel for a NY State agency- again, still a good gig, but with more reasonable hours and work stress. Neither of these situations would be described as demotions or new careers, rather shifts that opened up more time for family and life.

> For the past five years, I worked at a great job at a great place, but the commute to way downtown Manhattan – a short drive, a long commuter train ride, and grabbing a subway – every day was too much. I have four kids, and they are all into sports and activities. I coach a few of their teams, and it was running me ragged. For a long time, our family decision was for my wife to work part time close to home – she has a consulting business with a few very loyal clients.
>
> After some careful planning and saving, I left my job and am now starting up my own consultancy, doing much of the same tasks as I did at my former employer. But, this allows me to be home more, and allows my wife to get

her turn to expand her career. So far, it is so great to be so much more involved at home.

Self-Employers - Many folks choose to get off a corporate track and go into business for themselves. This process isn't easy, and involves a lot of financial risk. But if you become your own boss without letting your business take over your life, self-employment can give you the autonomy to lead a better work-life balance. In a guest post on my blog, *Fathers, Work and Family*, one dad explained how he became achieved better work-family balance by becoming an entrepreneur:

> I wish I had done it sooner. I have the freedom to make my own schedule and prioritize my time. I've been able to coach my daughter's basketball and soccer teams, catch most of her swim meets, cheer on my wife as she completed her first marathon, and become an active member of my church and my community. I also made it to my daughter's play performances, a father-daughter dance, and some great dinners in town with my wife. During my thirties, I missed many of these events. And when I was there, my mind was somewhere else – getting a project done, meeting my deadline, frustrated with my boss or senior management or struggling with politics.
>
> Now, my time is mine and it's never wasted. I only sell my time at a premium. I spend time with my family and my community, and make time for myself to play basketball and work out. The life of an entrepreneur is stressful, and you're on 100% of the time – except when you're not. You control the on and off switch.

One note of caution, this dad's experience is not universal. I know many entrepreneurs who are far more demanding of themselves than any boss would be. Plus, for many entrepreneurs, time not spent working can feel like time spent not earning, and there can be constant pressure to do more and more. In fact, back in grad school, I assisted in a study of work-life balance among small business owners, and many reported more imbalance and stress than those who worked for others. If you pursue this path, be sure you can create and maintain boundaries.

Urban Escapees - The cost of living in the orbit of large affluent coastal US cities pretty much precludes downshifting. $900,000 can get you a one-bedroom apartment in NYC, but $200,000 can buy you a beautiful house in many other parts of the country.

I remember when I was first hired at Fairleigh Dickinson University. One of my friends from grad school took a similar job at a college in a small town in the Midwest. He bought a big house his first semester. It took me a decade to save up for the down payment on my modest house in the suburbs of New York City. I'm a life-long overly-proud New Yorker, but if I wasn't so committed to my homeland, and if Amy didn't need to be near Manhattan for her career, my salary would go *a lot* further in most other parts of the country.

Because of the wide variation in cost of living throughout the US, lots of people who can work remotely, or have shifted their careers to be more flexible, have chosen to move out of the city to where the lifestyle is slower and more affordable. Taking a similar but less stressful but lower paying job in a more affordable area can actually be a financial net positive, and can alleviate a lot of stress. As Billy Joel once sang, "Good luck moving up, cuz' I'm moving out."

Saying "No" To More - Of course, there are financial consequences to downshifting. You'll earn less and you have to be sure your family will still be OK. In the case of my plateauing, my plateau still pays pretty well, Amy and I have been very conservative with our finances, and I am blessed to have a wife who shares my priorities and life goals. Not everyone is so lucky. As discussed in

Chapter 2, financial prioritization and simplification are critical. Beyond finances, the greatest barrier to downshifting is often that of our own making. According to Salzman:

> Getting over the idea that they will be cast as failures is the greatest challenge facing backtrackers... stepping back is often the culmination of a painful battle between personal needs and professional expectations.

Society sends many repeated signals, especially to men, that MORE success, MORE money and MORE power are the keys to being seen as a success, a man in full. Most of us have been receiving this signal for virtually our whole lives. It takes a strong sense of self to turn away from more. Swimming against the tide isn't easy, but it might just be worth it. Before you consider downshifting, you need to go back to Chapter 2 and start planning your finances to allow you the freedom so that you can decide to downshift – if it fits with your work and family priorities.

▌ Active Management Needed

The luckiest among us have a great work situation that allows us to achieve success in our careers and at home. For others, adding flexibility to our jobs is the solution to our work-family imbalance. Some of us would find that a new employer would be life changing. But, for some, there is a need to make a more dramatic shift in their careers to allow for a more fulfilled life.

No matter your situation, we need to actively manage our careers so that we stay true to our work and family priorities. Too many dads get stuck on a treadmill. Too many remain on a career path we chose twenty years ago when we were just out of college and free of family and parenting responsibilities.

We need to reassess our careers periodically so we do not drift along a path that may no longer make sense for us and our families.

The exercises at the end of the chapter can help.

There's one more overlooked action we can take to help our family dynamics and set ourselves up for work-family success – paternity leave. We'll explore the ins and outs of paternity leave in the next chapter.

Chapter 7 Exercises

1. Allocating Points to Career Priorities

The nine career priorities reported by the respondents to Boston College's "New Dad" study all received very high ratings and were, in general, seen as equally important. I'd like you to rate the importance of these characteristics to you, but am not letting you off so easy. You are going to have to choose. To do so, I am giving you 30 points you can distribute among the three categories of job factors. A 10 for each category means equal importance. Anything above a 10 means that the category is more important than the others and at least one other category must get a rating lower than 10. Also, I'm going to ask you to fill this out for various stages in your life.

Please distribute your 30 points among these 3 categories for each stage of your life:

1. Just starting out in your career

Security, Income, Advancement	Interesting Work, Accomplishment, Beneficial to Others	Flexible Work with Independence and Time for Life

2. Five years into your career path

Security, Income, Advancement	Interesting Work, Accomplishment, Beneficial to Others	Flexible Work with Independence and Time for Life

3. Where you are in your life now

Security, Income, Advancement	Interesting Work, Accomplishment, Beneficial to Others	Flexible Work with Independence and Time for Life

Reflection Questions:

- Are these priorities the same?
- How have they changed over time?
- Are you in a job or career path that reflects your priorities?
- If not, what can you do about it?

2. Envisioning Downshifting

Before we can successfully downshift, we need to look at the pros and cons of each strategy and envision how we would downshift. In this space, choose one of the 5 varieties of downshifting and imagine what that might be like, and what could pose obstacles to this change. Importantly, we need to consider how the rest of our life and our finances would have to change.

If I were to become a _____ :

This is what my new career path would look like:

This is what would be good about my new path:

This is what would be bad about my new path:

This is what would have to change in my life or my finances to enable this to happen:

How feasible is this in the next 6 months, the next 3 years:

CHAPTER 8

A Dad's Guide to Paternity Leave

On my blog, *Fathers, Work and Family*, I asked dads to share their paternity leave experiences. A few had supportive employers with generous policies, some had nightmare situations that led to them find employment elsewhere, and most were unsupported and left to rely on their accumulated time off. Here are some of their experiences:

> They call it paternity leave in the employee handbook but then I was forced to use vacation time, of which I only had five days. My daughter ended up having to be in the hospital the first week so I took another week unpaid just to be at home with her and my wife.

. . . .

> I'm really thankful for my work and their stance on paternity leave. HR actually reached out to me ahead of time to let me know that I could take 2 weeks paid time off, but any more would be unpaid. I ended up just taking the two weeks and it was an extremely smooth experience.

. . . .

> I had to take two weeks' vacation when my son was born because my workplace doesn't provide paternity leave beyond what the FMLA legally requires. Once I returned to work everyone asked me how my vacation was and I

had to correct them, it was a lot of work introducing a new little person into our home and extended family. I was also greeted by many complaints about how I had taken "time off" during a "busy season." It was one of the most frustrating experiences of my life. Had I been provided with paternity leave and a more understanding work environment my son's birth would not have been such a stressful undertaking.

· ·

I have to say, my employer was wonderful with the birth of my daughter. I had paid leave for 4 weeks and used my vacation for an additional 2 weeks. It's one of the reasons why I turned down another job that offered me more money.

· ·

My daughter was in the NICU for 22 days. I was allowed to work from the hospital for a few weeks, then told I had to come into the office at least three days a week. I was told I was "like a kid in high school smoking the restroom" and they were covering for me. Even though my job could be done from anywhere, they wouldn't let me work remotely. I quit a few days later.

· ·

My company at the time handled it informally, which was kind of a double-edged sword. They were cool with letting me take some time off when my son was born, but without an official policy, it was hard to know what was acceptable and where the leeway ended.

· ·

What's paternity leave?

You have probably heard the statistic that the United States is the only industrialized country, and one of only four countries in the entire world (Lesotho, Swaziland and Papua New Guinea being the others), to not guarantee women any paid maternity leave.

We're not quite as far behind the rest of the world when it comes to paternity leave – for the simple and pathetic reason that we have more company in not providing it; only about fifty nations currently do so. However, we are still way behind most industrialized nations, especially compared to Europe. For example, in Iceland new dads get eighteen weeks of paternity leave at eighty percent wage replacement. It's thirteen weeks in Italy, and twelve in Norway. These countries also allow for additional parental leave to be divided up by spouses as they see fit. But Sweden takes the cake. Swedish dads can take an incredible 16 *months* of paternity leave, with a wage replacement level that starts at 77% and declines over time.

I do not expect the U.S. to start offering Sweden-style benefits anytime soon. However, I see little reason why we can't keep up with the policies of our closest "cultural cousins," the UK, Australia and Canada. In Quebec, dads get five weeks at seventy percent pay, plus the option for more. In the rest of Canada, dads and moms share up to thirty-five weeks of partially-paid family leave. In Australia and the UK, dads are entitled to two weeks at a fairly low flat rate of wage replacement. In a show of support for working dads, Prince William made an important public stance when he took his full two week paternity leave from the Royal Air Force when the Royal Baby was born in 2013.

Any way you look at us compared to the rest of the world, American working dads are not in a great situation.

What US Dads Are Entitled To

In the U.S., many workers[12] are entitled to take up to twelve unpaid weeks of family and medical leave, including paternity leave, thanks to the Family and Medical Leave Act (FMLA). However, the fact is that very few new dads take FMLA leave. The main reason is that it only provides for unpaid leave, making it hard for many to afford to use it. Also, while we might be legally entitled to this leave, many workplace cultures are resistant to this idea. This can lead to subtle (and not-so-subtle) career consequences for those who assert their rights.

Currently, three states – California, New Jersey and Rhode Island – have programs in which new parents, both moms and dads, are entitled to a few weeks of parental leave, including wage replacement of up to two-thirds salary. Liza Mundy recently reported about California's program in the *Atlantic*:

> Since California instituted its program, the percentage of "bonding leaves" claimed by men has risen from 18.7 in 2005 and 2006 to 31.3 in 2012 and 2013. A study by the economist Eileen Appelbaum and the sociologist Ruth Milkman showed that initial concerns that the California law would be a "job killer" were unfounded, and that workplaces have figured out effective and creative ways to cover for leave-taking parents. The biggest hurdle seems to be getting the word out, particularly among lower-income families that could benefit enormously from the program. (Part of the beauty of the California policy is that it extends leave to men in non-white-collar jobs.)

The same study showed that, while many families were helped by this program, many were unaware of the available benefit, and others were afraid of consequences if they made use of it. If you live in one of these states, you should check with your employer's HR department or look for the information on your state's website.

Good news – The FAMILY Act was introduced in Congress in 2014, and, if passed, it would extend the system used in these three states nationwide. Bad news – It has no chance of being passed in the foreseeable future. For the majority of dads in the U.S., our lack of public policy means that, more than dads in any other country, we are dependent on our employers for paternity leave.

▌ Employer Options

Unfortunately, as reported by the Families and Work Institute, only about fourteen percent of U.S. companies offer paid paternity leave. Yeah, well, so much for that.

However, progressive employers are starting to catch on that paternity leave is a great way to retain employees during a time in their lives when workplace support can be the difference between them staying long-term or looking around for a better place to work. Here's a quick list, compiled by Care.com, of major employers, many of whom are in very macho, high-pressure industries, that offer paid paternity leave policies to full-time salaried employees:

- Reddit: 17 weeks
- Facebook: 16 weeks
- Bank of America: 12 weeks
- Yahoo: eight weeks
- Patagonia: eight weeks
- Google: seven weeks
- Twitter: six weeks
- Arnold and Porter: the primary caregiver gets 18 weeks of paid time off and the secondary caregiver gets six weeks
- Comcast: four weeks (with the option of an additional eight without pay)
- Microsoft: four weeks
- Trip Advisor: four weeks
- McKinsey and Company: four weeks
- Covington and Burling LLP: four weeks for non-primary caregivers
- PricewaterhouseCoopers: three weeks
- McGraw-Hill Financial: three weeks
- Deloitte: three weeks
- Discovery Communications: three weeks

- Fannie Mae: 20 days
- Wal-Mart: 2 weeks (with an option for an additional six without pay)
- Ernst & Young: two weeks (six weeks for primary caregivers)

Yes, Silicon Valley leads the way, but there are lots of other, more mainstream employers offering paternity leave. Industries known for intense work cultures, like management consulting, finance, accounting, telecommunications and publishing are all represented. And many are not just "Johnny-come-latelys." In fact, Ernst & Young has had a paid paternity leave policy for over twelve years, and reports that somewhere between 500 and 600 dads take paternity leave each year.

But, even at these progressive employers, cultural and supervisory attitudes mean that most dads do not take all the paternity leave available to them. Here's the experience of one dad at a company that is known for having one of the most generous paternity leave policies in the country:

> With about 6 months before my wife was due, I talked to my employer about paternity leave. I wanted to be up-front and give everyone, my boss, my team, the higher-ups as much time as we could to prepare for my absence, and that they had what they needed to carry one without me for a while. I wanted to do this the right way. I was a high-performing VP at this firm, with three years of excellent performance reviews, and I wanted to make sure there wouldn't be any problems during my leave that could reflect poorly on me down the line.
>
> When I had a one to one with my boss he asked how much time I was planning to take. The company policy is 10 paid weeks, and I said I'd use it all. This was clearly not what he was expecting, or wanted to hear. He told me that most guys take 2 weeks and that seemed more appropriate. He wasn't a jerk about it, but it was an early sign that even though the policy was on the books, taking leave might be problematic for my future.

Leading up to my leave, I spent a lot of time working ahead and preparing my team, but the higher-ups kept pressuring me. It was clear that taking my long leave was not OK with everyone. I was on the radar for making wrong decision and worried what this would mean after I returned. The fact that they'd hold me personally responsible for any production loss caused me a lot of stress. So much so that I actually got shingles the week before the baby was due! In the delivery room, I was only allowed to hold my baby with these thick plastic hazmat-like gloves. It shouldn't have been like that.

That being said, I don't regret taking the full 10 paid weeks. When my daughter was born, I let all that stress go, soaked her in and fully shared all those moments. My dad wasn't around when I was growing up and I so wanted to be there for my girl. My paternity leave time was so incredible to create our bond, to be constantly around her, and to introduce her to the world.

Coming back to work, I did fear getting blackballed. I had heard tales of guys being marginalized and subtle things like that. But, it was definitely worth the gamble. I mean, I had three years of great performance reviews and had made the firm a LOT of money. What's the worst that could happen, especially considering how amazing getting 10 paid weeks was?

Well, when I got back, there was nothing overt, but the vibe wasn't great. Another opportunity came for me a few months later and I took it. The company having this policy is phenomenal, but it got lost in the translation with managers and the pressures they face for short-term performance. Our industry has such high turnover rates, it would really help the company, and dads, if they really supported their own policies. But, we operate so "lean and mean" that there's no slack in the system for leave without consequences, I guess.

And I'm the phenomenally lucky one. Most dads I know use up their sick days and vacation time. And I know so many non-white-collar dads have it so much harder than us.

Just like this dad said, most new fathers cobble together a week or less of accumulated time off, usually sick and vacation days, when their children are born. In fact, seventy-five percent of Boston College's "New Dads" sample of mostly affluent, white collar dads took off one week or less and sixteen percent did not take any time off at all following the birth of their most recent child. And it is likely these white-collar dads have it much easier than their working class counterparts.

This represents an enormous missed opportunity for fathers to spend time bonding with and caring for their newborns. And it is a shame, as I believe that this early chance to transition to fatherhood as a fully involved parent yields benefits that last a lifetime. Why do I believe this to be the case? Because I'm living proof.

Sports lead the way

Do you remember the big controversy at the beginning of last baseball season, when the Mets' Daniel Murphy took a two day paternity leave? Some sports radio personalities crudely criticized him. But the outcry that followed showed that their opinions were no longer the norm. As the story made it to national newscasts, Twitter lit up with reactions – over 95% of them rallying behind Murphy and his family.

Also in sports, last year, pro golfer Hunter Mahan left a $1 million tournament he was leading when his wife went into early labor. Over a hundred Major League Baseball players have made use of MLB's paternity leave policy, which was instituted in 2011. Several football players publicly declared they'd miss games to be at the birth of their children.

■ My Paternity Leave Experience

I didn't *exactly* take a paternity leave. Nick was born three days after my last final exam of the spring semester. Perfect timing (although we didn't actually plan it that way). I was able to spend the summer on a "de-facto" paternity leave, and Amy, Nick and I got to learn how this whole "baby makes three" thing would shake out.

For me, bonding with Nick was immediate. Amy had to have an emergency C-section, so while she was in recovery, the first hour of Nick's life was just me and him. I spent that hour touching his little fingers and toes and vowing to him I would do all I could to be sure he would have a happy life.

My bond with Nick grew even stronger as, thanks to my ability to be at home, I was there to soothe him when he cried, feed him when he was hungry, cuddle with him when he slept and comfort him when he was sick. I experienced so many firsts with him. He sometimes drove me ragged and seemed to enjoy depriving me of sleep and personal hygiene, but even then, suffering through it all for his benefit just made me feel closer to him. There is something primal about caring for a little ball of possibility who is so utterly and completely dependent on you. For me, it created a love and devotion that is hard to describe.

Before Nick, I had never changed a diaper, mixed a bottle of formula, dressed a squirming baby or put one down for a nap – to me, it was a brave new world. Amy read all the books (I skimmed a few parts of one or two of them), and we attended a class or two, but I really wasn't prepared. However, by being around and actively involved, I quickly caught on.

Taking care of a baby is *hard* because it is unrelenting and because of all the sleep deprivation. But I never found it difficult to figure out diapers, feeding, snuggling and all the other basic blocking and tackling of new parenthood. These early experiences served me well as Nick got older. I'm fine being on solo dad duty, taking him outside armed only with a diaper bag and what was left of my wits (the sleep deprivation again). But I never felt like anything less than a capable parent, and I credit my early climb up the learning curve with my earned sense of confidence.

My "paternity leave" was not just a bonding experience for me and Nick, it was also one for me and Amy. I always knew she was the right partner for me, but our first few months of working together caring for Nick reinforced for us that we are a great team and that we can always rely on each other to step up when needed. Caring for a newborn is a crucible, and sharing an experience that is so maddening, wonderful, awful, exhilarating, depressing and inspirational as equal partners and true team-mates can't help but make you a stronger couple. To this day, we are on the same page as parents, and I believe our shared early struggles helped get us there.

Because we shared so much of the parenting load and each got to see how wonderful the other was with Nick, we became very confident in each other as parents. I know Amy's a great mom. I'm pretty sure she thinks I'm a great dad. She knows I can do all the parenting that she is capable of – well, except breastfeeding. I have never felt like "the helper" as opposed to an equal parent. This was essential for our desire for a shared-care approach to parenting. Further, the fact that I was a fully capable parent allowed Amy to return to work with confidence. She was back on stage three months after Nick as born, and she was able to do so with peace of mind because she knew I had it covered.

I see how important being home for the first few weeks of Nick's life was for my development as a father and for setting the stage for my family's dynamics. It makes me angry that more dads don't have the opportunity I did. This opportunity to develop as a person, a parent and spouse should not be reserved just for new moms, or just for the lucky few new dads with ultra-flexible jobs or awesomely progressive employers.

I believe all dads deserve this opportunity, and that dads, moms, kids, families and our society all benefit when dads get to immerse themselves in the life of their children in such a uniquely intimate and transformative way. I'm not just an advocate for working dads because of my professional interests. For me, paternity leave is personal.

I have seen how being able to take a sizeable paternity leave brought so many benefits to my family. Some recent studies back up my personal observation. Researchers compared the kids of dads who took a paternity leave of two weeks or longer to those whose dads could or did not. They found a strong link between paternity leave and subsequent paternal involvement in their children's lives, including feeding, changing diapers, getting up during the night, bathing and reading. They also found some evidence that the children of fathers who take long leave after their birth performed better on cognitive development tests and were more prepared as they entered school.

Paternity leave is also an important opportunity to take care of one's wife and other kids during a physically and emotionally draining time. Being able to take time to care for a newborn can give unconfident dads the experience they need for future childcare and parental involvement. In short, the whole family benefits – dad, mom and baby[13].

Further, if paternity leave is linked to greater paternal involvement later on in life, there's an entire library of research that shows that in almost any way a child can be better off, they are better off for having an involved father. Kids with involved dads stay in school, do better in school, get into less trouble, get arrested less, get divorced less and are physically healthier.

So, now that I have you all fired up to take paternity leave when your next kid is born, here are some things to consider as you weigh your options:

■ Does Paternity Leave Fit Your Priorities?

Earlier in the book, you laid out your work and family priorities and assessed your financial situation. Would a paternity leave help you act more in accordance with these priorities? Do you have the financial resources to allow for leave? As much as I advocate for the availability of paternity leave, I also believe that dads should be free to choose the path that works best for them and their families.

Just a few months ago, my best friend became a dad for the first time. He sheepishly admitted to me he only took one day off after his daughter was born. He knows I'm "the work-family guy" and thought I might judge him. Even though I made a different choice when Nick was born, I did not question his decision. After all, who am I to criticize anyone who considers his family's needs and priorities and makes a thoughtful decision as to what's best?

My friend works at a prestigious boutique consultancy with many high-end clients, and there was pressure for him to stay connected to the office. Plus, he's a really hard worker and takes pride in being a good provider. Further, his father-in-law came to stay with them to help out with the baby. So, my friend worked from home the next week and somehow, even with all the sleep deprivation, hit his goal for billable hours. He was back in the office the next week.

So far, my friend has proven to be an awesome, loving, involved, hands-on dad. His decision to get right back to work is one I do not question, as it was in line with his priority to be a good provider.

He did what he needed to do to support them by supporting his career. His family was also smart in lining up help from extended family, which enabled him to continue at work.

■ Understand What Options Are Available to You

The first step is to contact your employer's HR department to learn what parental leave benefits you may be entitled to. Some have a paternity leave policy collecting dust in the policy manual. Perhaps you can be a role model and make use of it. Some employers have a parental leave policy, equally applicable for new moms and new dads. Most, however, only have a maternity leave policy. If so, you may still have a legal right to a paternity leave.

In 2014, the EEOC issued new guidelines concerning pregnancy and family-related issues in the workplace[14]. The guidelines state:

> Parental leave must be provided to similarly situated men and women on the same terms. If, for example, an employer extends leave to new mothers beyond the period of recuperation from childbirth (e.g. to provide the mothers time to bond with and/or care for the baby), it cannot lawfully fail to provide an equivalent amount of leave to new fathers for the same purpose.

To clarify the EEOC's language- a lot of the time, employer maternity leave policies actually consist of two types of leave: time for physical recovery (sometimes put in language of short-term disability leave), and time for care and bonding. The guideline makes it clear that dads are legally entitled to the same parental leave offered to new moms, excepting leave specifically for physical recovery. That's only fair- I shudder to think how difficult pregnancy and childbirth must be. A company that offers women 8 weeks of paid leave (2 for recovery and 6 for care/bonding) should offer dads 6 weeks of paid leave. If they do not, they risk discriminating based on gender and exposing itself to potential legal liability.

If your employer currently offers maternity leave, this new guideline may help you, especially in that many more employers offer maternity leave than paternity leave. If they offer maternity leave beyond "pregnancy and childbirth-related medical leave," you are equally entitled to that portion of parental leave. More dads have been exerting their rights, and paternity leave related lawsuits are on the rise – and we're generally winning.

In one recent high-profile case, CNN journalist and author, Josh Levs, filed an EEOC action against Time Warner because of the disparity between parental leave offered moms and dads. As a result, Time Warner changed its policy. Score one for the dads.

However, the new guidelines do not obligate employers to offer maternity, paternity or any parental leave at all, beyond the 12 weeks of unpaid leave under FMLA (unless they are in California, New Jersey and Rhode Island). Further, these guidelines do not obligate employers to who offer maternity leave to offer anything beyond medical leave, and if your employer does not, then the EEOC guidelines do not affect you.

■ Understand your Culture

Finally, please understand that while you may be legally entitled to leave, there is still the potential for career consequences against men who use these policies. This could mean that, even if you are acting fully within your rights, depending on your company culture and the attitudes of your supervisors, you may not feel able to do so without damaging your career. The compelling story of the dad who took the full 10 weeks clearly illustrates this point.

The best way to know if this is the case at your workplace is to ask around. First, try to find men who have taken paternity leave and dads you have seen be up front about family concerns at work. Women who recently took maternity leave may also be good sources. I would also ask around with supervisors, coworkers and others you trust about the possible consequences or support for you potentially taking a paternity leave. Bear in mind, many will be supportive because it is the "socially correct" thing to do, even if they think a paternity leave would be career suicide. So take extra care to go to people you trust to be honest with you.

▌ Ready to Leave?

The fact that so few dads are given the opportunity to take paternity leave is a shame. But I encourage you not to compound our predicament. If you are able, take all the leave you can. I can almost guarantee you'll be glad you did.

I think a fitting way to end this chapter is an excerpt from a fantastic article written by Aaron Gouveia on his blog, *Daddy Files*.

> I soaked Sam in, totally and completely…. It was so worth it to me to have that initial time to get to know my son. It's the foundation of a solid father-son relationship and I can't imagine what it would've been like to try to fit that all in while I'm gone for work 12 hours a day.
>
> It's my sincere hope more companies start offering dads paid leave, while more dads realize the importance of using every available bit of it without fear of corporate retribution.

Amen, brother.

And with that, we are ready to transition the focus of the book from the workplace into the home.

Chapter 8 Exercises

1. What Was Your Paternity Leave Experience?

Much like the dads whose quotes opened the chapter, every dad has some sort of experience related to paternity leave and his transition to fatherhood. What's yours?

These following questions will help you write your own narrative:

- Were you able to take paid time off? Unpaid time? Accumulated vacation days?
- How could your employer have made it easier on you?
- What was especially hard about this experience?
- What was especially awesome about this experience?
- How involved were you able to be from the beginning?
- What did you learn about yourself and about parenting during those first few weeks?
- What would you do differently if you were to have another child? What would you be sure to do again?

Here's some space for your story:

2. What Are Your Options?

1. Are you eligible to make use of the Family and Medical Leave Act's provision of up to 12 weeks of unpaid leave? Generally, one must be a full-time employee with 12 months with your employer (which must have 50 or more employees). See http://www.dol.gov/whd/fmla/employeeguide.pdf for more.

2. Do you live in California, New Jersey or Rhode Island?

3. Does your employer offer paternity leave? If so, copy down the policy here:

```



```

Does your employer offer maternity leave beyond physical recovery? If so, you are entitled to this as well. Copy down your policy here:

```



```

Would there be adverse career consequences for you if you took paternity leave? Describe:

```



```

PART 3

———

Success at Home

On the morning of July 27th, 2013, professional golfer Hunter Mahan was warming up for the third round of the RBC Canadian Open. He was thirteen strokes under par, two shots ahead of the field and just 36 holes away from a potential $1 million payday. As he took his first few practice swings, his cellphone rang. His wife had unexpectedly gone into labor back home in Texas. Mahan immediately packed up his golf bag and left the tournament to be with his wife for their birth of their daughter.

A little after noon on September 16th, 2013, NFL quarterback Joe Flacco was warming up for the Ravens' early-season matchup against the Cleveland Browns. He was riding high as the reigning Super Bowl MVP, but his team was struggling early that season. As he tossed the football around, he also got a call. His wife had unexpectedly gone into labor and had just arrived at a local hospital. Flacco talked with his wife and other family members, but decided to stay at the stadium. He led the Ravens to a victory and joined his wife and baby a few hours after the birth.

As an advocate for fathers, I admit my initial reaction to Flacco's decision was disappointment. But then I realized that _this_ is what progress for dads looks like. Real progress for working dads comes when we have choices and can thoughtfully make work-family decisions that fit our lives.

Mahan and Flacco made different decisions. They both made the right decision.

They both made the right decision because they both took fatherhood responsibilities seriously and both made considered decisions based on communication with their spouses about what was right for their families. I will never criticize a dad for doing that. Who am I to judge? In fact, thinking about these situations led me to adopt three personal guidelines about dads and their family decisions:

1. I will never know the whole story from the outside, so I will not criticize dads on their parenting or work-family decisions, unless they do something particularly egregious or harmful. This goes double for dads who don't have the financial security or work flexibility that some lucky dads have.

2. When a dad is trying his best, I will support him.

3. If I can help a fellow dad, I will.

In this section of the book, I'll describe ways we can open up more time with our families and how we can make good use of this time. We'll explore ways to take care of ourselves so we can better take care of others and how we can build networks of friendship and support with fellow dads.

In researching this section of the book, I confronted the fact that there were areas in which I needed to improve (put down the stinkin' smartphone, for one), and found the ideas and techniques I discovered really helpful. Even good dads need to be open to new ideas. If you do find an area where you see a need for improvement, don't feel too bad. If you care enough to try to improve, you are already winning the battle. There's no one best way to be an effective father.

I'll be sharing ideas that work for me and for other dads I know, with a little dash of research thrown in for good measure. No one has all the answers. I certainly don't. I hope that, after reading this section, you will feel more equipped to make thoughtful decisions about your role as a father, and then choose what is best for you and your family. There are many different ways to get to that place – just ask Hunter Mahan and Joe Flacco.

CHAPTER 9

Uncovering and Protecting Family Time

When I was in law school, the competition for grades was fierce. The best exam scores after first year get you in Law Review and the inside track for the best clerkships. Leading up to exams, I was part of a study group. We met a few times a week, but I always skipped Fridays to take my son to the Natural History Museum. The group thought I was crazy.

The week before exams, I begged off a study session. I told them that instead, I'd be watching the tigers with my boy at the Bronx Zoo. Things were getting really intense and busy, and I hadn't seen my son as much as I wanted. The group stared at me as if I had two heads – they couldn't believe it.

I suppose I could have scored a point or two better had I studied that day, but I have zero regrets. I did well enough on the exams, and, years later, have a great career. In the long run, studying a little less didn't really matter. The day at the Bronx Zoo with my son did. It's a day that is forever etched in my memory, and one my son and I still talk about.

In my line of work, I ask a lot of dads how they want their kids to look back on their childhoods with them. How do they want to be remembered? Almost universally, their answers gravitate to a single theme:

> I want them to remember that I was a constant, involved loving presence in their lives.

It's a seemingly straightforward answer, but there's actually a lot going on in that sentence.

First, it means that we need to be *present*, that is, spend enough time with our kids so that they know we are a constant, foundational part of their lives. This is sometimes really hard, given our careers, the pressure to provide, and other extenuating circumstances[15].

That's why the dad in the quote above leaves me in awe. He's facing an unbelievably difficult and important work-related challenge. Most lawyers consider their first-year exams second only to the bar exam in terms of the long-term consequences on their lifetime earnings and career trajectories. His study partners sure saw things that way. But this dad made sure that he remained a constant presence in his son's life, even through the crucible of law school exam preparation.

The second part of our common aspiration is not just to be present, but also to be *remembered as an involved, loving presence* in our kids' lives. Law school dad could have been physically present at home with his nose in a book or distracted by studying, with his son sitting at the other end of the room. That is, in one sense, being present. But it wouldn't be *presence*. Instead, he carved out time chunks for memorable days at the Bronx Zoo and Natural History Museum. That'll get you remembered.

Taken together, this means, beyond providing for our families through work, or task is to be present and to be *present*. We need to ensure we spend enough time with our families, and then make great use of that time. In this chapter, we'll explore ways to create, discover and protect time so that we spend enough time with our children. In the next chapter, we'll consider ways to maximize the impact we can have during family time.

◼ 168 Hours

There are 168 hours in a week; this is immutable truth. Of course, all our situations differ, and some face more challenges and time commitments than others, but knowing that we have 168 hours gives us a jumping off point for examining our time use and making positive changes.

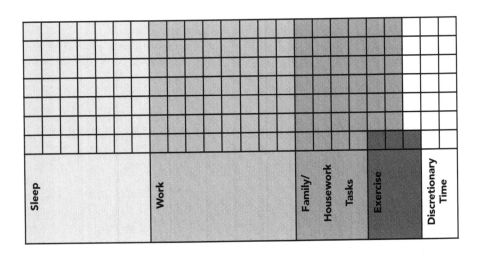

168 hours sounds like a lot, but is it enough for everything we have to do? Let's do a back-of-the-envelope calculation.

First, let's take away 49 for sleep. Don't try to cheat on this. If you are getting less than seven hours a night, you are probably not resting enough, and your decreased energy will take its toll on the rest of your week.

So you've really got 119 hours. Let's assume you're an ambitious professional and subtract 56 for work. This means working eight hours a day, seven days a week – or, if your weekends are off-limits, 11+ hours a day on weekdays only. I know some of you put in more time than this. However, outside of very few professions (and peak times at others) no one really needs to. If you do, you are probably working inefficiently or being pressured to uphold unrealistic expectations. You should go back and re-read Chapter 6 on time management and chronic overwork.

Subtracting 56 hours, that leaves you with 63. Now let's take out two more chunks of non-fun activity: 7 hours per week of commuting, and 33 hours per week of errands and housework, ranging from cleaning to shopping to changing diapers to cooking. A decent slice of this time represents time with family, but more the "have to do" stuff rather than the "want to do" stuff. At this point, you still have a full 23 hours remaining.

Maybe you think you don't have time for exercise, but it seems you do. As we'll discuss further in Chapter 11, exercise makes you more effective the rest of your week at work and at home. Let's devote 3 hours to that. This leaves you with 20 hours of free time to do whatever else makes you happy and healthy, and/or pour this time into your relationship with your children. Twenty hours a week is a lot – just about three hours a day. But it hardly ever feels like a lot of time. Where does this time go?

Remember the time diary I asked you to keep back in Chapter 6? At the end of this chapter, I'm going to ask you to do this again, this time for the hours you are not at work. Many of the same principles apply.

Regularly Scheduled Time Chunks of Unstructured Activity

In Chapter 6, we discussed why and how time chunks are important for focus and productivity at the office. It also works at home. A few hours dedicated to a single father-kid activity is better than several distracted twenty minute snippets scattered throughout the day.

When I first started writing this book, for example, Nick would often ask me to play. I didn't want to disappoint him, so I'd set aside my laptop and join him for ten minutes of *Wii LEGO Harry Potter*. Then, I'd go back to my writing. Invariably, he'd be back asking me to play a half-hour later, and we'd repeat the cycle.

However, this was actually a poor pattern. Nick was unsatisfied with the small scraps of my time and attention, and I was constantly interrupted from my task. In the words of Brigid Schulte (whose book, *Overwhelmed*, gave us the term *time chunk*), I shredded my chunk into "time confetti." The sporadic ten minutes of play time wasn't enough for Nick and wasn't doing me much good. This leads to a third Schulte-ism: "Contaminated time." One of the reasons my ten minutes of play were unsatisfying is that my interrupted writing was still on my mind. My attention wasn't focused on Nick or on using the Patronas spell against the Dementors; it was split between Nick and all the work I still had to do.

So here's how I adjusted: Nick and I set a time the next few nights when I would stop writing and join him to complete two full levels of the Harry Potter game. This usually took about 45 minutes, and represented a satisfying, completed task. I stayed focused on the game until we finished the levels, knowing I had just spent a productive time chunk writing, and had another one waiting for me later that night. As a result, our playtime was less contaminated by thoughts of work. I had more fun with Nick (and he with me), and by the end of the night, I got more accomplished. Bedtime hugs became debriefs of the levels we completed and "Easter eggs" we uncovered.

■ Family Dinner

For many families, the most important instance of regularly-occurring unstructured family time is family dinner. Here's what two dads had to say about it:

I think dinner is the most important part of the day for my family; it's our daily reinforcement. Families that don't have this may be lacking in structuring enough time together. Family dinner also represents prioritization. If Dad and Mom can't make it, then how can the kids prioritize this dinner, especially when they are teenagers?

· ·

When you are all seated together at the table, there are no distractions or interruptions, you can sit quietly and have a conversation directly with your spouse or your kids. You can ask specific questions that pertain to their day to day life... friends, activities, school work, etc. The less time you spend with your children, the less time you have to instill in them the morals and values that you feel are important for them to have.

Family dinners are great because they represent unstructured time for families to talk about their days, and I suspect there is also something primal about sharing meals. As these dads correctly note, meal time can also help us communicate our values and priorities to our kids. In fact, as reported by Nancy Gibbs in a great *Time Magazine* article,

Studies show that the more often families eat together, the less likely kids are to smoke, drink, do drugs, get depressed, develop eating disorders and consider suicide, and the more likely they are to do well in school, delay having sex, eat their vegetables, learn big words and know which fork to use.

However, the fact is, there are lots of us who travel for work, who work long hours, and who work non-traditional schedules. We need to provide for our families, but work obligations often preclude us from consistently having family dinners. Does this mean we're depriving our kids of the myriad benefits of family meals? Should we be feeling guilty about this?

Doctors and nutritionists have a saying, "It doesn't really matter if you take vitamins, but it matters if you live your life like someone who takes vitamins." Basically, people who take vitamins also tend to eat better, exercise more and think about their health on a daily basis – and this is what leads to better health. The research on the efficacy of vitamins is inconclusive at best, but the evidence for these other healthy practices is rock solid. I contend that family dinners are a lot like vitamins. Family dinners are ideal, but as long as we build in consistent unstructured time with our kids and families, I think we can still gain most of the benefits.

Remember my brother-in-law from Chapter 1? For many years, his travel schedule precluded four family dinners a week. However, when he was home, he prioritized unstructured time with his kids and made sure to have daily phone calls while away. Of course, I'm sure my sister, niece and nephew would rather have had dad home for dinner every night, but they still received all the benefits of having a great dad and lots of time together.

Regardless of your ability for consistent dinners together, there are ways to ensure your family gets enough unstructured time with you. Remember the dad from Chapter 5 who negotiated with his boss for "Daddy-Daughter Wednesdays?" Even though he worked long hours, he was able to carve out four hours every Wednesday morning just for him and his little girl. Another dad I know who works long hours is in charge of the bath and bedtime routines for his kids, spending time talking and reading with them every night. Another dad I know goes for a long bike ride with his son every Saturday morning.

However you do it, I highly recommend carving out a regularly scheduled time to be present with your kids. If this does not become an inviolable part of our weekly schedules, the urgent demands of work and life sometimes get in the way. Specifically, we need to be aware of five recurrent obstacles that can prevent regularly-scheduled unstructured family time.

- Too many structured activities
- Unproductive "time sucks"
- Unrealistic standards
- The creeping demands of work
- The distraction of technology

▌ Too Many Structured Activities

Two years ago, when Nick first started on his path towards competitive gymnastics, I wrote a post about the dangers of over-scheduling our kids on *Fathers, Work and Family*. Here's an excerpt:

> Most dads I know feel incredible pressure to schedule their kids in activities. Often without realizing it, we end up over-scheduling them, which is good for no one. Especially because over-scheduling cuts into the very limited time we can carve out for incredibly valuable unstructured time.
>
> Instead of quality time with their dads, our kids get to see the backs of our heads in the car as we shuttle them from thing to thing. Then, when we do get to the activity- art, music, dance, sports, what have you- we're often dropping the kid off to go have quality time with peers, a coach or a teacher. Unless we are directly involved in coaching or volunteering to help, we're often just standing on the sidelines, sucking down coffee and checking in on work.
>
> I don't mean to harsh on scheduled activities for kids. After all, part of our responsibility as good dads is to provide our kids with opportunities to try out lots of different things, discover their interests and talents, and encourage them to develop their abilities. Signing the kids up for sports, music, etc. represents an effective way to achieve these goals.
>
> But, these activities have a way of becoming too much of a good thing. There's a lot of subtle pressure out there in the culture to sign kids up for more and more. I say enough! One activity, maybe two. Two, three hours

a week, tops. That's all I'm willing to do with my seven year old (Nick's gymnastics coaches are grooming him for the competitive travel team, so I'll have to put these principles to the test soon). I don't know how families with multiple kids juggle it all.

Rather than getting caught up in the pressure of signing them up for a second travel team, your kids will be better off with a healthy relationship with you—and soccer just once or twice a week. Because, in the end, what your kid needs more than time with a piano teacher or a soccer coach (or even a college scholarship or his face on a Wheaties box) is time with you.

This is perhaps the most obvious area in which I have let my life slip very far away from my own advice. Hello "good in theory" versus "doable in practice."

Nick's gym is about 40 minutes away, and he currently goes twice a week for two-hour sessions. This means that most Wednesdays and Fridays I pick Nick up from school and drive him to gymnastics. Where I once used our long car-rides for introducing him to music and having long chats, he now spends the car ride doing homework or obsessively playing *Minecraft* on the iPad. By the time we get home, it is nearly 7pm, and we haven't yet spent any meaningful time together. We still need to have dinner and he has some homework left to complete. This doesn't leave much time to play or talk until his bedtime routine begins at around 8:30.

Structured time basically gobbles up unstructured time two days a week. But, perhaps we can be forgiven as this is his major activity, and as his coach told me, "If he wants, Nick really has a future." Proud parent alert: Just a few weeks before this book went to press, Nick competed in his first regional tournament. He won the silver medal in the all-around (just 0.3 off the gold!), won the gold on the vault, the bronze on the rings, and 4th place in the other four events. So, yeah, he could have a future.

But Nick is interested in many other activities, and, I confess, I haven't done my job in setting limitations. He wanted to take the after-school computer class on Thursdays. We want to feed his interests, so we signed him up. Another day with a structured activity. He came home a while back with a flyer stating that the local high school was holding auditions for their production of "The Music Man" and needed several third through fifth graders for the show. Of course, Nick wanted to audition (and follow in his mom's footsteps), so we let him. Now, he has rehearsal once or twice a week, plus the week before the show will involve long rehearsals every day. Oh, yeah, and Little League baseball season will start right after the play is over.

How did this nine-year-old get so busy? It's my fault. In the coming year, and especially as gymnastics gets more demanding, we're going to need to limit his structured time with coaches and directors. We need the unstructured time together.

▌ Avoiding Time Sucks

Urban Dictionary defines "Time Suck" as "something that's engrossing and addictive, but that keeps you from doing things that are actually important, like earning a living, or eating meals, or caring for your children."

The number one killer of available time is wasted time. It is important that we all take some time for ourselves, but we need to do this purposefully, as we will discuss in Chapter 11. I confess that I was once a terrible time-waster, but I've (mostly) broken this habit since adding blogging, book-writing and other professional endeavors on top of career and family involvement. If I was going to get to everything on my plate, and do them well, something had to give. The lowest-hanging fruit were my time sucks. Here's a list of common time sucks, and why and how we should avoid them:

Television - I really enjoy watching TV. I have hundreds of channels and there are a lot of good shows out there. But too many good (or even deliciously bad "guilty pleasures") options can lead to a problem. In my opinion, the worst thing to do is to just turn on the TV and start flipping around. We usually start channel surfing with the intent on finding something to watch, but invariably we watch a bit of something, realize there must be better things on, and flip around to find them, repeating the process ad nauseum. Two hours have flown by, and we didn't even enjoy it.

Thank goodness for DVRs! Now I almost never watch live TV, except for sports. After Nick goes to bed, Amy and I often snuggle up on the couch for a mini-date, watching a show or two we enjoy together (there's nothing like watching *Game of Thrones* with a glass of wine curled up with my Khalessi). A happy consequence of using the DVR is that I watch far less TV, and when I do, it is almost always with the purpose of watching something specific. Other side benefits include pausing (I can pause the Yankee game when it is time to tuck Nick into bed or take out the recycling, avoiding time conflicts and stupid arguments), and circumventing kids' TV I hate. No *Barney*, *Caillou* or *Dora* in my house, ever!!!!!

Social Media- How many of us have gone to Facebook intending to spend just a few minutes checking in with friends and seeing whose birthday it is – and then looked up to see that ninety minutes have passed? Yeah, I thought so.

Facebook and other social media can be fantastic. It keeps me connected with so many people with whom I would have lost touch long ago, I get exposed to new information and articles and cat videos on an-almost daily basis, and I even use it to promote my writing and advocacy for working dads. However, there is a real downside. Facebook may just be the ultimate time-suck. Checking in with friends is great, but too often Facebook time devolves into getting suckered into "clickbait" or yelling with guy you barely knew in high school about how the other political party is ruining America. Even worse, with cellphone alerts, now we can get a "ding" every time someone in our network does something. This creates temptation to shred our time chunks into contaminated confetti.

Fantasy Sports - I used to love playing fantasy football. Then I became a dad and I needed to open up more time. For me, fantasy sports were the first to go. Twenty hours a week on a non-work, non-family activity that causes stress and borderline psychotic behavior? No thank you. For me, this was a no-brainer.

There's nothing wrong with having fun in a friendly league with some buddies. But fantasy sports are deceptively addictive, and, if left uncontrolled, can suck up a ton of time. The addictive nature of fantasy football gives it a very specific kind of enjoyment. Game day induces a lot of stress, losing causes misery, and winning doesn't really cause happiness as much as it provides a temporary reprieve from misery. Especially for fantasy football, some dads I know put in so much time preparing for their fantasy drafts (of course, the unpredictable nature of football and sports injuries means that these obsessively-made plans get upended right away, defeating the purpose).

But the most insidious aspect of fantasy football is that it gives you an incentive to follow every game, not just the big game of the week or those involving your favorite team. Fantasy players are way more likely to watch all 15 hours of weekly live NFL programming. Add in extra games on Thanksgiving plus the daily media coverage, and my wife's not that far off when she quips that "the NFL seems to have been designed to ruin marriages."

So, play in a friendly league, and even involve your older kids with you. But please don't be the guy who obsessively checks updates while at his wife's cousin's wedding or the guy who bores his friends to death with stories of how you lost by two points because of a bad call by the refs. Don't be the guy who refuses to go apple-picking with his family on a Sunday because football is on TV. And, please don't, as one of my dad friends does, play in eight different money-based fantasy football leagues, mostly against strangers. Everything in moderation, my friends.

Golf and Other All-Day Activities - We all need time for exercise and relaxation. In fact, I devote the entirety of Chapter 11 to discussing this imperative. However, we need to make sure our "me time" activities are chosen carefully so that we get the most benefit without having them suck away too much time away from work or family.

Many of my friends love golf, citing the exercise, relaxation and time with friends. Frankly, I just see a "good walked spoiled" and six hours of weekend time away from family. I know mine is a minority view, but I think golf takes up too much time relative to its benefits. I'd much rather play tennis for ninety minutes or take an hour's bike ride – you get most of the same benefits without all the time and expense. Golf clubs are expensive, as are greens fees, driving ranges and lessons.

If golf is your thing, I apologize. Just be careful that it is not keeping you from getting as much family time as you need. Also, please don't buy those ugly pants. And please know that I'm not just singling out golf. Fishing with your buddies is awesome, but spending six hours every Saturday doing that? Training for Tough Mudder races? Too much time away. We need to balance out the psychic and physical benefits we get from our activities with the commitments of time they demand of us. Recharge, but choose carefully. We'll explore much more on this issue in Chapter 11.

It takes real resolve to limit yourself to just a few hours of TV a week, or just one fantasy sports team, or just 30 minutes a day on

Facebook. The exercises at the end of the chapter are designed to help.

Unrealistic Standards

If you pay attention to marketing or the signals from society of what it means to be a good parent, you will invariably come away feeling inadequate. Perfectly trimmed lawns, beautifully waxed cars, floors so clean you can eat off them – are we really expected to live up to all that? Me, I like the old expression, "this house is clean enough to be healthy, but dirty enough to be happy." We shouldn't live like pigs, but making sure our showers are immaculate, our shirts are perfectly pressed, and our home-made gourmet hamburgers include twelve herbs and spices seem like reaches to me. The time required to live up to those standards takes us away from more important things, like work and family time.

Have you ever been to one of those over-the-top birthday parties? Clowns, pony rides, bounce-houses and gourmet birthday cake for the precious four year old and every kid from pre-school? I guess if you have the time, resources and inclination, go for it. But for me, I wonder why on earth anyone would do that to themselves. All the kids want is something fun to do and some sugar. Two bowling lanes and a store-bought cake for your kid and six friends should do the trick.

Admittedly, moms tend to face more pressure to be "perfect parents," and uphold some unrealistic notion of motherhood. Mommy wars and expectations from extended family can cause unremitting stress. But, as we dads continue to expand our involvement in family duties, the external pressure will start building up for us. Before we accept societal pressure, we should remember to "Calm the * down" and understand the benefits of a "lazy marriage." (Check out the Sources section for this chapter for information on these vitally important and entertaining viral sensations.)

▌ The Creeping Demands of Work

> Sure, I'm valuable at work. But at work, everyone is replaceable. The only place I'm not replaceable is in my family's eyes.

Smartphones, email, and other communication technology are great assets in the quest to get the most out of a day, but they can also create the perceived need to be accessible to work 24/7. This is especially true for those of us who are integrators rather than segmenters, as discussed in Chapter 4. If left unchecked, work demands tend to creep in around the edges of family time, often so gradually that we do not even notice. We need to limit our exposure to work during family time. Here's one dad with a plan.

> One day, I told my co-workers and my supervisor that, from now on, I would be checking my work email only once each night at 9:30pm after my kids were in bed, and that I'd only reply to any that require immediate attention – the rest can wait until morning. I wasn't sure how they'd react, but after a pretty short learning curve, they respect my decision, and many adopted this practice themselves.

Here's a dad who runs his company largely from home, but strictly during non-family time. Work demands try to push their way into his family time, but he doesn't even give them a chance.

> I slowly went from being a 24/7 at-home dad, to part-time work, to running a growing web venture. But I only work on my business during my kids' school hours. I squeeze all my conference calls, meetings, publicity, work with brands and everything into the 6 hours a day I'm free and clear of family. I'm being very intentional about my time. The venture is doing great, but it is not growing as quickly as it could if I was "all in." But that's OK. Turning down some opportunities because of work hours is not always easy. But I do, because I want to be there for my kids and wife.

Of course, connectivity to the office isn't just a challenge of keeping work from entering family time. We also need to fight the temptations to allow phones, email, texts and other electronics to contaminate our family time.

◼ The Distraction of Technology

My New Year's Resolution is to severely limit screen time when I'm with my family. A little while ago, I was in the living room with my wife and daughters. I took out my phone to check if a text had come just when my youngest started to ask me a question. I didn't even hear her, and she was right next to me. My wife jumped in – "Hello... she's asking you something!" I didn't even realize my daughter was there. A real wake-up call for me.

Like this dad, I often struggle with the distractions of technology. Unlike many of you, I really don't have a boss to blame; frankly, I often do it to myself.

Last year, my family and I flew down to Orlando the first week of January, which is a slow time at work for me – just after the holidays and still two weeks from the beginning of the spring semester. We're a Disney family and love being in the happiest place on Earth. I was filling in for our department chair during her sabbatical, so I did have things to get done, but there was nothing pressing for me to finish until I got back from Florida and back on campus.

However, while waiting in lines with Amy and Nick, I found myself checking for work emails on my phone. That's not so bad; I'm just waiting in line. But then I was checking the phone while walking through the park. I even found myself pulling the phone out at dinnertime. Lots of people do this, but I was with my family, my in-laws and two family friends. Pretty rude. Worse still, Tigger and Eeyore were coming to our table and I almost missed it!

And, you know what? I didn't even have very many emails. I confess I was also checking in on my blog and my blog twitter account – talk about a time suck! And even if I did have emails, it's not like I work in a nuclear power plant. I could reply to student queries at night, and everything else could wait a few days for me to return. People knew I was away, and no one at work would have cared that much.

I'm sure I'm not alone in checking the smartphone for work emails and texts when I really should be focused on family time. Most of you have more demanding work situations than I do, and I understand sometimes this is necessary. However, I'm convinced we do this to ourselves, sometimes even more than our employers. Sometimes, we are our own strictest taskmasters. I think this dad has it right:

> Have a look in the mirror before you lay blame on the boss or the corporate culture. It's been my experience that most men who have worked hard to build the reputation of being a hard worker have a substantial amount of difficulty dealing with the inevitable by-products of working more flexibly.

After my two and a half days in the parks checking emails on my cellphone- I took a long look in the mirror (no, not that one- I know I'm the fairest of them all!) and kept the phone in my pocket, where it belonged, for the rest of the trip.

Here are some really great ideas from dads who have been able to counter the siren song of technology:

- One dad I know set "no screen hours" for everyone in his family from 6pm until 8pm. All phones, iPads, TVs and computers are off. This way family dinner and other unstructured time is protected.
- There's a fun trend I read about called "phone stacking" in which when people go out to dinner, everyone stacks up their phones into a single pile. The first person who reaches for their phone has to pick up the tab.
- One family I know bans all electronic devices from the living and dining rooms.

- One dad brilliantly puts his iPhone into a docking station as soon as he gets home from work. He sets it to Pandora so the house gets nice ambient music. But, best of all, his phone is never in his hands or his pocket, so he does not feel the temptation to check texts and emails when at home.

The problem with technology is that it can keep us from being mentally present when we are physically with our families. Being there, but not being *there* means that neither you nor your family get the benefits of being together. Even worse, we send a signal that work or other distractions come before paying attention to family. None of us would intentionally send that message; we need to stop doing so unintentionally.

The advice and exercises from the earlier "Work" section of this book can also help us with this challenge. If we can find ways to work more flexibly, maximize our productivity and efficiency while at work, and build family considerations into our career plans, we'll be much more capable of carving out and protecting family time, and better able to block out distractions.

Now that we have some ideas of how to create and protect regularly scheduled time chunks of unstructured activity, we'll continue our discussion of family time in the next chapter. There, we'll focus on how we can maximize the time we've set aside, so that it is fun and memorable for everyone.

Chapter 9 Exercises

1. Time Sucks

Let's take some time to think about the time sucks that are most challenging to us, and brainstorm two ways we can cut down (or eliminate) that activity

Time Suck	Ways to Eliminate
Television	
Social Media	

2. Revisiting Fatherhood Goals

Based on the content in this chapter, let's take a minute to revisit our fatherhood goals from Chapter 3. Do you have anything to add or change? Any new ideas for building in time for renewal, hobbies, interests or spirituality? For eliminating time sucks?

Fatherhood goals
6 month goals
3-Week "To-Dos"
1 Thing to Stop Doing

3. Time Diaries

Like we did with work time, let's keep track of our non-work time use for a week. Where can we eliminate time sucks? Create time chunks? Keep our goals more realistic? Keep work from creeping in?

Week of [Dates]

	Monday	Tuesday	Wednesday	Thursday	Friday
6					
7					
8					
9					
10					
11					
Saturday:					
Sunday:					

4. Avoiding Technology

Let's brainstorm a quick list of how we can avoid the constant temptation of connectivity through technology:

1. _____
2. _____
3. _____
4. _____
5. _____
6. _____
7. _____

CHAPTER 10

———

Making Family Time Memorable

As a teacher, my hours are long and, at times, stressful. There have been times when I came home from work with a pile of papers to grade and tired as hell, but when my little girl wants me to play with her I put it all down and give her 100%. That's what I want her and her brother to remember, that I always put them before anything and did everything in my power to make sure they were happy and taken care of.

. . . .

I want my kids to remember the time we spent doing activities, trips to the zoo, watching cartoons together, working with them on hands-on projects, cooking, building a ground floor cubby, watching sports on TV, playing with them, and just basically having that all important balance so they know and remember I was there during these all important years.

Now that we have opened up and defended our family time, and figured out some ways to be in the moment with our families, our final task is figuring out how to fill up our present and *present* family time with memorable, fun activities. The dads in the above quote seem to have things figured out. Let's see how we can emulate them.

▌ Nick's Winter Coat

A few years ago, I was in a big, fat stinking hurry for some *thing* that I am sure I thought was important at the time. Nick was just old enough to get his coat, hat, gloves and shoes on by himself, and I needed him to do so *quickly* or else we'd be late for the *thing* that was soooo super-important that now I can't even remember what it was.

So, of course I see Nick presumably fooling around and taking his sweet time getting his jacket on. We're running late. This *thing* is very important. We *need* to get going. So, I snap at him about his jacket.

He's a great kid and I hardly ever raise my voice to him, so he is struck by my tone, and he sheepishly says that he can't get his sleeve on. "Of course you can," I bark at him as I start to shove his sleeve onto his arm. But his arm won't go through- something was blocking the sleeve. That's when I realized I had put his hat and gloves in his sleeve earlier that day.

Nick was trying to do the right thing, but couldn't get past an obstacle.

I apologized, tried to make him feel better, and slowed down to his speed. Somehow it turned out perfectly ok that we were ten minutes late for that super-important *thing*.

My mistake was a powerful lesson that taught me to be a better dad. I was injecting unnecessary stress into my time with Nick. I wasn't being present with him. Instead, I was so focused on my schedule and on a fleeting, unimportant thing that seemed so pressing at the time. My time with Nick shouldn't have gotten contaminated. While I'm not always successful, I'm getting better about being in the moment.

This lesson on fatherhood also helped me in other facets of my life. Ever since becoming a father, I've learned to be more patient, more tolerant, and less of a "type-A" person. I'm far happier, more relaxed, and have learned to better separate what's worth worrying about and what isn't. I've also learned to listen better, to empathize more, and to see things from other's perspectives. I have a better understanding that what comes easily to me does not always come easily to others. I've learned how to be more precise when communicating and giving instructions, and, perhaps most importantly, learned how to help people handle change and other stressful situations. (Thank you, Nick, for making me a better, happier person!)

All of these fatherhood-acquired skills and perspectives also serve me well at work. My college students usually try to do the right thing, but get stuck by real and self-imposed obstacles. They are just being introduced to information and perspectives that I've been focusing on for almost two decades. They have different learning styles, and come to my classroom from all over the world with different experiences and perspectives. I now better understand my students, and have gotten better at reaching them. Thanks to being a father, I am a far more effective college professor.

At work, I have also had opportunities to supervise other professors as department chair, run committees, and be an informal leader on team project work. As a tenured professor, I have also been called on to mentor new faculty.

My work colleagues also usually try to do the right thing, but get stuck by real or self-imposed obstacles. They have different specializations, personalities and communication styles. Some of my colleagues have a difficult time trying new things or working in new ways. I now better understand my colleagues, and have gotten better working with them. Thanks to being a father, I am more effective as an informal leader at work.

I suspect many of you have similar experiences, in that the perspectives and skills you acquire as a father spill over into your performance at work. Through fatherhood, many of us have learned to be more organized, efficient, empathetic, and to better differentiate what is/is not truly important. These skills apply to all aspects of life, including at work.

Work-Family Synergy

Over the past few chapters, I've been emphasizing the need to protect family time from the interference of work. Of course, as there are only 24 hours in a day and 168 in a week, work and family compete with each other for our two most valuable resources, time and energy. Time is non-renewable, and energy only renews itself slowly over time. It is only natural to focus on the conflict between work and family.

However, it isn't always that simple. In many ways, work and family enhance each other. In fact, they are two of the main components of a full, meaningful life – success in both is vitally important. In fact, time and energy spent at work can make us more effective at home, and time and energy spent on parenting can make us more effective at work. There is actual evidence that fatherhood enhances and enriches us in our work roles. According to the tremendous study by the Boston College Center for Work and Family:

- 64% of working dads agreed that involvement with their family gave them knowledge/skills that made them better employees
- 61% agreed that family life made them use their time more efficiently, helping them be better employees
- 82% agreed that family life made them feel happier, helping them be better employees

A more recent follow-up study by the folks at Boston College also shows that men who, because of workplace flexibility, have more time with their kids are:

- Happier at work
- Less likely to voluntarily leave their company
- More engaged at work
- Report that their work performance is improved by having enough time with family

So, it also works both ways. Conflict and synergy. We often neglect to mention how our work and family lives can enhance and enrich the other. I bet that, like me, most of us are better employees because of our fatherhood experiences.

To go back to the "balanced diet" metaphor from Chapter 3, we shouldn't have to choose between work and family. We can choose enough of each to be successful in each. There's no sense in choosing just steak or just potatoes; let's take enough of each to make a great, balanced meal.

And, just as a balanced diet requires more than two food groups, a balanced approach to life means time and attention devoted to the full range of life activities, not just work and family. A full, balanced life means attention to work, family, self, exercise, religion, community, extended family, friends, social needs, relationships and relaxation (more on this in the next two chapters).

A balanced diet extends far beyond steak and potatoes, or bacon and eggs, or spaghetti and meatballs, or PB&J (or any other yummy two-food combination). It's more like Thanksgiving dinner. Turkey and stuffing and cranberry sauce and sweet potatoes and corn and green beans and some weird Jello-fruit thing and wine and beer and water and mashed potatoes and my wife's awesome lemon-poppy seed cake and far too many other desserts to list.

So, please spend your time at work productively and efficiently. Support your family the best way you can. But be sure to balance career aspirations with spending lots of time with those you love. Soak in family time and be fully present with your kids. Take all the lessons you learn in your life, no matter where you've learned them, and apply them to be as effective as possible in all your roles.

Perhaps, most importantly, we need an occasional reminder that the whole point of family time is to enjoy being with your family, even if they take a little longer than you'd like putting on their jackets.

■ Making Memories

Flying in an airplane is much safer than covering the same distance riding in a car. Yet, most people are more afraid of flying than driving. One of the main reasons for this is *availability bias*, in which things that are easier to call to mind are given greater weight than things that are less memorable. Availability bias is why we remember the rare plane crash that is all over the news rather than the thousands of car rides every day.

Most of the time, availability bias is a problem that leads us to make faulty decisions regarding risk. For example, at the beach, we may be more concerned with shark attacks than skin cancer; after watching *Law & Order SVU*, we vastly overestimate the incidence of child abduction. But we can also use this quirk of human memory to our advantage.

The universal aspiration of fathers, articulated in Chapter 9, involves being a constant presence and also being remembered as a constant presence. The former involves being a good father. The latter can be helped by consciously activating availability bias in our kids. In short, we have to:

1. Do all the everyday, sometimes unnoticed work of being a good father

2. Punctuate the everyday with occasional bursts of something memorable

My dad was a constant loving presence throughout my childhood. Upon reflection, I know he did all the grunt work of being a good father—providing for our family, maintaining the house, buying the presents Santa gave us, reading to me, teaching me to brush my teeth, disciplining me when I needed it, etc. This is far and away the most important work he did for me and my family.

However, when I think back to my childhood, I don't remember those things. I remember the above-ground pool he built in our back yard and swimming with him. I remember my summers at Great Kills Little League with him as my team's manager. I remember us watching Dave Righetti's July 4th no-hitter. I remember the Galoonky-rides (our silly version of a piggy-back ride) when it was bedtime. I remember our camping trips in Bucks County, Pennsylvania, in the tiny Shasta trailer. These are the fun, memorable events that, thanks to availability bias, are in the front of my mind.

I try to do the same for Nick. Like my dad, I put in the thankless everyday work – providing for the family, packing lunch, buying Santa's presents, helping Nick with homework, restricting his screen-time, driving him to gymnastics, etc. But, perhaps because I teach stuff like the availability bias in my management courses, I am very mindful about also building fun, memorable traditions with Nick. Like my dad did for me, I coach Nick's little league team. When Amy has to work nights, especially during the summer, Nick and I spend evenings at the town pool or at the local minor-league stadium.

▮ Feeding Common Interests

I share all things Star Wars with Nick; we spend a lot of time watching the movies, engaging in elaborate light-saber battles (we even developed characters- I am evil Sith Lord Darth Taraco, he is Jedi Qui-Son), and playing the *Wii LEGO Star Wars* games together. I decorate his birthday cakes with elaborate Star Wars scenes, we march in Nyack's Halloween parade as a group of Star Wars characters (me: Boba Fett, him: Darth Vader, Amy: a very regal Queen Amidala), and Nick and I even built the Lego Millennium Falcon together. The payoff for all of this – last year, his hand-made Father's Day card to me read "The galaxy is better with you and me, Dad!"

Amy does similar things with Nick. They share all things Harry Potter, including the books, movies, Wii game, and even a trip to Universal Florida (mmmm butter beer!). When I work nights, Amy and Nick bake cookies. They share a love of YouTube "epic fail" videos and those funny "Sign Spotting" books. Nick loves going backstage at the theaters where Amy works. And that's just a small part of their shared activities.

When Nick looks back on his childhood, I think he will remember feeling secure that both his parents were constant loving presences in his life. But he won't remember how great his mom was when he was sick with the stomach flu or how I picked up a summer class to get a little extra money for the vacation fund.

I do think he will remember Star Wars, baseball and swimming with dad. I think he will remember reading Harry Potter, baking cookies, going backstage at the Madison Square Garden Theater, and laughing the night away with mom.

While it is definitely more important that we do the less-memorable, less-glamorous hard work of being a good dad, creating happy lifelong memories is important too – for us and our kids. Thank you, availability bias.

To create a childhood full of happy memories, all we need is a little creativity and an open mind. Homer Simpson once quipped that one of the perks of fatherhood is that you get to teach your kids to hate the things you hate. Let me invert that. One of the best things about fatherhood is getting your kids to love the things you love. I had a specific plan to get Nick into Star Wars, but I was lucky that he really took to it right away.

However, it's not always so easy. Your kids will also be interested in things that you are not at all interested in, and they will reject some things you love. In these cases, we have to find a way to get interested in their stuff, or work to find some middle ground. There is a universe of things to try – art, science, reading, travel, cooking, photography, music, fashion, outdoors, sports, etc. There are so many ways to build fun memorable events or common hobbies into our kids' childhoods. Sometimes, it just takes a little extra effort to get started:

> I wouldn't trade my daughters for the world, but sometimes, I do need to push myself to keep me into what they are interested in. They love princesses, dresses and things that aren't up my alley. "Will you play Magic Clips with me?" But I push myself to do it, and do it happily, because, well, it makes them so happy. I never thought I'd go to "Frozen on Ice," but there I am. Because I love them and have to meet them where they are at. My long-term plan of getting them into punk rock and tennis, however, is working perfectly.

■ Buying Experiences, Not Things

The best gift you can give your kids is your consistent presence. Happily, instead of buying your kids the latest junky plastic thingamabob they have their eye on, we can use Christmas or

Hanukkah or birthdays as excuses to purchase things that create opportunities for time together. Research shows that money buys far more happiness if it is spent on experiences instead of things, especially when purchased in advance, as looking forward to something adds to the fun.

Every year at Christmas, my present to Nick (the rest come from Santa, although, sadly, I think Nick sees through this now) is an envelope with some pre-purchased tickets. A few years ago, it was kids' ski lessons at Mt. Peter, a tiny ski mountain about 40 minutes north of our house. Last year, it was tickets to four games at our local minor-league baseball stadium. Next year, I think I might book us a few sessions at an indoor rock climbing gym.

If you are a dad who likes the outdoors, buying a small tent for Christmas and attaching a note about when your first camping vacation will be would make for a cool present and a way to lock in a weekend dad-and-kids adventure (plus, the tent can be used in the living room for a test run after the tree is put to the curb). Family memberships at many cultural institutions pay for themselves in two visits. In my neck of the woods, family memberships to Storm King Arts Center, the Norwalk Aquarium, the Bronx Zoo and the NYC Botanical Gardens are very reasonable, right around the cost of two admissions. By buying a membership, you are much more likely to spend a few Sundays over the course of the year out on a family trip, as opposed to spending the day watching your football teams lose.

Toys and games are great, and I'm not advocating taking the thrill of ripping wrapping paper from our kids, but perhaps we would all be better served by shifting the types of presents we give – less stuff more dad-and-kid experiences. They'll remember the gift of your constant loving presence more than any present under the tree.

The right kinds of gifts also open up opportunities for experiences together. I have a friend whose son is very mechanically inclined, and every birthday, he gets his son one of those gonzo mechanized Lego sets for them to work on together. The hours they spend working on these is great bonding time, and they also get a tangible reminder of their work together after the project is finished. Legos are great, but Lego sets that become father-son projects and then are proudly displayed are gifts that keep on giving.

Another good idea is to buy fun board and card games for a regularly scheduled family game night. Our current favorite board/card games to play are Telestrations (a combination of Pictionary and the telephone game), Apples to Apples, Sorry! and Uno. One dad also relates the joys of family game night:

> I know it sounds corny, but we really try to have "family game night" every Friday. Me, my wife, and our kids break out the popcorn and play a bunch of board games. The 25-year old bachelor version of me would consider this a nightmare, but I actually look forward to it after a long week of work.

▌ Saying "Yes" To Rituals

I like how this dad has made game night part of the family schedule. It is a weekly family ritual, much like family dinner or the other forms of "regularly-scheduled unstructured family time" I advocated for in the previous chapter. No doubt, you've picked up on one of this book's recurring themes – my insistence that, if we do not make important things part of our regular schedules, life gets in the way with 100 little excuses for us to say, "well, this one time, I can skip it and make it up later."

But here's a sobering thought. Our kids grow up and grow out of things all the time. You never really know when the last time you do something with your kid is the last time you'll do that specific thing with him. This passage from my favorite writer, Bill Bryson, always gets to me:

> This may get a little sentimental, and I'm sorry, but yesterday evening I was working at my desk when my youngest child came up to me, a baseball bat perched on his shoulder and a cap on his head, and asked me if I felt like playing a little ball with him. I was trying to get some important work done before going away on a long trip, and I very nearly declined with regrets, but then it occurred to me that never again would he be seven years, one month, and six days old, so we had better catch these moments while we can.

My son is now in fourth grade and there are lots of things I "used to do" with him that he's now grown out of. It's not like, one night before bedtime, we agreed that tonight would be the last "Nicky, the Skunk and the Dinosaur" story we'd make up together (based on my son and two of his favorite stuffed animals). Instead, the stories just gradually ended, replaced by reading a chapter of a Roald Dahl classic each night, recapping the Yankees game or quizzing each other on *Star Wars* characters.

I loved co-creating and telling these stories, especially as we expanded the cast of characters to many other stuffed animals and his real-life best friends, Jesse and Lucas. But some nights, I bristled and resisted. Some nights, I grew impatient when Nick would "correct" my story by insisting on some detail or another. Sometimes, I was just tired and wanted a quick hug before turning out the lights.

Most of the time, I stayed for a quick story and was glad I did. But now I look back and miss the Skunk and the Dinosaur, and I kick myself for not fully appreciating the stories at the time. I miss "Nicky" too – for some time now, he has insisted on the more grown-up sounding "Nick." I miss Buzz Lightyear, Curious George and lots of other Nicky stuff, too.

There are still lots of fun things we do together, and many things we'll always remember. However, I will try to be more conscious of our dad-and-son rituals, less likely to put Nick off when he asks me to play light sabers or record his silly videos or work on his batting stance or help him put together the Lego version of Jabba's Sail Barge. I resolve to say yes to his requests, and to soak it in every time (I can almost always make up the half hour of work or writing after he goes to bed). After all, skunks and dinosaurs don't live forever. You never know when the next time you do something together is the last time you do that thing together. Perhaps we all could resolve to catch these moments while we can.

Presence from a Distance

Finally, with our career demands, we can't always be present as much as we'd like. Long hours, shifting schedules and business travel can get in the way. One dad describes how he tries to minimize the impact of business travel on his family time:

> I've lost count of how many times I've opted for the 6am flight that gets me to the 9am meeting just in time, just so I can have the prior evening with my wife and kids. It takes a toll sometimes, but the benefits more than justify the lost zzz's.

However, if we do need to be away for long stretches of time, there are lots of things we can do to help our children be connected to us. I know we've been criticizing the use of technology in these past few chapters, but technology is a fantastic tool for long-distance communication. FaceTime and Skype are free and add visual contact to what was once an expensive long-distance phone call. One dad I know takes his kids' favorite stuffed animals with him when he travels and makes sure to take funny pictures with them each day when on the road. Thanks to smartphone cameras and texting capabilities, his kids receive these in real time, feeling connected with dad. Another recorded himself reading his son's favorite bedtime story and has his wife play it on the iPad each night he's away. Finally, you may remember how my brother-in-law bought a second cellphone with a dedicated, family-only line so his kids could be assured their dad was always available to them.

Jason Swann wrote a guest post on *Fathers, Work and Family* with some great advice about staying connected with your kids while traveling for work.

> The point is, dads, we are missed. A lot. A WHOLE lot. We're all rock stars to our children, and we can take care of our "fans" by taking a bit of care with how we leave them for our work trips. It will pay dividends in the end to pay attention to how we deal with being gone, as our little ones are dealing with us being gone. So I've looked around the web, read, asked, cajoled, and uncovered to find what we can do when we have to be away. The list is organic, so use or don't, add to or take away.
>
> 1. Don't overdo it, or under do it on the explanation. They need to know that you'll be gone, but don't freak them out about it.
>
> 2. Leave some notes, in the open and hidden where they'll find them later. I've done this with The Wife and my Wee ones and they LOVE it.
>
> 3. Use the technology you have. Skype, FaceTime, MMS pics, text, and so on. I was at training for two weeks and created a blog, just to upload videos I made for the home team. You can get to the mini bar later.
>
> 4. Ask for a project to be done when you return. A drawing, craft piece, marble statue, or whatever. They'll put their all into it, just waiting for you to go nuts over it when you get back.
>
> 5. For heaven's sake, don't forget to bring them something home. We all remember wanting that small token that said we were missed. It can be small and cheap. Just don't forget it.

When I travel for work, I try to follow Jason's advice. Many years ago, when Nick was three, I accompanied a group of MBA students on a two-week travel course in Beijing and Shanghai. Before I left, I bought 14 little toys at the dollar bin at the local toy store and had Amy hide one each day for Nick's "daddy toy." It went over great. About a year ago, Nick and I downloaded a fun free app that turns pictures into memes by adding captions. Now, when I travel, Nick and I exchange memes back and forth – the sillier the better. It's really fun, and the memes made sure he knew I was always thinking of him. That's all any kid can ask for. Even better than a LOLcat!

So far, this book has focused on talking care of work responsibilities and taking care of our families. Starting in the next chapter, let's start focusing on taking care of ourselves.

Chapter 10 Exercises

1. Common (and Uncommon) Interests

Please fill out the following chart, indicating your interests, your kids' interests and where they two sets may or may not overlap. Where they overlap, your action step can be a way to spend time together on that common interest. For interests that do not overlap, your action step can be a way to reach common ground, something you can do to better embrace their interests, or something you can do to get them more interested in your stuff.

My Interests	Common Interests	My Kids' Interests

Action Steps:

1.

2.

3.

4.

CHAPTER 11

Taking Care of Yourself

Honestly, taking care of myself has been a low priority. I'm 45, overweight and don't exercise. My knees and back aren't great. There's always something more pressing to do, or I'm just stressed and exhausted from working and being the primary parent. When I do get some time for myself, I tend to crash on the couch with some mindless TV.

· ·

My problem is I have so many priorities. I never get to a point of doing everything I want to do or the way I want. There's just not enough time. I let go of my own goals and hobbies, and my health has suffered, too. Also, time with my wife often gets pushed aside because of all the things we have to get done.

Being a working dad is hard. Like these dads, and like you, I spend much of the time working and putting my family's needs first. That's just part of the deal in being a good, involved father. After taking care of others, we often have limited time and energy to spend on taking care of ourselves. If there was one common theme through all the interviews I conducted with dads for this book, it was that we struggle for time spent on their own needs. However, listen to this dad:

It's wonderful to have your kids as the center of your life but at the same time, part of their growth is to see how dad is as a man. How he interacts in the world outside the home is in part how they learn to be an adult. As a working dad, my struggle is that because my job requires so many hours outside the home, the time I have at home is focused on the kids and their lives. Now, how do I balance my social life, work, and home without feeling that I'm neglecting my kids? Man, it's not easy.

He makes a crucially important point. Sometimes, it has to be about you. If we never get away, they'll never get the chance to miss us. If we never put ourselves first, they'll take for granted we're always there. If we don't, as the flight attendants always remind us, put our oxygen masks on first, we can't help our families with theirs.

It would be better for everyone if we took just a little bit of time to focus on ourselves. In his classic book, *The Seven Habits of Highly Effective People,* Steven Covey suggests that we schedule in some time every week for renewing ourselves in the various facets of our lives. In this way, we'll be more effective as fathers and in our careers. In this chapter, we'll explore how we can take care of ourselves by taking time to meet our needs to:

- Stay physically active and reasonably healthy
- Tend to our mental and spiritual well-being
- Nurture the relationship with our spouse or significant others
- Contribute to our communities

And we'll do so in a way that gives us the time we need without taking too much time away from our work or family responsibilities.

Before moving on in this chapter, you should take a quick check back to Chapter 3 – "Goals for a Balanced Life." In the exercises at the end of that chapter, you already thought through how you can better attend to various priorities. We'll revisit those goals and to-do lists throughout this chapter. Also, please note that our social and friendship needs are also paramount. So much so, that I give them their own separate treatment in the next, and final, chapter.

▌ The Formula for Parenting Effectiveness? (A Little Bit Less is More)

Being a bit of a geek, I've come to expressing my orientation towards my own "me time" and social time with this snappy little formula.

X-2 hours a week of effective, involved parenting > X hours of distracted or stressed-out parenting, as long as X is big enough[16].

In previous chapters, I rang the warning bell against "time sucks"- activities that, in my opinion, take up too much away from work or family relative to their psychological and social benefits. Your mileage may vary, but spending all weekend on the golf course, watching all 15 hours a week of NFL programming, or playing in 8 fantasy sports leagues takes us away from work and family duties for too long. I recommended that dads find other outlets that don't take up so much valuable time.

Now, I'm not pulling a 180 here and I do not advocate neglecting our responsibilities. But I recommend that we involved dads cordon off some time on a regular basis for our own needs. If things are not regularly scheduled, they tend to get put off. Relaxation is important, so much so that what we do with that time should be chosen with a purpose and then regularly scheduled. A short dose of something mindless like channel surfing can be OK, but there are much better choices.

In my life, my weekly 2 hours of volleyball is a haven – I can just concentrate on the game, get into a flow, get some good exercise, and enjoy the company of fun group of people who are not involved in the other aspects of my life. And it means I get out of parenting duties on Monday evenings, and sometimes it means we hire a sitter. While I love Nick more than anything, I think it is healthy that he knows that he is not always the center of the universe.

I even maintain my commitment to my volleyball league when Amy is out of town or working on a show. I'm a much better dad when I get to take breaks. I think we all are. To me, getting that break is worth hiring a sitter, arranging what we call a "half-sleepover" (in which Nick goes to bed at a friend's house, but I pick him up later that night instead of him staying until morning) or calling in a favor from friends.

▌Taking Care of Our Physical Health

Another reason volleyball is important to me is that it is regularly scheduled exercise. We are far more likely to commit to time to something if we make it a set part of our weekly schedules. Otherwise, it is easy to put off these important activities because something more urgent pops up or because we're feeling lazy that day. The fact that Monday night is volleyball night means that Amy and I schedule our other plans around it, making it much more likely that I make almost every session. Without structure, it is easy to backslide:

> I've struggled with my weight ever since I was a kid. In college, I got thin through the not-very-healthy combination of starving myself and working out like a demon. I've always had an all or nothing personality like that. After college, I worked at a start-up, 70-80 hour weeks where they ordered in dinner for us every night. The job paid well, but my health really suffered. When I took a more regular job, I got back into fitness and was even running half-marathons.

The last race I ran was two weeks before my son was born. I went from running 30-40 miles a week to virtually none. I'm back to being overweight. My blood pressure is high and I'm temporarily on medication. It's hard to find the two-hour chunks of time needed to run, plus our busy schedules means my family eats out or orders in more than we cook.

Like this dad, a lot of us feel too busy to regularly exercise. After all, there's so much to do, and, especially with young children, when it's all done there's little time or energy for much more than sleep. I confess this is sometimes a problem for me.

But, as Stephen Covey reminds us in *Seven Habits of Highly Effective People*:

Most of us think we don't have enough time to exercise. What a distorted paradigm! We don't have time not to. We're talking about three to six hours a week, or a minimum of thirty minutes a day, every other day. That hardly seems an inordinate amount of time considering the tremendous benefits in terms of impact on the other 162-165 hours of the week.

Exercise gives you more energy to tackle the other 165 hours of your week. And is the single best thing you can do for your health.

In short, studies have shown[17] that a few hours a week of moderate exercise lowers pain and disability among those with arthritis, slows the progression of dementia among Alzheimer's patients, reduces the progression of diabetes, prevents hip fractures, lowers anxiety and depression symptoms, and lowers blood pressure and hypertension. Lack of basic cardio fitness is the No. 1 predictor of death. Beyond the big-picture health benefits, regular exercise gives us more energy to be better at the rest of our lives. We can be more productive at work and more energetic and involved at home.

And you don't have to lift weights or do anything extreme, like train for a Spartan Race, to get immediate benefits. My friend who is a personal trainer always says a little exercise is way better than none. Walking through your neighborhood or on a treadmill a half hour a day is so much better than being sedentary.

For a long time, my commitment to exercise and eating well was sporadic. I'd be conscientious for a while, and then slip into bad habits. But, as I discussed in Chapter 3, I've become much more focused and consistent in my approach. Not to sound too dramatic, but as I've gotten to mid-life, I've begun to recognize my own mortality. I have so much to live for and want to be part of Amy's and Nick's lives as long as I can. That's the motivation that gets me on the elliptical machine even on days I'm feeling slothful.

Still, I envy those who have a more natural affinity toward fitness:

> I'm actually pretty good at this. I get up early to go swimming at the Y at 6am. I shower there and then come back home to check in with the family before we're all off to school or work. A half an hour swim five days a week gets me the exercise I need – and an opportunity for some quiet time for myself.

But, as this dad also told me, once swimming became his morning routine for a few months, he no longer felt any struggle to maintain this part of his schedule. Conscious choices can, over time, become consistent good habits. I'm trying to get to that point. For now, my fitness tracking app and its goal of 10,000 steps per day, along with a weekly dose of volleyball, are keeping me on track.

Now is a good time to revisit the health and exercise goals we identified in Chapter 3. Do you have anything to add or change? More ways to make exercise a routine part of your weekly calendar?

Health/exercise goals
6 month goals
3-Week "To-Dos"
1 Thing to Stop Doing

"Me Time" can become "We Time"

While this chapter is focused on ways we can use alone time, there's no rule that you cannot include your family or friends in your activities.

I've come to learn that it's not just time alone that recharges me. Two years ago I told my 10 year old I was going for a run, and he asked to come with me. While we didn't keep to my regular pace, it was fun, and now I look for ways to involve him is staying active and doing the things I like to do.

Here are a few more ideas of how we can incorporate our kids and others in what we do to recharge:

- Community service as a family
- Family bike rides
- An age-appropriate show on Netflix to watch together
- A big Lego or K-Nex set and work on it together over a period of a few weeks

- Nature walks, fishing, camping
- A video game or two you can enjoy with your kids – Just Dance or Guitar Hero may be good choices
- Turn "boring car ride time" into a time you can expose your kids to the music you love. I did this during the 40 minute drive to Nick's ski lessons and now he's a life-long fan of Elvis, Pat Benatar and punk rock (Although he now also likes Kidz Bop and hates grunge. So sad)

Tending to Our Mental, Spiritual and Relaxation Needs

Grace Naessens[18] wrote an inspirational poem that begins:

I got up early one morning

and rushed right into the day;

I had so much to accomplish

that I didn't have time to pray.

The poem continues with how she was so rushed and frantic that she lost sight of what was most important. She lost her center and was far less effective. She then ends the poem with this beautiful line:

I woke up early this morning,

And paused before entering the day,

I had so much to accomplish,

That I had to take time to pray

I'm not a particularly religious person, but this poem resonates with me. Sometimes I'm so busy with what's urgent that my day becomes a blur of largely ineffective hustle and contaminated time. Taking some time to pray, or to relax, or to get into a good "head space" usually pays dividends. By clearing out our mental clutter, we can better identify what we should be doing. Slowing down allows us to be more effective. Here's how one dad describes the role of religion in his and his family's life:

> Faith is an essential part of my life. It grounds me intellectually, mentally, morally. It informs what I choose to do with my life and keeps me asking myself whether I'm acting the way I want to be in my family, with friends and at work.
>
> I think going to Mass each week with my family is the most important thing. No matter what we are doing, or if we've been butting heads, we have to stop and be at peace together. I especially like the "peace be with you" towards the end of mass. This ritual really challenges us – it doesn't matter if my wife and I had sharp words that morning or if my son is mad at me. In the moment, we are called to get over those things and make peace. This moment of reconciliation is priceless, and helps remind us what is important.
>
> My religion also calls me to service, and I've been able to meet so many people and feed my soul by serving the less fortunate. It is also a great way to pass on these values to my children. That the world needs them to help others.

This dad, and so many others find that their faith and regular observance of rituals like Sunday mass reminds them of what is most important in life, helps guide their decision making, and brings them peace and calm.

If, like me, organized religion is not your thing, you should be sure to make space in your life for contemplation or renewal. Many people find peace in meditation or yoga, in being outdoors, in artistic expression, or in simple acts of cooking or gardening. If you have an activity that allows you to lose yourself, relax and find your center, please be sure to set aside and protect the time needed for regular immersion. Rituals and regular practice are important, or else the time we need slips away in the rush of little things life throws at us.

I'm an academic, so it is natural for me to find renewal through reading and writing. There are occasional stresses in writing a blog, an article for *Harvard Business Review* or (especially) a book, but I must admit that I derive a lot of joy and satisfaction from the process of writing and then of seeing my words out in the wider world. Labors of love can be self-renewing.

But even with that, I sometimes get into a mental rut. Because I read academic journal articles, business periodicals, textbooks, and (worst of all) student papers for a living, I'll sometimes go stretches of time in which I am only mentally focused on things relating to my work.

A year or so ago, my mother told me a little fact that completely changed my thinking about reading. She said that if you just read 10 pages every night before going to sleep, you'll wind up reading 12 books a year. That's not too much to ask. So, most nights, even if I've used my brain all day, I'll pull out a book and spend just a few minutes reading something unrelated to my work.

I look at a new book as a chance to spend a few weeks in a long story, or an opportunity to learn from someone else's life and perspective. I read some novels, and spent a recent summer devouring the entire "Song of Ice and Fire" series (aka *Game of Thrones*), but I mostly read non-fiction, often about baseball, and anything written by Joe Posnanski, Michael Lewis or Bill Bryson. Reading about different topics helps me activate parts of my brain and think about issues that had been shunted aside for academicy-jargony stuff like "The Importance of the Critical Psychological States in the Job Characteristics Model: A Meta-Analytic and Structural Equations Modeling Examination" (the actual title of a journal article I wrote), or, to be honest, yet another *Fathers, Work and Family* blog post.

Another mental activity I enjoy is doing crossword puzzles. I subscribe to *Games Magazine*, which is full of crosswords, cryptics, acrostics, soduku, kenken, logic puzzles, wordplay and trivia. Almost every day, I take 15 minutes or so to do a puzzle or two to exercise different parts of my brain. Nick and I do the kid's page together. Sporcle.com is a good alternative, with lots of fun quizzes on a variety of topics.

There are many other ways to exercise the mind. One of my good friends sets aside a couple of hours every weekend to pluck away at a new tune on his guitar. Another dad gets renewal and social time as part of a singing group:

Every Sunday, I sing in a chorus. As I work from home, it is so important for me to get out of the house and be with adult friends. My husband is totally supportive of this. I actually worry about him and his lack of social life sometimes. He works really hard for really long hours. I'll have to give him this book when you've finished writing it.

Whatever your preferred activity, the important thing is to spend some time thinking about something other than your immediate concerns, or, perhaps, even thinking about nothing at all. Sometimes it's good to just shut off your brain for a while. So veg out with some TV or Facebook every now and again. Just try not to time suck for too long!

And, yes, make sure your spouse gets the time she or he needs, too. They deserve this time every bit as much as you do.

Finally, as this dad says, it is not always so hard to find some time for yourself:

If your kids are going to bed at 8 or 9, that leaves anywhere from 2-3 hours, depending on your sleep needs, for YOU time. Get in a workout, have a beer with a buddy, or just curl up with a book; if you plan it out, you'll be surprised how much "me time" you can fit in.

As before, let's take a minute to revisit our goals from Chapter 3. Do you have anything to add or change? Any new ideas for building in time for renewal, hobbies, interests or spirituality?

Religious/spiritual goals
6 month goals
3-Week "To-Dos"
1 Thing to Stop Doing

Hobbies/interests/relaxation and renewal goals
6 month goals
3-Week "To-Dos"
1 Thing to Stop Doing

■ Nurturing Our Most Important Relationships[19]

> My wife and I struggle with drawing a line between work time and family time. We do all the things that need to be done: bath, dinner, play, bedtime for our two young girls. This leaves little time for us as a couple. Just some time to relax and talk about something other than coordinating our schedules would be heaven. But in the end, there's always something to do, a house to clean, kids to take care of.

As discussed in Chapter 3, one of the major struggles couples have is maintaining their bond in the face of work and parenting demands. Daily schedules and laundry and the piling up of tiny resentments can imperceptibly and over time alter our relationship. It is deceptively easy for the love of your life to become just a teammate or co-parent. These aspects of the relationship are important, but we sometimes need to be reminded about what brought us together in the first place and is at the core of a marriage – romantic love.

And, to do this, we have to schedule in the time. As I reported back in Chapter 3, I decided to practice what I preach about relationship goals, and now Amy and I schedule in one movie night a month, plus at least two lunches or dinners out alone each month. Nothing fancy – last week it was pancakes at a diner. After Nick goes to bed, we often savor some couple time on the couch with a blanket, two glasses of wine and one of our Tivo-recorded or Netflix shows. As of this writing, we're watching the last few episodes of *Parenthood* and are on season two of *Orange is the New Black*.

I also think it is important to make a big deal over things like anniversaries and Valentine's Day. Celebrating milestones and observing rituals are important reminders of what is important.

Yeah, yeah, I'm a schmaltzy, sentimental guy. Guilty as charged. I've heard lots of my friends, especially those who've been with their spouses for a long time, criticize Valentine's Day as a "Hallmark holiday" and as unfairly women-centric (they get jewelry and roses, and all we get is half a dinner out that we're paying for anyway). Many criticize Valentine's Day because they think setting aside one day to celebrate love is dumb – after all, we should recognize loving relationships every day, not just on some arbitrarily-picked date.

Yes, some parts of our culture have built Valentine's Day up into some over-the-top Hollywood fantasy. And I suppose we should make Valentine's Day gifts more egalitarian, but these seem like a trivial objections to me.

However, I strenuously disagree with those who dismiss "special days" as arbitrary and unnecessary. Hear me out: Your kids love you every day, but Father's Day is important as recognition for all you do. Celebrating birthdays is somewhat arbitrary (after all, mom did all the work), but it is important to gather to celebrate that someone important to us was, well, born. So, yes, love your wife every day, but use the ritual of Valentine's Day to reinforce the romantic side of your love.

There's another good reason to make a fuss. Comedian Bill Maher once quipped that Valentine's Day, anniversaries and birthdays represent the three days men in stagnant marriages get to have sex. I'm not prepared to put so blunt a point on it, but Valentine's Day should remind us that the romantic and physical parts of our marriage should not be neglected.

This being said, if you are not pulling your weight as a husband and a father, all the romance in the world won't paper over problems. Romance, rituals and special days are important, but only went built on a foundation of respect and working side-by-side in the trenches of work and family.

Finally, does this sound familiar?

My parents live about an hour away. They come to visit us, but are getting up in age. We probably see them maybe once a month, but I know they would want more than this. Family's important, and I've let this slip too much. In fact, they sometimes tease me that I only call when I need their help with the kids.

While I've been more focused on romantic relationships, I'd be remiss if I didn't at least mention the importance of nurturing our relationships with our own parents, siblings, cousins and friends. Once we all get so busy with life, it is deceptively easy to neglect these relationships. As a result, we have too many people in our lives we only see at holidays, and regretfully say that we'd been meaning to call. We should all set aside an hour a week to attend to the other neglected relationships in our lives. Take that time to call your mother. Make that trip to visit your sister whom you love but don't see often enough.

Let's revisit our goals from Chapter 3. Did this section spark any new ideas?

Relationship goals
6 month goals
3-Week "To-Dos"
1 Thing to Stop Doing

Extended family goals
6 month goals
3-Week "To-Dos"
1 Thing to Stop Doing

■ Contributing to Your Community

I must confess I didn't intend to write on this topic, and that my community involvement is not what it could be. But so many of the dads I interviewed for the book brought up how serving their communities was an important part of their lives and contributed to their mental and spiritual well-being. I figured it merited mention in the book. Talking with them also challenged me to go beyond writing an occasional check and start rolling up my sleeves to make a difference. In the meantime, here's what a few dads had to say about the importance of service and how it contributes to the fullness of their lives:

- When I moved to my town, I knew no one, but my wife got me involved with people at our community garden. I'm not much of a gardener, but as a contractor, I helped them with planning, schematics, etc. It was lots of fun, and allowed us to meet so many neighbors.

- I tell people that one of the best things about being a volunteer firefighter is the hours. Many of our calls are in the middle of the night - car accidents and alarms and the like - which doesn't interfere with family time, just a little sleep!

- One of the best ways to continue to give back to your community is to find a way to do it with or through your employer. As a family man, I appreciate the importance of maximizing my time. My firm is committed to corporate responsibility, and I've been encouraged to give back - even during "work hours."

- When we first moved to our town, my wife attended a town meeting and through that, got involved with a local cause. Through her, we all got involved in our new neighborhood right away. We've met so many friends through community projects.

- I started our coaching and now I'm on the board of the Little League. This way, I can stay involved with my son's favorite activity, but also give him his own space to grow.

- It's special when you can get your friends and family involved with you. My whole family walked together in a March of Dimes walkathon, and that was really special to me.

- I worked with a bunch of other dads on a long-term project to get a skate park built in our town. We did it! But the best part was to meet so many new friends, and exactly the kind of guys I used to hang out with in high school and college.

- I didn't do it for this reason, but all the relationships I made through various community groups really paid off when I left my job to start my own business. I developed some skills that were really important, and have a wide network of people locally who are happy to help me out with advice and connections. It has really helped my transition to starting my own business on the right foot.

I resolve to do more. Maybe you can, too.

▌ Marshalling Your Resources

Now that we recognize the need to take care of ourselves, we need to make it happen. If you need three hours a week for exercise and two more for community service, you have to cordon off that time with police tape and barbed wire – metaphorically, of course. One way to protect "me time" is to make sure we have others we can rely upon to watch our kids and make sure everything is ok while we take our needed breaks. We need to marshal our resources.

> I wish we had local extended family! This would help so much. "Here, take the kids for a few hours!!!" We have some friends who have this set-up and we are really jealous. Using your parents or in-laws would be much better and easier than always having to arrange for and pay sitters.

A few years ago, Amy was rehearsing a show on an extremely compressed time schedule, just three weeks to get the show up and running. Rehearsals were 1pm to 9pm, with tech week going even later. Considering the 75-minute ride each way to the theater, it pretty much meant that Amy was working the entire time Nick gets home from school until after he's asleep. And, of course, one of these weeks coincided with Nick's one week mid-winter break from school. I still had my full allotment of work activities.

Before she started rehearsal, though, Amy and I sat down and planned how we would make it work. The number one key was arranging for help so I could take care of Nick, fulfill my work duties, pace myself, and also defend my "me time." Here are a few things we did:

- There were a few days when Nick got off the bus and went home with one of his friends from around the corner. This meant I could be at work until four-thirty or so instead of rushing home by three. I made sure to be very focused at work on those days so when I was home, I could really be present.

- We scheduled our regular sitter in advance for my volleyball nights
- Nick had play-dates and a sleep-over with friends
- My mom and my in-laws each came for a weekend visit. I let them take the lead with Nick for large chunks of the time. This opened up time for me to relax and also to get ahead with work over the weekend.
- I actually had a last-minute really important work commitment on a Tuesday night. My hero, my dad, drove down from Albany to watch Nick that night.
- Nick spent 3 days during his "mid-winter break" at the local (and very reasonably priced) YMCA's kid's camp, along with two of his best friends. He had a blast. I *could* have managed and had Nick most of the time, but I would have been a distracted stressball, and Nick wouldn't have had nearly as much fun.
- For the other two days, Nick and I spent time at our town's indoor pool and spent unstructured time together. I arranged my work schedule to allow for this time. I didn't want to make him feel like he was being shuttled back and forth to things and that he was not my priority.

Even though this was a busy time for me, it worked out pretty well. Nick was well cared for, Amy knew I had it covered, and I still managed to protect some time for my own mental and physical help. This couldn't have happened unless we made our plan to call in for reinforcements. Extended family is usually the first line of defense.

> Thank goodness for my in-laws. They take my son every Saturday night, and my wife and I can have an evening to relax – and sometimes we even go out, like, on an actual date!

Friends and neighbors, and especially the parents of your kid's friends can also be really helpful.

> There's nothing my son and his friends love more than sleepovers at each other's houses. We make sure to invite his friends over on weekends when we don't have a lot planned. This way, their parents are happy to reciprocate when we need a night out. In fact, one year, we hosted a New Year's Eve party for our son and three of his friends- popcorn, games, YouTube videos of last year's ball drop and fireworks from Australia up on the widescreen TV at 10pm, and then bed for them. It was actually a lot of fun, and we built up so much good will from our friends who actually got to have a big night out that now we can call on them for help when we need it, no worries.

Enrolling Your Spouse in Your Need for Your Own Time

Finally, the other key element in getting enough time for yourself is getting your spouse on board. If she recognizes all the work you do and your need for occasional breaks, life gets a lot easier. As this dad says:

> I get the "me time" I need because wife is fantastic. My dad and I have had season tickets to the Patriots my whole life. This is an all-day commitment for 8 Sundays every winter- plus all those playoff wins. Aren't you jealous, Scott! I also get a night out every month or so with friends, so while I don't feel like I take too much time out for just me, I get the time I need to recharge and really be there as a dad.
>
> It's funny though, about half the dads I talk to say the same thing that their wives are awesome and support their need for time away, while the other half have given up on asking because their wives are consistently opposed. I don't get it.

Like this dad, I am lucky in that Amy is awesome and supportive of my "me time" (though not so lucky in being a fan of the New

York Jets). I know not all dads are as fortunate. But I believe that time to recharge is so important that we need to plan for it, use it wisely, and yes, sometimes even take a stand to get what we need. We need to make sure our family members recognize and support our need to occasionally take care of ourselves. In the long run, this makes you better able to take care of others – your work, kids, and spouse will all benefit.

Gotta put on our oxygen masks first.

CHAPTER 12

Building Your Fatherhood Network

On my mind recently has been my impending 40th birthday. As a NY Times article suggested, I took stock of what a hypothetical guest list might look like for a hypothetical party and the result was, well… pathetic.

There are certainly people who play a regular role in my life, but none of those acquaintanceships seem to have the potency of the friends I made in my youth. And of those "real" friends I made when I was younger, none of them are part of my daily life anymore. I don't need friendships now any less than I did then, and I certainly feel their absence in my life today, sometimes very acutely. But the realities of being an adult, which to my thinking is synonymous with being a dad, seem to preclude the "real," emotionally sustaining friendships that I had in my youth. So it begs the question: Where do dads get friends?

- Sam Christensen on his blog, *Dork Daddy*

Like Sam, many dads don't have an extensive friendship and support network of other fathers. This is largely due to our crazy time commitments to our careers, and to being both a good provider and a good dad. If you're doing it right, there isn't that much time for socializing and comparing notes. Further, while society tends to support and promote "mommy groups", there's little cultural support for dads. Women just seem to be wired to do this better than we do. Men who are new to their neighborhoods, live in spread-out suburbs where neighbors are not that physically close-by, who work long hours, and who commute long distances are at an even further disadvantage.

It is a sad but true fact that, for most men over 30, making new friends can be difficult. Sure, we have co-workers we like, and we chat with the other dads we see at our kids' events, but we often find it hard to make new *friends*. We're busy with work and being involved fathers. Many of us feel guilty about our long hours; so much so that we devote our non-work time to our kids and to giving our wives some well-deserved free time.

It even becomes increasingly difficult to see our older, longer-established friends as much as we'd like. High school and college friends scatter and move away. Most get married and have kids, greatly reducing their free time. A while back, I called a college friend to get together for dinner and a drink and he confessed, "I work such long hours at my firm, and I know my wife feels cooped up all day with our two girls. I just can't justify my own social time after work." Last year, Amy and Nick went to visit her brother in California and I stayed behind for work. I called every friend I had to try to arrange some bro time. Unfortunately, while I had free time that week, no one else did, and most of my plans fell by the wayside.

Sociological research demonstrates that the ability to make new strong friendships is dependent on three factors: proximity; repeated, unplanned interactions; and comfortable settings that allow people to get beyond superficial chit-chat. You can see why high school, college and early adulthood provide many opportunities for new friendships to develop. After all, lots of people live together in a dorm, you constantly run into new people (and run into them again and again on campus/at parties/in bars, etc.), and social time in college can be, well, very social. However, for many of us at this point in our lives, each of the components of making new friends can be a problem.

In terms of proximity, we often live in the 'burbs, and many of us commute decent distances to work, making it harder to see "work friends" outside of the office. The 2008 US General Social Survey found that fewer than 30 percent of Americans spend even an occasional social evening with neighbors (the lowest number they ever found), citing suburban and exurban sprawl as a major reason.

Repeated, unplanned interactions are difficult because of work and family demands and the overall lack of free, unscheduled time. Finally, comfortable environments are hard to come by at a chaotic youth soccer field, a (let's face it, not very talented) school talent show or, heaven forbid, a Chuck-E-Cheese. Also, many guys I know are uncomfortable getting beyond surface-level conversations when they are one of the few dads among a gathering of mostly moms. But, as Donkey once sang to Shrek, "You've got to have friends." What's a working dad to do?

▌ Beer Fire!

I am lucky that my friend and neighbor, Francesco, developed his own solution to this problem. He started a semi-regular tradition of inviting his local guy friends to hang out by the fire pit in his backyard with a cooler full of beer. We've come to calling this brilliant innovation BEER FIRE!

Beer Fire usually consists of a dozen or so thirty-to-forty-something guys, most of whom are balancing interesting and rewarding careers with the rigors of being fathers to young kids. Time is spent relaxing, hanging out, swapping stories, having a few beers, and getting to know each other. And it passes the tests of proximity, informal interaction, and comfortable setting.

Beer Fire is awesome, and I have benefitted greatly from attending – it's relaxing; it's fun, and I always learn a little something from everyone I talk to. For example, a neighbor and I discussed how much allowance is appropriate for our kids and how many chores our kids needed to do to earn it. In another conversation, I learned about local swimming and fencing programs. I even helped a dad develop a strategy for asking his boss for more work flexibility (see Chapter 5). The beer was pretty good, too.

Francesco explains his motivation for starting Beer Fire:

> Finding a way to be able to relax with friends and neighbors while still being able to fulfill putting-to-bed obligations is a key challenge for fathers. I know many of us feel a constant desire to be as present as possible in our children's rituals, and to be equal partners in their upbringing. For me, that meant figuring out how to get my friends together after 8:30 pm, mostly on week nights. Beer Fire and its summer equivalent, Porch Beer, were perfect ways to make this happen, and some of my favorite moments in Nyack sprang from these sessions. The group that gathered was a little different each time, and soon I started mixing in friends from different parts of my life intentionally to change the dynamic. Soon friends of friends started to become friends, and the network grew bigger and tighter. Kinda like a LinkedIn, with alcohol. A DrinkedIn, if you will. Strangest part of it all – I don't really like beer. Wine Fire didn't have the same bro-jo, however.

Part of the success of Beer Fire is that it is not a formal group. No one distributes an agenda ahead of time, and the conversations flow organically. Yes, we talk about cars, sports and women. But, because the attendees are mostly of the same age group, live locally, and have kids of around the same age, the conversation naturally gravitates to what we all share in common – our careers, our kids, and how we try to juggle it all.

Another part of Beer Fire's success is that it is represents a "guys' night out." We're not a John Birch Society, the Little Rascals' "He-Man Woman Hater's Club" or Al Bundy's "No Ma'am" group (from *Married with Children*). No drum circles or hazing rituals for us. However, I think it is important that Beer Fire is a comfortable place just for guys. This allows folks to open up a little more, and to discuss family issues more readily. I think that because even today's modern dad sometimes sees "family issues" as a primarily women's concern, we self-censor our discussion when moms are around. "After all", we may think to ourselves, "my wife has it even tougher than me. What right to I have to complain?"

Even more than that, while I am a sensitive modern guy, I think there is something primal to gathering around something that is explicitly masculine every now and then. After diapers and tea parties and far too many episodes of *BubbleGuppies*, it's nice to take a small vacation away from the somewhat domesticated life of a husband and father. It doesn't need to involve beer or fire (although what is more bro-tastic than that?). I know folks who run occasional very-low-stakes poker nights, or get people to gather at a local pool hall. Some even play online video games together (which, while fun and a release, may not have as many opportunities for unstructured conversations).

Whatever you are interested in, there's probably a group of your peers eager for the opportunity to join you and buddy up. In fact, Sam Christensen, whose quote started off this chapter, has been able to assemble a group of "dorky dads" (his words) who get together for opening nights of various superhero and sci-fi movies. Way to go, Sam!

▌ Networking for Fatherhood

It is also important to note that Beer Fire could not have taken off unless Francesco first laid the groundwork. He is an incredibly personable guy, has work colleagues who live locally, is well known in our neighborhood, and plays in a local soccer league. As a result, he built a sizable social network of local dads before he started gathering us together.

Many of us are working professionals, and we understand the importance of networking to our careers. I would gather that most of us are quite good at professional networking too. We should use these skills to start building our own Beer Fires (or equivalents – of course beer is not everyone's thing). Whatever its form, we can all take steps to build and maintain an informal friendship network of fellow dads.

I'd wager that if we spent just a little bit of time on a consistent basis to develop and maintain a network of local dads, we'd all be happier and better off. Obviously, we can't walk up to random guys in the street with business cards labeled "Father of three" (or maybe we can?[20]), but we can and should put in the work to developing our "fatherhood networks." Beer Fire is great, but you have to build the network first.

And there's ample opportunity to get started building our own Beer Fire (or whatever two cool words you use to describe your group). Here are a few ideas:

> Once a month, the dads at our preschool get together for a happy hour. I've been able to make some friends that way.

First, our kids almost certainly go to school. At school, there are often events and organizations for parents to attend and/or get involved. Society is changing, so now the PTA is often only 75 percent women, and many men volunteer and attend school functions held at night. Most schools would be happy to host a "Dad's Group" if a dad or two decided to start one.

Many dads also wait with their kids for the morning school bus. I do, and I look forward to my 10 minutes of chatting with Joe and Francesco and the other parents. These are great opportunities to be social and meet the other dads in your kid's school and the local area. Further, our kids are often participating in some sport or activity. Those other kids have dads too.

These are all opportunities to *gasp* exchange emails and phone numbers and then organize a guy's night. I know it may feel a bit uncomfortable at first, but fighting through the initial awkwardness is well worth it. As this dad says:

> I think fatherhood is the ultimate bonding opportunity for men, at least for those who are fortunate enough to experience it. I don't know whether to call it a club or a fraternity or whatever, but there's something bonding about fatherhood.

I never met so many parents of 6 year olds than when I volunteered to help out Nick's coaches when he joined Little League. Now, many of these dads are my friends, and, in fact, some even attend Beer Fire.

■ Church and Community

Perhaps one overlooked aspect of church or community service, which we discussed last chapter, is the opportunity they provide for building and maintaining friendship networks. As this dad explains;

> It all started at Church. It was my entry point for meeting so may fellow dads. Now I'm involved with the Knights of Columbus one or two nights a week. We do a lot of good, which is very fulfilling, but it also gets me out of the apartment and keeps me from feeling isolated.

> Also, now I know so many good dads – some my own age, others older, others younger, and we can share advice and learn from each other. I've been helped so much by their words in being a better dad and a better husband and even balancing my finances.

Actually, a few years ago, I got laid off. These guys rallied around me. Everyone offered a hand and an ear, and several even came to me with checks! I didn't take them up on that, but it was deeply moving. Being part of a fraternal organization is a real source of strength and can feed your soul as well as provide a social life.

The best part about networking is that you don't just help yourself, you establish mutually beneficial relationships. After all, we're all in this thing together.

A note from my wife:

One of the troubles with men and their friendships is that you'll see your friend and ask him about getting together for a specific thing – "Hey, want to go out and grab a beer for Monday Night Football?" Yet, if the guy can't do it, "Can't do it man, I have my daughter's recital that night," you say "OK, another time" and let it go – end of story. There's no follow up.

Look at it this way, if you were asking a girl you really liked out and said, "Hey, how about we go out Saturday night?" and she replies, "I'd love to go out with you, but I'm going away with my family this weekend." You wouldn't just let that drop – you'd be on that and say, "Well, what night next week works for you?" and nail it down.

The way I see it, friendships should be just as important as that, and they require follow-up. So, guys, don't just float out a date for your bro time. Set a date, follow up with friends. Gotta put in the work to get the ball rolling.

Then, perhaps set up a schedule – the first Saturday of every month for backyard football or whatever.

▌ Getting Spouses on Board

In most cases, your spouse will be very supportive of these efforts. I know my wife and the wives of my friends fret that we don't get enough social time away from our responsibilities. Amy worries I don't get out enough and constantly reminds me to call my friends. And Francesco's wife even arranged a surprise Beer Fire party for his birthday!

Yes, of course, there are husbands/dads who are selfish with their time. However, they are not reading this book. You are, and you deserve the time and space to build a friendship network- I bet your family recognizes this. Also, remember that social time is an important part of personal renewal and is vital for your physical and mental health. Finally, be sure to reciprocate and support your wife when she needs social time or a well-earned girls' night out. She works really hard too and also deserves occasional breaks.

▌ Beyond Beer Fire

Besides informal neighborhood gatherings, there are many other ways we can meaningfully connect with fellow dads. I am friends with Lance Somerfeld and Matt Schneider, who founded the City Dads Group network. Their efforts represent a somewhat more formalized approach to addressing the need so many busy dads have to connect with fellow dads.

The network started with the NYC Dads Group, which now has more than 1,100 members. The group runs a variety of events. Some are meet-ups in which dads and their kids gather together at a designated playground at certain times, or get discounted group admission to a children's museum or new movie. Some events are simply social events for the dads – I had a blast joining them for a March Madness happy hour at a midtown bar. They even run "new dad boot camps" in which "veteran dads" with young children give advice and help to expectant dads, including actual instruction on how to change diapers.

Based on the success of the NYC group, their network now extends to 15 cities across the country, including Boston, Chicago, Los Angeles, Denver and even Albuquerque (Go, Isotopes!). If you live in or near any of these metro areas, I encourage you to reach out and join. The link for the group is listed at the end of the chapter and is just a quick Google-search away.

I spoke with Matt and Lance about how they and their fellow local dads have benefitted from their membership. Lance discussed the origins of the group:

> We decided after we had our son that I would stay home. My wife had a generous maternity leave, and after three months of tag team partnering, I realized I was now largely going to be on my own. Where was I going to turn?
>
> There just aren't as many resources for dads. I live near the 92nd Street Y, which has regular new parent get-togethers. But, when I went, it was 25 moms and me. While I liked the group and found it helpful, I felt there needed to be more for dads. So the initial vision came about that way.
>
> My first thought for myself is that I needed to get out with other dads at least one a week. I knew Matt from when we worked together, and we had kids about same age. It started just meeting him out for burger, to a museum-something interesting once a week. Our kids were so young the events weren't really for them, they were for us. Both socially and for advice- for example, I remember talking to Matt about how I was going to survive as my son was transitioning from two naps to one.
>
> The circle expanded to a handful of other dads, and our get-togethers became every Wednesday morning at 10am. We then got the idea to use a website to make our meet-up plans public, so that other dads could join. I started blogging about our meet-ups, and over time, the group began to grow. We realized we were addressing an

unmet need for many dads to connect with other dads, share ideas, and not feel so isolated. Now we're helping thousands of dads in 15 cities. It's really amazing.

Matt adds that both he and many other dads have benefitted by seeing how other dads handle their kids and their different situations.

For the dad of a newborn, it is great to see dads of toddlers and older children on a playground together. Kind of like a preview of the challenges you'll face later on, so you are more prepared.

Being an at-home or very hands-on dad can be an isolating experience, so sometimes just being out and social with other dads is a huge benefit to itself- we make sure to offer dad's only events and happy hours to feed this.

Finally, during our "new dad boot camps" we have such a variety of dads- those that come with detailed birthing plans and others who haven't thought much about how life was going to change. The sharing of experiences and role modeling has been a huge benefit. Very different people are able to bond and grow through their shared value of involved fatherhood.

Finally, it is also possible to re-create some of the benefits of a Beer Fire in a work context (probably with less beer and no fire, however). If you work for a smaller employer, this might involve a dads' happy hour every few weeks, or a semi-regular group to go out for lunch with every now and again.

Most larger employers have various workplace interest groups (often called "diversity and inclusion" groups). Many have specific groups for moms or for working parents. While these may be helpful to you, for several of the reasons explained earlier in the chapter, a group specific to dads may be more valuable. A few notable employers even have groups specifically for working dads. I encourage you to inquire about whether there is a group at your workplace, and, if not, consider how you can start one.

In fact, the international accounting and financial firm, Deloitte & Touche, was one of the first to establish a formalized Dads' Group. The group's mission is to foster a more inclusive work environment to help fathers achieve success at home and in the workplace. Andrew Hamer, one of the co-founders of "Deloitte Dads" explained to the *Globe and Mail* that he launched the group in 2010 because he was "unwilling to believe that it is impossible to have an active co-parenting role and a successful career path in management consulting." The member dads discuss their challenges, time management techniques, and the need to be proactive and flexible. They have also developed materials and cases to help their fellow working dads. Unfortunately, they do not mention beer or fire.

Chapter 12 Exercises

1. Brainstorm the names of 10 guys in reasonably similar circumstances to you (age, kids, location, employer).

1. _____
2. _____
3. _____
4. _____
5. _____
6. _____
7. _____
8. _____
9. _____
10. _____

This is your first list of guys to contact for a "Guys' Night Out"

2. Brainstorm 3-5 somewhat "manly" activities you can do with them;

1. ____Beer Fire_____
2. _____
3. _____
4. _____
5. _____

Write down two days/times within the next 4 weeks you will set aside to get your fatherhood network going:

1. _____

2. _____

Over at http://WorkingDadsSurvivalGuide.com, I have set up a page for folks to share pictures and stories from their beer fires or related events. Once you hold your first event, please visit the site and add yours.

CONCLUSION

The Joys and Sacrifices of Fatherhood

Last year, I attended a reception for Honor Students at my university. I had served as a Senior Thesis mentor for a promising young man named James, whom I am certain will leave his mark on the world. It was a great night where we acknowledged the efforts and intellectual endeavors of our very best students, and I was in awe of how preternaturally mature and composed these future leaders were. In contrast, the 21-year-old Scott was nowhere near as together as these students.

But the highlight of the night for me was meeting James' parents. James' mother is from Guatemala and speaks very little English. But you could see how proud she was of her son, and how close they were. James' dad was also proud and loving. Years ago, he had emigrated from Argentina, and has worked tirelessly to provide his son with a better life and the opportunities he never had.

James' father worked three jobs most of his adult life – real, physically and psychologically demanding manual labor. He wasn't always there to be with his son growing up – he was too busy doing the most important job of a father – sacrificing himself so his son could get what he needed. James' parents worked incredibly hard to be able to send him to college, and James was the first in his family to go. What an evening it must have been for James' father, seeing his soon-to-be-college-graduate son receiving his academic honors in the ballroom of a fancy hotel. How proud he must have felt to see the payoff for all his work and sacrifice. As a college professor, I keep fathers like him in mind. I owe it to them to give their children my best.

Speaking with James' father, my thoughts started drifting to my relationship with Nick. While I have made sacrifices and work hard to be a good father, I couldn't help but feel lucky to have had things so much easier. My single job pays well and affords me lots of time flexibility and autonomy. I never felt the stress of deciding whether to spend time with my son or take on another job so I could feed him. Most of the time, what is best for Nick is also what I want to do – spend quality time with him, and serve as his life coach and mentor.

Back in Chapter 9, I mentioned Nick's triumph at his first gymnastics meet. It was such a special moment for me. Not that he performed so well (although that was a nice perk), but rather that I got to see my son grow from the infant for whom no crib or baby gate could deter, to the toddler who couldn't walk ten steps without doing a cartwheel, to the young man who worked his butt off for two years training for that moment. The fact that he was there, confident, and having fun was enough to bring tears to my eyes as he approached the parallel bars for his first ever event. I felt so blessed to have been able to be with him, *really* with him, every step of the way.

On the drive home that afternoon, my thoughts again drifted to James' father. It would break my heart to have had to miss out on a day like that. To miss Nick's birthdays, light-saber battles and little league games. Heck, it would pain me to miss out on celebrating my own birthdays, enjoying lazy weekend days, and having the leisure time to read, relax and recharge. James' father gave up all those experiences out of love for his family. I am in awe of his love and sacrifice, and wondered if, had I been in a similar situation, I would be man enough to always do what was needed instead of what I wanted. I also think about all the single parents who have made sacrifices and faced a much harder road than mine.

James' father sacrificed much of his life and poured that life into his son. He's my inspiration. I try to keep James' father in mind whenever I write or speak about fatherhood. He reminds me that while work-family concerns are most commonly addressed in white collar companies with middle- and upper-class workers, work-family concerns actually hit those in blue collar and working class jobs the hardest.

But even from my fortunate perch, I struggle with work and family pressures. We all have our challenges. We all could use some help. That's why I wrote this book. It is my sincerest hope that all fathers can experience joyful moments like the one I experienced at Nick's tournament. My wish for you and for all fathers is that you can succeed in your career, provide for your family, and spend vast quantities of high quality time with those you love.

I began this book bemoaning the fact that the challenges faced by working dads had not received the attention they deserve, and that there is not enough support for us. However, I want to end this book on a more optimistic note about how our society is changing. Yes, we need to be brave and smart in order to work within the world as it is, but you should know that things are getting better. Recent developments at many progressive workplaces, in public policy, in the media, and across kitchen tables all over the country give me hope that momentum is finally building for the concerns of working fathers.

CEOs are on the record that work and family challenges are not just a woman's issue, and affect men as well. Some have made working father's issues an organizational priority. Those advocating for increased access to parental leave have been very clear that they wish to include all parents in these programs, not just moms. Every week, there is some news event, covered by business or popular press, that deals with work and family. Public figures, celebrities and sports stars have been raising the profile of what it means to be a modern man and modern father. Academic research on men, work and family is increasing exponentially. In my mind, I can see the smoke from beer fires igniting all over the country!

I have the sense that this increased attention on working fathers will only pick up speed. A groundswell is starting. It is indeed great news that, despite the challenges, in some ways it is more possible than ever before to have a great career and be a great dad.

I don't believe we can "have it all" in terms of work and family, certainly not all at once. We are adults, we have to set priorities and understand the trade-offs involved. However, I do believe that if we adopt the mindset of this book, prioritize, develop strategies and put them into action, we can get what is most important for us and for our families. We can get what we need. We can be successful both at work and at home.

Thank you so much for reading this book. Let's keep the discussion going at http://WorkingDadsSurvivalGuide.com and http://FathersWorkandFamily.com.

SOURCES AND RESOURCES

▌Resources for Fathers, Work and Family Concerns

Some of my go-to sources for information and help regarding the concerns of Working Dads are:

- 1 Million for Work Flexibility
- A Better Balance
- Boston College's Center for Work and Family
- Center for Legal and Social Policy (CLASP)
- Center for Work-Life Law
- City Dads Group
- Family Values @ Work
- Good Men Project
- National Fatherhood Initiative
- Thirdpath Institute
- Wharton Work-Life Integration Project and Total Leadership Program
- Work and Family Researchers Network
- Working Mother Research Institute

▌Sources by Chapter

Introduction

Breadwinner Moms | Pew Research Center's Social & Demographic Trends Project. (March 2013). Retrieved from http://www.pewsocialtrends.org/2013/05/29/breadwinner-moms/

Dorment, R. (2013, May 28). *Why Men Still Can't Have It All - Esquire.* Retrieved from http://www.esquire.com/features/why-men-still-cant-have-it-all-0613

Father's Day: The Benefits for the Involved Dad. Parenting at More4kids: Raising Children in a Complex World. Retrieved from http://www.more4kids. info/2590/fathers-day-benefits-for-the-involved-dad/

Harrington, Van Deusen, & Humberd, (2011). Boston College Center for Work and Family. *The New Dad: Caring, Committed & Conflicted.* Retrieved from http://www.bc.edu/content/dam/files/centers/cwf/pdf/FH-Study-Web-2. pdf

Harrison, J. (2012, March 14). *Huggies Pulls Ads After Dads Insulted - ABC News.* Retrieved from http://abcnews.go.com/blogs/lifestyle/2012/03/ huggies-pulls-ads-after-dads-insulted/

Lewis, M. (2009). *Home Game: An Accidental Guide to Fatherhood.* Norton.

Modern Parenthood | Pew Research Center's Social & Demographic Trends Project. (March 2013). Retrieved from http://www.pewsocialtrends. org/2013/03/14/modern-parenthood-roles-of-moms-and-dads-converge-as-they-balance-work-and-family/

Smith, J. (2013, June 12). *Five Reasons Why It's a Good Time to be a Dad |* Greater Good: The Science of a Meaningful Life. Retrieved from http://greatergood. berkeley.edu/article/item/five_reasons_why_its_a_good_time_to_be_a_dad

Chapter 1

Breadwinner Moms | Pew Research Center's Social & Demographic Trends Project. (March 2013). Retrieved from http://www.pewsocialtrends. org/2013/05/29/breadwinner-moms/

Lobel, S. & St. Clair, L. (1992). Effects of Family Responsibilities, Gender, and Career Identity Salience on Performance Outcomes. *The Academy of Management Journal,* Vol. 35, No. 5, pp. 1057-1069.

Meers, S. & Strober, J. (2009). *Getting to 50/50: How Working Couples Can Have It All by Sharing It All.* Bantam.

Chapter 2

Behson, S. (2013). *A Dad's Dilemma: Prioritizing Time Versus Money | Fathers, Work and Family.* Retrieved from http://fathersworkandfamily. com/2013/12/03/a-dads-dilemma-prioritizing-time-versus-money/

Doise, D. (2010). *Essential Wealth Building Strategies: Your Guide to Ultimate Financial Freedom and Abundance.* Motivational Press.

Farrell, W,(2005). *Why Men Earn More: The Startling Truth Behind the Pay Gap -- and What Women Can Do About It.* AMACOM.

Katepoo, P. (n.d.). *How to Ask for Flexible Work at Your Current Job. Are Your Finances Foiling Your Job Flexibility?.* Retrieved from http://www. workoptions.com/finances-foiling-flexibility

Whyte, D. (1996). *The Heart Aroused: Poetry and the Preservation of the Soul in Corporate America.* Crown Business.

Chapter 3

Behson, S. (2013, February 15). *Five Things I Did in My Twenties and How They Have Changed, Now That I'm 40 -. The Good Men Project - The Conversation No One Else Is Having*. Retrieved from http://goodmenproject.com/the-good-life/five-things-i-did-in-my-twenties-and-how-they-have-changed-now-that-im-40/

Behson, S. (2014, May 4). *The Best Way to Think About Work-Family Balance (Balanced Diet, Not a See-Saw) | Fathers, Work and Family*. Retrieved from http://fathersworkandfamily.com/2014/05/05/the-best-way-to-think-about-work-family-balance-balanced-diet/

Covey, S. (2013). *The 7 Habits of Highly Effective People: Powerful Lessons in Personal Change* (Anniversary ed.). Simon & Schuster.

Friedman, S. D. (2008). *Don't Leave Your Personal Life at Home, Harvard Business Review*. Retrieved from https://hbr.org/2008/03/dont-leave-your-personal-life

Friedman, S. D. (2008). *Total Leadership: Be a Better Leader, Have a Richer Life*. Harvard Business Press.

Locke, E., Latham, G., & Smith, K. (1990). *A Theory of Goal Setting & Task Performance* . Prentice Hall.

Loehr, J., & Schwartz, T. (2011, January). *The Making of a Corporate Athlete - Harvard Business Review - Ideas and Advice for Leaders.*. Retrieved from http://hbr.org/2001/01/the-making-of-a-corporate-athlete/ar/1

Teller, D., & Teller, A. (2014, September 30). *How American parenting is killing the American marriage. Quartz*. Retrieved from http://qz.com/273255/how-american-parenting-is-killing-the-american-marriage/

Chapter 4

Behson, S. (2013, August 21). *What's a Working Dad to Do? - Harvard Business Review - Ideas and Advice for Leaders.*. Retrieved from http://hbr.org/2013/08/whats-a-working-dad-to-do

Bock, L. (2014, March 27). *Google's Scientific Approach to Work-Life Balance (and Much More) - Harvard Business Review - Ideas and Advice for Leaders*. Retrieved from http://hbr.org/2014/03/googles-scientific-approach-to-work-life-balance-and-much-more/

Kossek, E. & Lautsch, P. (2007). *CEO of Me: Creating a Life That Works in the Flexible Job Age*. Financial Times Press.

Macy's Worker Addresses White House Summit | RWDSU. (2014, June 23). Retrieved from http://rwdsu.info/media--and--press/news--and--events/macys-worker-addresses-white-house-summit

National Study of the Changing Workforce | Families and Work Institute | Research to Live, Learn and Work By. Retrieved from http://www.familiesandwork.org/national-study-for-the-changing-workforce/

Pearce, J. (2014, January 20). *The 14 Step Commute: Making it Work from Home*

| *Musings of a serial teleworker. Walking the dog, and other productivity killers | The 14 Step Commute: Making it Work from Home. Retrieved from* http://14stepcommute.net/2014/01/20/walkingthedog/

WorkLifeLaw. WorkLifeLaw | Jumpstarting the Stalled Gender Revolution. Retrieved from http://worklifelaw.org/work-life-issues/workplace-flexibility/

Chapter 5

Behson, S. (2012, December 10). Negotiating for Work Flexibility | Fathers, Work and Family. Retrieved from http://fathersworkandfamily.com/2012/12/10/negotiating-for-work-flexibility/

Carnegie, D. (1998). How to Win Friends & Influence People (Special Anniversary ed.). Pocket Books.

Fisher, R., & Ury, W. Getting to Yes: Negotiating Agreement Without Giving In. 1991: Penguin.

Global Workplace Analytics. (2008, January 30). Global Workplace Analytics - Making The Case For Place Flexibility. Retrieved from http://globalworkplaceanalytics.com/telecommuting-common-at-84-of-fortune-top-100/107

Haidt, J. (2012, October 8). Obama, Romney and the War to Define Fairness, Moral Vision of America | TIME.com. Retrieved from http://ideas.time.com/2012/10/08/the-new-culture-war-ove-fairness/

Levine, J., & Pittinsky, T. (1998). Working Fathers: New Strategies for Balancing Work and Family. Mariner.

Lewis, K. (2014). How Men Flex | Working Mother. Retrieved from http://www.workingmother.com/content/how-men-flex

Porter, T. (2013, July 31). Bill Parcells got most of his players, some times not kindly - News - The Repository - Canton, OH. Retrieved from http://www.cantonrep.com/article/20130731/News/307319888#ixzz3P7BdkkEr

Telecommuting Has Mostly Positive Consequences For Employees and Employers, Say Researchers. American Psychological Association (APA). (2007, November 17). Retrieved from http://www.apa.org/news/press/releases/2007/11/telecommuting.aspx

Weinfuss, J. (2014, February 5). Hot Read - Recovering from an NFL season is physical and mental - ESPN. Retrieved from http://espn.go.com/nfl/story/_/id/10396406/hot-read-recovering-nfl-season-physical-mental

Chapter 6

BBC News - Volkswagen turns off Blackberry email after work hours. (2011, December 23). Retrieved from http://www.bbc.com/news/technology-16314901

Behson, S. (2013, February 25). How to Cope with Work-Family Conflict and Stress (part 2) | Fathers, Work and Family. Retrieved from http://fathersworkandfamily.com/2013/02/25/how-to-cope-with-work-family-conflict-and-stress-part-2/

Behson, S.J. (2002). Coping with Family to Work Conflict: The Role of Informal Work Accommodations to Family. Journal of Occupational Health Psychology, 7(4), 324-341.

Folkman, S., Lazarus, R. S., Dunkel-Schetter, C., DeLongis, A., & Gruen, R. (1986). The dynamics of a stressful encounter: Cognitive appraisal, coping and encounter outcomes. Journal of Personality and Social Psychology, 50, 992-1003.

Leland, K. (2012, June 8). New Study Shows We Are Overworked and Overwhelmed | Psychology Today. Retrieved from http://www.psychologytoday.com/blog/the-perfect-blend/201206/new-study-shows-we-are-overworked-and-overwhelmed

Marcus, G. (2014). Busting Your Corporate Idol: Self-Help for the Chronically Overworked. The Idolbuster Coaching Institute.

Schulte, B. (2014). Overwhelmed: Work, Love, and Play When No One Has the Time . Sarah Chricton Books.

Tracy, B. (2007). Eat That Frog!: 21 Great Ways to Stop Procrastinating and Get More Done in Less Time (second ed.). Berrett-Koehler.

Chapter 7

Bersin by Deloitte: The Flexible Workplace Delivers Results How Ryan, LLC, Transformed Its Workplace Culture to Increase Earnings and Retain Its Highly Skilled Employees. Retrieved from http://www.bersin.com/Practice/Detail.aspx?docid=16746&mode=search&p=Human-Resources

Covert, B. (2014, March 21). The Burger Chain That Pays $10 An Hour With Benefits | ThinkProgress. Retrieved from http://thinkprogress.org/economy/2014/03/21/3417056/shake-shack-wages-benefits/

Feloni, R. (2014, July 1). Why Ernst & Young Believes So Strongly In Paid Paternity Leave. Business Insider. Retrieved from http://ernst-and-young-paid-paternity-leave-policy-2014-7

Franklin, M. (2014, December 30). Will Shake Shack's IPO Affect Wages, Benefits for Workers? | The Braiser. Retrieved from http://www.thebraiser.com/heres-the-one-bad-thing-that-no-one-will-say-about-shake-shacks-ipo-filing/

Gaddis, J. (2012, November 18). Why Guys Get Trapped in Soul Sucking Jobs - The Good Men Project - The Conversation No One Else Is Having.. Retrieved from http://goodmenproject.com/featured-content/jayson-gaddis-why-guys-get-trapped-in-soul-sucking-jobs/

Harrington, Van Deusen, & Humberd, (2011). Boston College Center for Work and Family. The New Dad: Caring, Committed & Conflicted. Retrieved from http://www.bc.edu/content/dam/files/centers/cwf/pdf/FH-Study-Web-2.pdf

Saltzman, A. (1992). Downshifting: Reinventing Success on a Slower Track . Perennial.

Weiler Reynolds, B. (2015, January 20). Telecommuting Jobs & Professional Part-Time Jobs. 100 Top Companies with Remote Jobs in 2015 - FlexJobs. Retrieved *from* http://www.flexjobs.com/blog/post/100-top-companies-with-remote-jobs-in-2015/

Chapter 8

Behson, S. (2014, August 10). *16 Dads 16 Experiences: This Is What Paternity Leave Looks Like in 2014 | Fathers, Work and Family*. Retrieved from http://fathersworkandfamily.com/2014/08/12/16-dads-16-experiences-this-is-what-paternity-leave-looks-like-in-2014/

Behson, S. (2014, July 28). *How Paternity Leave Shaped Me As a Father and Strengthened My Family | Fathers, Work and Family*. Retrieved from http://fathersworkandfamily.com/2014/07/28/how-paternity-leave-shaped-me-as-a-father-and-strengthened-my-family/

Devlin, D. (2015, February 5). *The cost of having mandatory paid parental leave - Fortune*. Retrieved from http://fortune.com/2015/02/05/paid-parental-leave-costs/

Dumas, D. (2013, October 12). *From career to paternity: A labour of love. Australian Breaking News Headlines & World News Online | SMH.com.au*. Retrieved from http://www.smh.com.au/national/from-career-to-paternity-a-labour-of-love-20131011-2vdxg.html?fb

Enforcement Guidance: Pregnancy Discrimination And Related Issues. EEOC Home Page Retrieved from http://www.eeoc.gov/laws/guidance/pregnancy_guidance.cfm#parental

Gouveia, A. (2013, August 21). *Daddy Files. Paternity Leave is Essential (And It's Not a Vacation)*. Retrieved from http://paternity-leave-is-essential-and-its-not-a-vacation

Hall, K., & Spurlock, C. (2013, February 4). *Paid Parental Leave: U.S. vs. The World (INFOGRAPHIC). Huffington Post Canada - Canadian News Stories, Breaking News, Opinion*. Retrieved from http://www.huffingtonpost.com/2013/02/04/maternity-leave-paid-parental-leave-_n_2617284.html

Infographic: Paternity Leave Around the World. GOOD.is | Infographic: Paternity Leave Around the World. Retrieved from http://awesome.good.is/transparency/web/1206/papa-don-t-leave/flash.html

Mundy, L. (2013, December 22). *Daddy Track: The Case for Paternity Leave - The Atlantic*. Retrieved from http://www.theatlantic.com/magazine/archive/2014/01/the-daddy-track/355746/

Quinn-Szcesuil , J. (2014, September 30). *20 Companies With Great Paternity Leave. Care.com Workplace Solutions Blog for HR Professionals.* Retrieved from http://workplace.care.com/20-companies-with-great-paternity-leave

Chapter 9

Behson, S. (2012, October 10). *The Dangers of Over-Scheduling (or, relax, Scott, Nicky will almost certainly not be an Olympic gymnast) | Fathers, Work and Family*. Retrieved from http://fathersworkandfamily.com/2012/10/10/the-dangers-of-over-scheduling-or-relax-scott-nicky-will-almost-certainly-not-be-an-olympic-gymnast/

Behson, S. (2014, August 1). Relax, You Have 168 Hours This Week - Harvard Business Review - Ideas and Advice for Leaders. Retrieved from http://hbr.org/2014/08/relax-you-have-168-hours-this-week/http://lauravanderkam.com/books/168-hours/

Friedman, S. D. (2008). Total Leadership: Be a Better Leader, Have a Richer Life. Harvard Business Press.

Gibbs, N. (2006, June 4). The Magic of the Family Meal - TIME. Retrieved from http://content.time.com/time/magazine/article/0,9171,1200760,00.html

Ravishly. (2015, February 2). Virtues of a Lazy Marriage. Huffington Post. Retrieved from http://www.huffingtonpost.com/ravishly/the-virtues-of-a-lazy-marriage_b_6584110.html

Schwartz, T. (2012, November 27). Fatigue Is Your Enemy - Harvard Business Review - Ideas and Advice for Leaders.. Retrieved from http://hbr.org/2012/11/fatigue-is-your-enemy/

Schulte, B. (2014). Overwhelmed: Work, Love, and Play When No One Has the Time . Sarah Chricton Books.

Vanderkam, L. (2010). 168 Hours: You Have More Time Than You Think. Portfolio.

Vienna, D. (2013, July 7). Latest Parenting Trend: The CTFD Method | David Vienna. Huffington Post Retrieved from http://www.huffingtonpost.com/david-vienna/latest-parenting-trend-ctfd-method_b_3588031.html

Westring, A. and Friedman, S. (June 13, 2014) Working Dads Need "Me Time" Too. Retrieved from https://hbr.org/2014/06/working-dads-need-me-time-too

Chapter 10

Behson, S. (2013, January 12). Being a Father Makes You Better at Your Job | Fathers, Work and Family. Retrieved from http://fathersworkandfamily.com/2013/01/14/being-a-father-makes-you-better-at-your-job/

Behson, S. (2014, December 15). Hey Dads: Year-Long Presence Is the Best Christmas Present | Fathers, Work and Family. Retrieved from http://fathersworkandfamily.com/2014/12/15/hey-dads-year-long-presence-is-the-best-christmas-present/

Bryson, B. (2000). On Losing a Son (To College). I'm a Stranger Here Myself: Notes on Returning to America After 20 Years Away. Broadway Books.

Harrington, Van Deusen, & Humberd, (2011). Boston College Center for Work and Family. The New Dad: Caring, Committed & Conflicted. Retrieved from http://www.bc.edu/content/dam/files/centers/cwf/pdf/FH-Study-Web-2.pdf

Singletary, M. (2013, October 4). Five ways money can buy you happiness - The Washington Post. Retrieved from http://www.washingtonpost.com/business/five-ways-money-can-buy-you-happiness/2013/10/03/029339b2-2c72-11e3-97a3-ff2758228523_story.html

Swann, J. (2013, March 29). The Cheeky Daddy. The Cheeky Daddy: Work Life -

Traveling Dad. Retrieved from http://thecheekydaddy.blogspot.com/2013/03/work-life-traveling-dad.html?m=1

Chapter 11

Covey, S. (2013). *The 7 Habits of Highly Effective People: Powerful Lessons in Personal Change* (Anniversary ed.). *Simon & Schuster*.

Evans, M. (2011, December 2). *23 and 1/2 hours: What is the single best thing we can do for our health? - YouTube. Retrieved from* http://www.youtube.com/watch?v=aUaInS6HIGo

Chapter 12

Behson, S. (2012, September 19). *Networking for Fatherhood (or, in praise of BEER FIRE!) | Fathers, Work and Family. Retrieved from* http://fathersworkandfamily.com/2012/09/19/networking-for-fatherhood-or-in-praise-of-beer-fire/

Christensen, S. (2014, July 17). *Where Do Dads Get Friends? | Dorkdaddy.com | misadventures in raising two... wait, no THREE well-adjusted kids in the grandest dork-tradition. Retrieved from* http://dorkdaddy.com/2012/07/17/where-do-dads-get-friends/

City Dads Group – Navigating Fatherhood Together. Retrieved from http://www.citydadsgroup.com/

Eichler, L. (2013, March 1). *Double duty: The plight of the working dad - The Globe and Mail. Retrieved from* http://www.theglobeandmail.com/report-on-business/careers/career-advice/life-at-work/double-duty-the-plight-of-the-working-dad/article9213833/

Socialising in America: The decline of an American institution | The Economist. (2012, September 28). *Retrieved from* http://www.economist.com/blogs/democracyinamerica/2012/09/socialising-america

Williams, A. (2012, July 13). *Why Is It Hard to Make Friends Over 30? - NYTimes.com. Retrieved from* http://www.nytimes.com/2012/07/15/fashion/the-challenge-of-making-friends-as-an-adult.html?pagewanted=all&_r=0

Conclusion

Behson, S. (2014, August 13). *James' Father - Daily Plate of Crazy. Retrieved from* http://dailyplateofcrazy.com/2014/08/13/james-father-by-scott-behson/

ENDNOTES

1   I do not mean to minimize the obstacles faced by women in the workplace. In fact, I have often stated that the progress for women in the workplace is linked to progress of men in the home, and that when work-family issues are seen as issues facing both men and women, we will see more progress for working moms. There are many awesome writers, thinkers and advocates for working moms, and I recommend some of their work in my list of resources at the end of this book.

2   To their credit, Huggies responded to customer outcry and the negative media attention and has now become a company that is very positive and realistic in their depiction of involved dads.

3   All quotes are a result of dozens of interviews I conducted with dads from all over the country, reflect the conversations I had with friends, or are comments and content from my blog, *Fathers, Work and Family*. Quotes and anecdotes are real and were selected to reflect the diverse set of challenges modern dads face. I only altered the quotes for readability and to take out identifying details, ensuring anonymity.

4   Both Sheryl Sandberg's "Lean In" and Lisa Belkin, in her investigations of the "Opt-out generation," write compellingly about the struggles of women who subjugated their careers for families. In sort, by making even temporary concessions, they face considerable, long-range financial and career consequences. This is a book for working fathers, but we have to recognize that so many of the unfair consequences of balancing work and family land harder on working moms.

5   I list a few recommended books and articles on financial planning in the Sources and Resources section at the end of the book

6   These are commonly referred to as SMART goals- specific, measureable, aspirational, realistic and time-bound.

7   More on Ryan LLC and other family-supportive employers in Chapter 7

8   References to this study and lots more information on telework is included in the Sources and Resources section at the end of the book

9   I tell managers that the ultimate question regarding flexibility, and really any other managerial consideration, should always be, "how do I get the best work out of this person in this job?" For many jobs, flexibility either enhances or is neutral for performance. Plus, it is usually a make plus for employee loyalty and engagement.

10 Just be careful here. Remember anything you do on a company computer or email account is their property, and some employers seriously track this stuff. Since pretty much everyone has a smartphone now, you may as well use a different email account and use your phone for personal messages and stuff.

11 Some smart employers are indeed catching on. The Boston Consulting Group, a high-octane workplace in a demanding industry, recently started its "Redzone" (as in when a car engine overheats when revving too long) program to identify employees who put in a string of long work weeks, and then limit their workload for the next few weeks. This is done to prevent burnout, and is often done over the objection of the employee who has bought into the culture of overwork.

12 There are many caveats attached to eligibility under the FMLA. In general, full-time employees who have been working for more than a year at a company with fifty or more employees are eligible. Others, including freelancers and contract employees, are generally not covered, and it is estimated that 40% of the workforce is ineligible

13 There are lots of studies that show that wives of men who take paternity leave earn more over time and are less likely to interrupt their careers. There's even a study that shows that Swedish men who take longer paternity leaves also live longer!

14 I am not a lawyer. Although I consulted with a lawyer who specializes in work-life law when writing this section of the book, please do not take this section as legal advice. I recommend speaking with your employer's HR department or legal counsel before acting on these new guidelines.

15 When I wrote about this topic on *Fathers, Work and Family*, I received a gut-wrenching comment from a reader who was a soldier stationed far away from his family. He regretted the fact he was rarely present, but he was doing what he needed to do both the support his family and serve his country. I thanked him for his service and tried to reassure him that having the right priorities was half the battle and that he was teaching his son about sacrifice and service. If you know anyone in this position, the National Fatherhood Initiative works with the Department of Defense to provide information, counseling and services to our dads in uniform.

16 If X is not a big enough number, please go back to the beginning of this book and start again! ;)

17 Much of the information in this paragraph comes from this amazing nine-minute long YouTube video. Please take the time to watch it: http://www.youtube.com/watch?v=aUaInS6HIGo

18 For many years this poem was found, unattributed, in books, plaques, greeting cards and all matter of inspirational tchotchkes. It was only in the past few years that Grace Naessens stepped forward as the author. The fascinating story of the poem and its timeless wisdom can be found here: http://www.darkblueknight.com/thedifference.html

19 Many apologies to the unmarried dads out there. Feel free to skip to the last paragraph of this section, or to apply these ideas to other relationships in your life

20 From a female reader of my blog: I'm not so sure you can't just walk up to random guys and give them a business card that says "Father of three." Why not? When I first started staying at home, I wanted to build up a network of

friends, so I had mini "business cards" made up for myself, with my name, followed by "Mother of Henry" (because it's the kid's name they're more likely to remember than mine), my phone number, and email address. The cards came with their own case that attached to my keychain, so I had them with me wherever I went. When I met someone I liked at the library, kiddie gym, etc., I had a card to give them so that we could stay in contact and continue to get to know each other. Much easier, faster, and frankly, cooler than searching for a pen and an old Costco receipt on which I could scribble my name and number. The same strategies we employ for professional networking can work very well in purely social situations, as well!

ACKNOWLEDGEMENTS

When you see my wife on stage, you do not see the many other folks working behind the scenes to be sure she is put in the best position to knock your socks off.

Writing a book is quite a bit like that. I may be the one with my name on the cover, but so many people contributed to this effort. Writing this book has long been a dream of mine. To all who helped, I am eternally grateful. I'd like to highlight some of the amazing people who helped make this book a reality.

About three years ago, I spoke with my friend, Anjanette Harper, who is an incredible writer and editor. When I told her of my idea for this book, she wisely told me, "If you want to write a book in two years, start a blog now." Taking her advice has made all the difference.

I started *Fathers, Work and Family* in September 2012, and through my sojourn into social media, I met so many great people in the world of blogging, in the world of human resources, in the world of work-family advocacy, in the business world, and in the brotherhood of fathers around the country. I was afforded the opportunity to work with reporters, producers and editors at some of the best academic, business and news outlets on earth. Thanks to your support, I've had the opportunity to appear on CBS, MSNBC, Fox News, NPR and Bloomberg Radio. Heck, I even got to speak at the White House!

Thanks to the blog, so many doors opened to me, and I want to thank Dr. Suzanne deJanasz, Dr. Monique Valcour, Julia Kirby, Gint Aras, Robert Duffer, Justin Cascio, Lisa Hickey, Adam Auriemma and Tom Burns for opening doors for me at *Harvard*

Business Review, Good Men Project, Wall Street Journal and other amazing outlets.

Through my work at Harvard Business Review, I met literary agent extraordinaire Giles Anderson. He immediately saw the potential in this book, and shepherded this newbie author through the complex and ever-changing publishing world. Thanks to Giles and to friend and author Peter Danish, I was able to connect with Motivational Press. The MP team, led by publisher Justin Sachs, has been great to work with. Special thanks also to Beth Saulnier, Kerri Smith Majors, and especially the amazing Carter Gaddis for their tangible and emotional support in the development of the proposal and manuscript. I am also truly grateful to my publicity "dream team" of Ashley Bernardi and Lucinda Blumenfeld.

Beyond this book, my two years as fathers' work-family advocate brought so many others into my life. I was member #12 in the Dad Bloggers community, which was created out of the sheer force of will and generosity that is our founder Oren Miller. Membership is well above 1,000 now, proving that dads share a need for, and benefit greatly from, connecting with other dads. There are too many great dads and writers there to name, including several who lent their voices to the quotes and anecdotes throughout the book. Among so many, I want to give special thanks Brent Almond, Aaron Gouveia, Ryan E. Hamilton, Jeff Tepper, Zach Rosenberg, Sam Christensen, Dan Poore, John Pearce, Jason Swann, Larry Bernstein and John Kinnear.

I want to thank those I've worked with in advocating for fathers, and for work-family balance. These include leading academics Dr. Brad Harrington and Jennifer Fraone of Boston College, Dr. Stewart Friedman of Wharton, Dr. Nick Beutell of Iona College and Dr. Mark Promislo of Rider University, as well as Judi Casey and others at the Work and Family Researchers Network. Advocates for work-family balance whom I've had the pleasure to work with include Emma Plumb of #1MFWF, Rachael Ellison, Greg Marcus, Jessica DeGroot of Thirdpath, Liz Ben-Ishai of CLASP, Emily Seamone, and Jeremy Joseph of the Office of the Vice President of the United States. I'd like to thank fatherhood advocates Matt Schneider and Lance Sommerfeld of the NYC Dads Group, as well as Doug French, Dads 2.0, and the National Fatherhood Initiative. It is an honor to be in your company.

To my wide network of dads – my friends and neighbors – whether or not you've been to a Beer Fire, simply by sharing some part of my fatherhood journey, you have added to my life. Special thanks to Michael Montalto, Joe Ondrek, Francesco Fiondella, Joe Shatoff, Neil Berg, Dan Black, Alex Krolick, Brian Shields, Joe Villanueva, James Hamilton, Del Belfessa, Eric Baumes, Scott Evenson, Joe Marachino, Anthony Sweet and Jason Saltsberg. There are so many moms to thank as well. We couldn't be dads without you.

To my supportive colleagues at Fairleigh Dickinson University. I consider myself blessed to have a career that is so rewarding and a workplace that is so invigorating. If all employers could be as supportive, we'd have little need for books like mine! Special thanks to Drs. Andy Rosman, Chris Capuano, Gwen Jones, Steve Bear, Tiffany Keller-Hansbrough, J. Daniel Wischnevsky, Jim Hutton, Cathy Kelley and Kent Fairfield for your support. Drs. Bruce Tracey, Karyn Loscocco and Donald Schwartz were important early influences on my career.

Finally, to my amazing family, Amy and Nick, for, well, everything. I consider myself insanely lucky.

ABOUT THE AUTHOR

 **Scott Behson, PhD**, is a Professor of Management at Fairleigh Dickinson University, a busy involved dad, and an overall grateful guy. A national expert in work and family issues, Scott was a featured speaker at the recent White House Summit on Working Families.

Scott also founded and runs the popular blog, Fathers, Work, and Family, dedicated to helping working fathers and encouraging more supportive workplaces. He writes regularly for Harvard Business Review blog network, Huffington Post and Good Men Project, and has also written for Time and the Wall Street Journal. Scott has appeared on MSNBC, CBS, Fox News and Bloomberg Radio, as well as NPR's Morning Edition, Radio Times and All Things Considered. His work has been featured in such outlets as the Atlantic, Esquire, MSN Money, The Daily Beast, Salary.com, and Today.com.

At the Silberman College of Business at Fairleigh Dickinson University, Scott teaches, conducts research, and provides consulting services in Work-Family Balance and Workplace Flexibility. Scott earned a Ph.D. from the State University of New York at Albany and a B.S. from Cornell University. Scott has published numerous academic articles, has made over 40 presentations at prestigious national and international academic conferences, and has won multiple awards for his research and teaching.

Scott lives in Nyack, NY, with his wife, stage actress Amy Griffin, and son, Nick. Contact him @ScottBehson on Twitter and follow him on Fathers, Work, and Family.

Made in the USA
San Bernardino, CA
07 June 2016